Copyright © 2021 by Will Lar

All rights reserved. No part
in any manner without writte
cept for the use of quotations in a book review. For more information,
please address: will@lethain.com.

ISBN: 978-1-7364179-1-1

First edition

www.staffeng.com

Contents

Acknowledgments 3
Foreword 4
Preface 7

Overview 9
Staff engineer archetypes 12
What do Staff engineers actually do? 20
Does the title even matter? 27

Operating at Staff 32
Work on what matters 35
Writing engineering strategy 43
Managing technical quality 51
Stay aligned with authority 70
To lead, you have to follow 75
Learn to never be wrong 78
Create space for others 83
Build a network of peers 89
Present to executives 94

Getting the title where you are 100
Promotion packets 106
Find your sponsor 110
Staff projects 115
Get in the room, and stay there 121
Being visible 126

Deciding to switch companies 130
Finding the right company 135
Interviewing for Staff-plus roles 141
Negotiating your offer 145

Stories 147
Michelle Bu - Payments Products Tech Lead at Stripe 148
Ras Kasa Williams - Staff Engineer at Mailchimp 168
Keavy McMinn - Senior Principal Engineer at Fastly 178
Bert Fan - Senior Staff Engineer at Slack 184
Katie Sylor-Miller - Frontend Architect at Etsy 190
Ritu Vincent - Staff Engineer at Dropbox 203

Rick Boone - Strategic Advisor to Uber's VP of Infrastructure . . . 212
Nelson Elhage - Formerly Staff Engineer at Stripe 223
Diana Pojar - Staff Data Engineer at Slack 233
Dan Na - Staff Engineer and Team Lead at Squarespace 242
Joy Ebertz - Senior Staff Software Engineer at Split 249
Damian Schenkelman - Principal Engineer at Auth0 260
Dmitry Petrashko - Tech Advisor to the Head of Infra at Stripe . . . 272
Stephen Wan - Staff Engineer at Samsara 282

Ending words   294

Resources   296
Additional resources on Staff-plus engineering 296
Where do Staff-plus engineers fit into the org? 303
Managing Staff-plus engineers 307
Designing a Staff-plus interview loop 312
Staff-plus career ladders 318

References   319

Acknowledgments

This book took a village to write, especially when most of the work happened during the chaotic year that was 2020. There are so many people to acknowledge that it's hard to know where to start, but there's really only one place: with the folks who shared their stories.

Thank you, Michelle, Kasa, Keavy, Bert, Katie, Ritu, Rick, Nelson, Diana, Dan, Joy, Damian, Dmitry, and Stephen. I'm equally grateful to the folks who contributed stories to staffeng.com, whose stories aren't in this book. Every one of those stories is a unique voice and well worth reading.

Tanya Reilly's foreword is amazing, and I'm eagerly waiting for Tanya to publish the canonical book on Staff engineering that replaces this one. The cover illustration is by Luciana Guerra, harkening back to old nautical maps where sailors navigated through the same uncertainty that currently obscures the role of Staff engineer. Greglas on the TechWriters Discord is the only reason this book has reasonable fonts and formatting. The community in the TechWriters Discord gave endless suggestions and support, with particular thanks to Gergely, Shawn, and Uma. Laurel line-edited the entire book; if you're not throwing it into the fireplace after two chapters of inconsistent capitalization, it's thanks to her.

Many folks reviewed sections, with particular thanks to Sid, Gary, Pat, Gergely, Pete, and Tommy. I'm also indebted to everyone who wrote a blurb and the twenty-plus folks who've contributed pull requests.

Foreword

My copy of *An Elegant Puzzle*, Will Larson's first book, came with a side order of angst. No offence to the book – It's full of insights and I recommend it. But it's a book for *managers*, and I was reading it as part of the manager reading group in my office. I'm not a manager; I'm a principal engineer. I wasn't sure I was supposed to be there.

For engineers who have chosen the "technical leadership" career path, building skills can often mean feeling like you're in the wrong room. As our industry matures and tackles ever-bigger problems, more and more companies are recognising the need for engineers who have "seen some things" to drive technical strategies, lead projects that cross teams and organisations, and raise everybody's game by modeling what good engineering looks like. But thriving in any discipline means finding resources and communities to learn from – and that can require some creativity on the technical leadership track.

Oh, we have plenty of books, meetups and conferences about technology, but from around the "senior" level on (and arguably earlier), technical skills aren't enough. Success will often mean interpreting business needs, communicating a clear direction, defusing a looming crisis, convincing teams to agree on tradeoffs, or just being a good influence. Engineering bookshelves don't have a ton to say on these subjects. Instead, engineers read business or management books, picking out the topics that can apply to technical decision making, architecture, and so on, along with the techniques that can work without direct authority. For now, manager reading groups are often the best learning communities we have. (And, to be clear, we are grateful to be invited! Please keep inviting us, manager friends.)

The lack of resources for senior engineers is part of a larger problem: it's easy to lose track of what the job even is. Engineers promoted beyond "senior software engineer" can find themselves alone as they navigate an under-defined new role, grappling with the mysterious notion of "impact" to understand whether they're working on the right things, and struggling to adjust to feedback loops that come in quarters or years instead of sprints.

This isn't intentional neglect: managers just don't always know how to support their most senior engineers. How can you be sure your reports are working on the right things, when they're expected to advise you on the most important problems rather than the other way around? What are the skills and behaviours you should expect from the engineers who will be the role models for the rest of the organisation? And, the inevitable question, how much code should they be writing?

It doesn't help that there's no universal career ladder shared across companies, or that job titles aren't at all consistent. That's one reason it was such a relief when Will launched staffeng.com and encapsulated the various roles into the collective "staff-plus". Ok, we still have wildly divergent titles, but at least we now have a word to describe the sorts of roles we're talking about. I'm already hearing "staff-plus" in use where previously we'd have jumped through linguistic hoops to describe the engineers who are more senior than senior level.

staffeng.com was an immediate hit in tech circles. I've never seen a brand new site become the definitive resource on a topic so quickly. Will defines and describes the staff engineer role, offers clear advice on how to become one, and unpacks some of what he calls the "org-level chiropractics" needed to be effective at the job. He's adept at taking a familiar but ambiguous topic, drawing a clean circle around it, and explaining what the rest of us have been looking at without seeing all along. Along with the advice comes the beginning of the community we've needed. The many interviews (with staff engineers, principal engineers, senior principals, architects, tech leads, tech advisors and so on – I told you the titles are confusing) show a variety of paths to staff roles and beyond; most readers will be able to find someone whose path feels familiar and, I hope, achievable.

This is the kind of writing we need on staff engineering right now, and I'm delighted that Will has made it available in book form. Just like *An Elegant Puzzle*, the book you're about to read offers clear, pragmatic and practical leadership advice based on real life experiences. But this time, staff-plus engineers *are* the audience. Well, one of the audiences. Whether you're a staff engineer figuring out what the heck you should be working on, a mid-level engineer choosing between career paths, or a manager who wants to set their most senior engineers up for success, you'll find wisdom here.

The stakes in software engineering get higher every year, and that's not going to stop any time soon. As Will says, "Much as the Lorax speaks for the trees in his popular children's book, staff engineers speak for their companies' technology." The skills and behaviours we require from our role model engineers will have a direct impact on the code we write, the algorithms we deploy, the decisions we make, and the patterns we consider acceptable.

I'm delighted that leaders on the technical track finally have this kind of guidance. I hope that this is just the first of many books and resources for all of us who've ever felt a little out of place in the manager reading group.

Tanya Reilly
Principal Engineer, Squarespace.

Preface

When folks ask about writing my first book, *An Elegant Puzzle*, I say that I wrote half of it over ten years and the other half in six months. Its creation was a challenge at times, and there are many things I'd love to change in the final product, but creating it was a personal highlight. As an author, you're supposed to warn prospective authors away from writing a book, but I have no such warning, even to myself: I wanted to write another book.

The question was, what book? I might have more to say about engineering management at some point, but I certainly don't have much more to say there now. I've spent more time as a manager than as a developer, and there are other folks far better situated to write about effective development. I hope to write a book about infrastructure engineering one day, but I'm trying to spend *less* time thinking about infrastructure for the next few years.

Eventually, I came back to two core questions. What's an area that challenges me today? What's a topic where I believe a book could nudge the technology industry in a positive direction? One issue that fit both criteria was the role of Staff engineers. In most professions, folks become increasingly sure of their role as they become more senior, but it's been my experience that many engineers lose their sense of direction after reaching their first Staff role. It's horrifying to watch folks pursue a Staff engineer role for a decade or more, and then find that they despise the work or feel unequipped to succeed.

More than personally digging into the topic of finding and operating in these Staff-plus roles, I also recognized that different folks have a very different experience of reaching these roles. Some of the most talented folks I've worked with struggled to pass the Senior engineer level. Each time they tried, they encountered systematic barriers that pushed their promotion one performance cycle further out.

When I started working on this book, my first step was to outline the chapters and topics. Staring at that outline, I quickly realized that I couldn't write this book alone. That led to a series of interviews where I got to learn from the remarkable stories of folks reaching their first Staff engineer role and how they operated within those roles after the promotion. Those stories, combined with my own experience supporting, promoting, and hiring Staff-plus engineers as a manager, slowly became this book.

I hope *Staff Engineer* helps you refine your vision of what technical leadership can be, and how you can grow towards that vision.

Overview

At most technology companies, you'll reach Senior software engineer, the career level[1] for software engineers, in five to eight years. At the career level, your company's career ladder won't require that you work towards the next promotion; being promoted further is an exception rather than expected. This is also when many engineers are first given an opportunity to move into engineering management.

Over the past few years, we've seen a flurry of books unlocking the engineering management career path, like Camille Fournier's *The Manager's Path*[2], Julie Zhuo's *The Making of a Manager*[3], Lara Hogan's *Resilient Management*[4], and even my own *An Elegant Puzzle*[5]. The engineering management career isn't an easy one, but there are maps available to help navigate it.

What if you want to advance your career without becoming an engineering manager? Many companies will answer that question by excitedly telling you that they have a two-track software engineering career path. Engineering management is the first track, and the second is technical leadership. The technical leadership track is populated by titles like Staff engineer and Principal engineer. That this second track exists at all is a sign of progress, but there's much work left to make it both accessible and impactful.

This book standardizes on the most common sequence of titles: going from Senior to Staff, followed by Principal, and then Distinguished. It uses the term Staff-plus as an overarching label for Staff, Principal, and Distinguished titles. Many companies only have a subset of these

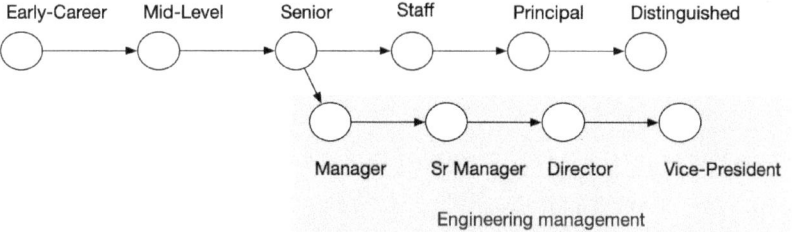

Typical dual-track engineering career ladder

titles, slowly adding more as their team grows, but companies that only have one technical leadership title almost always use Staff. A few companies use an alternative sequence, but they're in the minority.

There is pervasive ambiguity around the technical leadership career path, making it difficult to answer seemingly simple questions about Staff-plus roles. If you're a Senior engineer and want to reach Staff engineer, what skills should you develop? Are technical abilities alone sufficient? How do most folks move into one of these roles? What is your manager's role in helping you along the way? Will you enjoy being a Staff engineer, or will you toil for years to reach a role that doesn't suit you? This book will help you answer all those questions.

Given the broad confusion around these roles, I knew I couldn't write this book relying too heavily on my own experience. More than a dozen Staff-plus engineers across the industry were kind enough to share their experiences of reaching and operating in a Staff-plus role. Their wisdom has created something richer in nuance, breadth, and perspective than I could have ever written on my own.

If you're already in a Staff-plus role, I hope these writings will energize you in your journey as a leader outside the management track. If you aim for such a role, I hope this book will provide pragmatic aid in its pursuit.

You can read this book cover to cover, but please jump around if you want. There's no right or wrong way to read it.

Its sections are:

- **Overview** - a survey of the Staff engineer role, how it varies by company, and why the title matters
- **Operating at Staff** - how to do the work on the other side of the title
- **Getting the title where you are** - how to attain a Staff-plus role at your current company
- **Switching companies to get the title** - when and how changing companies can support the pursuit of a Staff-plus title
- **Stories** - collected stories from Staff-plus engineers about what they do and how they reached their role
- **Resources** - a collection of templates and further readings if you're looking for more

Every company puts its spin on Staff-plus roles, so it's likely that some parts won't map to your experience. If that's the case, please take what resonates and discard the rest!

Staff engineer archetypes

Most career ladders[6] define a single, uniform set of expectations for Staff engineers operating within the company. Everyone benefits from clear role expectations, but career ladders are a tool that applies better against populations than people. This is particularly true for Staff-plus engineers, whose career ladders often paper over several distinct roles hidden behind a single moniker.

The more folks I spoke with about the role of Staff-plus engineers at their company, the better their experiences began to cluster into four distinct patterns. Most companies emphasized one or two of the patterns, and one pattern only existed in companies with many hundreds or thousands of engineers. A few companies didn't feature any technical leadership pattern and pushed all their experienced engineers towards engineering management. In literature, recurring character patterns are called archetypes, such as the "hero" or the "trickster," and the archetype term is helpful for labeling these frequent variants of Staff-plus engineers.

The four common archetypes of Staff-plus roles I encountered are:

- The **Tech Lead** guides the approach and execution of a particular team. They partner closely with a single manager, but sometimes they partner with two or three managers within a focused area. Some companies also have a *Tech Lead Manager* role, which is similar to the *Tech Lead* archetype but exists on the engineering manager ladder and includes people management responsibilities.
- The **Architect** is responsible for the direction, quality, and approach within a critical area. They combine in-depth knowledge of technical constraints, user needs, and organization level leadership.
- The **Solver** digs deep into arbitrarily complex problems and

finds an appropriate path forward. Some focus on a given area for long periods. Others bounce from hotspot to hotspot as guided by organizational leadership.
- The **Right Hand** extends an executive's attention, borrowing their scope and authority to operate particularly complex organizations. They provide additional leadership bandwidth to leaders of large-scale organizations.

This taxonomy is more focused on being *useful* than *complete*, but so far, I've been able to fit every Staff-plus engineer I've spoken to into one of these categories. Admittedly, some folks are easier to classify than others.

Tech Lead

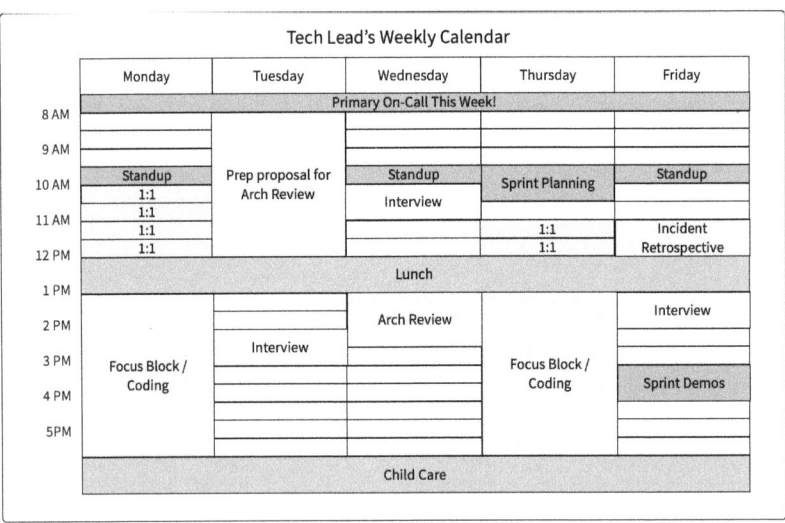

Example calendar for a Tech Lead archetype

Stories featuring Tech Lead archetpye: Diana Pojar, Dan Na, Ritu Vincent

Tech Leads are the most common Staff archetype and lead one team or a cluster of teams in their approach and execution. They're comfortable scoping complex tasks, coordinating their team towards solving them, and unblocking them along the way. *Tech Leads* often carry the team's context and maintain many of the essential cross-team and cross-functional relationships necessary for the team's success. They're a close partner to the team's product manager and the first person called when the roadmap needs to be shuffled.

Earlier in their career, they will have implemented their team's most complex technical projects, but at this point, they default to delegating such projects across the team. They do this both to grow their teammates and in acknowledgment that the team's impact grows as the *Tech Lead*'s coding blocks shrink. While they're coding less, they are still the person defining their team's technical vision, and stepping in to build alignment within the team on complex issues.

The *Tech Lead* role is, for many folks, their first experience as a Staff engineer. A few forces conspire towards that result. First, the *Tech Lead* role tends to develop early on within companies that have a strong concept of team, which is common among companies using agile methodologies, and most companies attempt an agile approach at some point. Another factor is that the day-to-day work of a *Tech Lead* is most similar to the work you'd already be doing as a Senior engineer, making it a fairly intuitive transition. Most importantly, an organization needs roughly one *Tech Lead* for every eight engineers, making it far more common than other archetypes.

Somewhat confusingly, some companies use *Tech Lead* as a title, and others use it as a role. In this list of archetypes, the *Tech Lead* is one approach to operating as a Staff engineer, but it's quite common to perform the *Tech Lead* role without having the impact expected of a Staff-level engineer. Indeed, you'll find non-Staff engineers acting with the behaviors of every archetype. Being a Staff-engineer is not just a role. It's the intersection of the role, your behaviors, your impact, and the organization's recognition of all those things.

Architect

Architect's Weekly Calendar					
	Monday	Tuesday	Wednesday	Thursday	Friday
8 AM					Technical discussion on potential acquisition
9 AM	Org Status Meeting	Prep proposal for Arch Review	Interview	Team Meeting	
10 AM	1:1			1:1	
11 AM	1:1			1:1	Incident Retrospective
12 PM	1:1			1:1	
1 PM	Lunch				
2 PM	Review and give feedback on proposals for this week's Arch Review	Interview	Arch Review	Work with pilot team on integration plan for new storage backend	Interview
3 PM			Share notes from Arch Review		Interview
4 PM		Urgent sync on scalability for upcoming enterprise launch			
5 PM					
			Child Care		

Example calendar for Architect archetype

Stories featuring Architect archetype: Joy Ebertz, Katie Sylor-Miller, Keavy McMinn

The *Architect* title has fallen out of style in many companies, but the *Architect* role remains alive and well for folks operating at Staff-plus levels. *Architects* are responsible for the success of a specific technical domain within their company, for example, the company's API design, frontend stack, storage strategy, or cloud infrastructure. For a domain to merit an *Architect*, it must be both complex and enduringly central to the company's success.

There is a toxic preconception that *Architects* design systems in isolation and then pass their designs to others to implement. That does happen in some cases, but reciting that stereotype would slander the architects I interviewed. Influential architects dedicate their energy to maintaining an intimate understanding of the business' needs, their users' goals, and the relevant technical constraints. They use that insight to identify and advocate for effective approaches within their area of focus, and do it with organizational authority that they've earned by demonstrating consistently good judgment.

The *Architect* role tends to evolve in relatively large companies, companies with exceptionally complex or coupled codebases, and companies that are struggling to repay the technical debt they created in their initial sprint to product-market fit. Some companies push for *Architects to* remain deep in the codebase, and others set a clear expectation that *Architects must not* write code: both models work for some companies.

Solver

	Monday	Tuesday	Wednesday	Thursday	Friday
8 AM					
9 AM			Scalability work		
10 AM		Deep dive into upcoming scalability issue for enterprise launch		Team Meeting	Scalability work
11 AM			Interview	1:1	
12 PM	1:1			1:1	Incident Retrospective
	1:1				
1 PM			Lunch		
2 PM	"Quick chat" about scalability				Interview
3 PM		Interview			Interview
4 PM	Deep dive into upcoming scalability issue for enterprise launch	Urgent sync on scalability for upcoming enterprise launch	Scalability work	Scalability work	
5 PM					Scalability work
			Child Care		

Solver's Weekly Calendar

Example calendar for Solver archetype

Stories featuring Solver archetype: Bert Fan, Nelson Elhage

The *Solver* is a trusted agent of the organization who goes deep into knotty problems, continuing to work on them until they're resolved. Folks in this role are moved onto problems identified by organizational leadership as critical and either lacking a clear approach or with a high degree of execution risk.

Where most Staff-level roles require a very heavy dose of organizational wrangling, the *Solver* generally operates on problems that are already identified as organizational priorities and thus are called on to do relatively little org-level chiropractics. On the other hand, they generally stop working on problems once they're contained, which can create the feeling of transience and requires a soft touch to avoid infuriating the teams left behind to maintain the "solved" problem.

The *Solver* is most common in companies that think of individuals, rather than teams, as the atomic unit of planning and ownership[7]. In such companies, it's common to see the *Solver* become prevalent in the place of the *Tech Lead*. You're less likely to encounter this role at traditionally managed sprint-centric companies until those companies become relatively large or long-lived enough to acquire their own varietal of technical debt.

Right Hand

Stories featuring Right Hand archetype: Michelle Bu, Rick Boone

The *Right Hand* is the least common of the archetypes, showing up as an organization reaches hundreds of engineers and is akin to operating as a senior organizational leader without direct managerial responsibilities. Rick Boone compared his role to the Hand of the King[8] in Game of Thrones and Leo McGarry[9] from The West Wing, operating with the borrowed authority of a senior leader. However, borrowing authority comes with the obligation of remaining deeply aligned[10] with that leader's approach, beliefs, and values.

Folks in this role attend their leader's staff meetings and work to scale that leader's impact by removing important problems from their plate. Problems addressed at this level are never purely technical and in-

	Monday	Tuesday	Wednesday	Thursday	Friday
8 AM					Technical discussion on potential acquisition
9 AM	Prep for Status	Deep dive into upcoming scalability issue for enterprise launch	Onboarding Working Group	Team Meeting	
10 AM	Org Status Meeting				
	1:1		Interview		
11 AM	1:1			1:1	
	1:1			1:1	Incident Retrospective
12 PM	1:1			1:1	
1 PM	Lunch				
2 PM	"Quick chat" about scalability		Arch Review	Quarterly Planning Offsite	Interview
3 PM		Interview			Interview
4 PM		Urgent sync on scalability for upcoming enterprise launch	Eng Budget Review		Scalability Status
5PM					Send Out Scalability Status Update
	Scalability Status		Scalability Status		
			Child Care		

Right Hand's Weekly Calendar

Example calendar for Right Hand archetype

stead involve the intersection of the business, technology, people, culture, and process. *Right Hands* often dive into a fire, edit the approach, delegate execution to the most appropriate team, and then pop over to the next fire elsewhere in the organization. The joy of these roles is that you only work on essential problems. The tragedy is that you're always on to the next issue by the time those problems are solved.

Which is right for you?

As you think about which of these archetypes would fit you, start by reflecting on the kinds of work that energize you, and then consider which roles are available within your company.

All companies develop a need for engineers who can fill the *Tech Lead* role, which makes it the most accessible archetype to attain your first Staff engineering role. Companies that emphasize individual ownership rather than team ownership often develop the *Solver* early. On the other hand, companies that operate under strict sprints or agile methodologies tend to develop that role late, if ever. In the recent crops of fast-growing technology companies, the *Architect* and *Right Hand* roles have generally emerged as the organizations reached one hundred and one thousand engineers, respectively, and simply don't exist beforehand. Companies with other strains of cultural DNA often develop them earlier, or sometimes never.

Success in these roles requires remaining engaged; it's essential to understand what kinds of work energize you. The *Tech Lead* and *Architect* tend to work with the same people on the same problems for years, developing a tight sense of team and shared purpose. Some months their focus will be a top company priority, and sometimes they'll be humming along so well that executives forget their team exists.

The *Solver* and *Right Hand* bounce from fire to fire, often having more transactional interactions with the folks they're working with on any given week. They're tightly aligned with executive priorities and are likely to receive recognition for addressing leadership's most pressing problems. On the other hand, while they'll nominally be on a team with other folks, there will generally be little-to-no overlap within their team's areas of focus, and they'll often have a limited sense of community.

For each archetype, you'll find folks who love it and find it deeply rewarding, along with folks who find the work despair-inspiring. While it's important to aim towards an archetype that fits you well, it's also worth remembering that over your thirty or forty-year career[11], you'll have long enough to spend some time sampling every archetype.

What do Staff engineers actually do?

> *The role of a Staff-plus engineer depends a lot on what the team needs and also what the particular engineer's strengths are. From my experience, the responsibilities of a Staff-plus engineer can change over time. Still, usually, their main focus is working on projects/efforts that have strategic value for the company while driving technical design and up-leveling their team. - Diana Pojar*

Anyone who has been cornered by relatives at a party and asked to explain what software engineers *actually do* knows that explaining the work can be challenging. Over time you may have created a compelling answer for your relatives, but many folks' minds go blank when their coworker leans over and asks, "What's a Staff engineer do?"

The most straightforward answer is that Staff engineers keep doing much of what made them successful as Senior engineers: building relationships, writing software, coordinating projects. However, that's a misleading answer. Staff engineers do those same tasks, but whereas previously they were the core of their work, now they're auxiliary tasks. Their daily schedule varies a bit by archetype, but there's a shared foundation across all archetypes: setting and editing technical direction, providing sponsorship and mentorship, injecting engineering context into organizational decisions, exploration, and what Tanya Reilly[12] calls being glue[13].

Setting technical direction

> *I feel most impactful when I can facilitate setting a technical vision for an area and get people moving toward that vision. I think we would all agree that we want our code to be better architected than it is or improved in some way. However, I've*

> *found that often people have some vague sense of wanting better without having a clear idea of what that thing they want is. I like to help the group decide on a shared understanding of where exactly they're trying to get (it's actually okay if we never get there) and come up with a general game plan of how to get there.*
> *- Joy Ebertz*

Much as the Lorax[14] speaks for the trees in his popular children's book, Staff engineers speak for their companies' technology. Technology cannot speak for itself and requires effective advocates on its behalf. Folks who successfully advance technology are pragmatic, deliberate, and focus more on the long-term trend of progress than viewing each individual decision as a make-or-break crisis. It can be helpful to think of this as being a part-time product manager for technology.

Some Staff-plus engineers are explicitly hired to lead a specific area such as API design, and in other cases, they find themselves editing and aligning approaches across a broad area. One constant across all roles is that the reality of setting technical direction is far more about understanding and solving the real needs of the organization around you and far less about prioritizing technology and approaches that you personally are excited to learn about. In earlier roles, you may have tried to influence decisions towards technology choices you were motivated by; in senior positions, you're accountable to the business and organization first and yourself second.

Mentorship and sponsorship

> *In my current role, I feel energized when someone I've sponsored sends an announcement that they've shipped their work, or when I see that I've helped shape or shift an engineering team's model of an important topic. It's these teams, not me, who are doing the hard work day-to-day of building and supporting their technology. I measure my impact based on*

> *their progress and, more importantly, the directionality of that progress and the alignment of their work to the company's goals. - Michelle Bu*

There's a popular vision of heroic leadership that centers on extraordinarily productive individuals whose decisions change their company's future. Most of those narratives are intentionally designed by public relations teams to create a good story. You're far more likely to change your company's long-term trajectory by growing the engineers around you than through personal heroics. The best way to grow those around you is by creating an active practice of mentorship and sponsorship.

Sometimes folks see a requirement for mentorship in their career ladder and try to mechanically check that box, which is a shame because mentorship is one of the most valuable activities in a Staff-plus role. Sharing your experience and advice, along with building an ongoing relationship to understand the recipient's context, is high impact work. The most effective Staff engineers pair a moderate amount of mentorship with considerably more sponsorship: putting your thumb directly on the scale to help advance and support those around you. If you haven't read it already, Lara Hogan has written the canonical piece on the distinction between sponsorship and mentorship, What does sponsorship look like?[15]

Providing engineering perspective

> *I have a seat at the table at higher level engineering discussions that occur at a level above individual projects and teams. We have recurring staff engineering meetings where we discuss problems that span teams which are both technical and non-technical in nature. - Dan Na*

Effective organizations streamline routine decision making. A good example of this is the process of reviewing contracts for potential enterprise customers. Early on, there will be some contracts signed that the product and engineering teams are uncomfortable supporting. After that happens a few times, the process will include more stakeholders in the review steps, and over time the right people will be in the right places at the right time.

Even companies that are great at making routine decisions often struggle when an unexpected decision shows up. The sort which is both time-sensitive and important, and it's challenging to even pull the right folks together before the decision needs to get made. It's frequent for an organizational restructure[16] to occur without valuable input that would have changed the outcome. Similarly, it's common for interview loops for infrequent roles–those where you might hire one person into them each year like executives or Staff-plus engineers in an early-stage company–to not evaluate the candidate on an important dimension. For some companies, even things like roadmap planning fall into this category.

Staff-plus engineers are the folks who will often get unexpectedly pulled into the room where this sort of decision is happening. This gives them the opportunity to inject the engineering context and perspective into a decision while it's still possible to change the outcome. These brief moments of input on critical decisions are unduly impactful and will allow you to inject an engineering perspective where it would otherwise be missed. Just remember that you're representing the interests of all of engineering, not just your own.

Exploration

> *In my current role within the incubator, I'm spending all day prototyping, but in my previous tech lead role, I did a lot of different things. - Ritu Vincent*

Hill-climbing[17] is a simple optimization algorithm. Imagine you're standing on a mountain somewhere and want to get to the top. You turn around in a circle, identify the highest nearby point, and then walk there. Once you get there, you turn around in a circle again, find the highest nearby point from your new location, and go there. If you keep doing this, you'll get to the top of whatever mountain you're on. However, imagine you tried this on a foggy day. Because you can't see very far, you might get to the highest nearby point and later realize there was a much higher point just out of sight.

Hill-climbing can't solve every problem, but it's so effective that many companies struggle to take other approaches. This can be a consumer-oriented company struggling to support enterprise deals or a mature company struggling to compete with a smaller competitor's release cadence. It can even be the case that your current business is so valuable that it's hard to prioritize new businesses[18], even though the valuable business' growth rate is trailing downwards.

In the long-term, companies either learn to explore, or they fade away; this isn't an ignorable challenge. Simply assigning a team that's mastered hill-climbing to do exploratory work[19] is far from a sure thing, so many companies take a different approach. They find a couple of trusted individuals with broad skills, allocate some resources, and check back in a few months later to see what they've discovered. One of those engineers is often a Staff engineer.

This isn't always a business problem either; it can be any ambiguous, important problem that the company's systems are ill-shaped to address. It might be reducing your infrastructure costs by an order of magnitude. It might be identifying a multi-region strategy that takes six months instead of three years. It might be addressing the sudden realization that your primary database only has three months of remaining disk space, and you can't upgrade to a larger size (in my experience, a surprisingly frequent problem at fast-growing startups).

This is some of the most rewarding and the riskiest work companies do. It takes a great deal of organizational trust to be trusted with this work, including having enough respect from the business that if you fail, it's a reflection on the problem and not you.

Being Glue

Tanya Reilly[12] wrote a wonderful post, Being Glue, which captures another core element of successful Staff engineers: doing the needed, but often invisible, tasks to keep the team moving forward and shipping its work. It's not glamorous, but high impact organizations often have one or more Staff engineer working behind the scenes expediting the most important work and ensuring it gets finished.

But will you still write software?

It's impolite to end any discussion of the Staff engineer role without opining on the first question that Staff engineers ask when they congregate in a room together: "Do you still find time to write software?" The answer is, of course, it depends!

Ras Kasa Williams said, "I still contributed code regularly—certainly less than the rest of the engineers on my team; but it was important that I sustained"hand to keyboard" work to ensure that my technical strategy (and other macro-level decision–making) was informed by the on–the–ground experiences of the rest of my team."

Katie Sylor-Miller said, "I'm a frontend architect, but by far the main thing I've been writing lately is SQL, because I'm doing a lot of data analysis. I've been looking at our performance metrics to figure out where the areas for improvement are, and what would be the most impactful issues to fix to improve performance and business metrics. I will write little bits of JS or PHP here and there, but it's mostly to help unblock teams or to run small performance-related experiments."

Joy Ebertz said, "The more senior you get, the less your job is about code. Sure, unlike a people manager, you still have a very technical slant, and even through principal, you'll likely be doing at least some coding. However, the higher you get, the more your job becomes about mentoring and growing the people around you (and more broadly), building your team through building your company's public tech brand, noticing larger technical trends that can be improved upon or corrected, helping to set the tech vision for your team or the company and advocating for resourcing for tech debt projects."

Most write some, some write none, but none write as much as they used to earlier in their career. There will be the occasional week that is purely coding, but those won't be the norm, and if they happen too often, it's usually a sign of working on something comfortable rather than important. Even if you're not writing much, you'll be reading *a ton* of your coworkers' code and doing a fair number of code reviews.

Slow but rewarding

One unifying theme across Staff-plus work is that the timeframes are longer. Early in your career, it's easy to get attached to software development's quick feedback cycle–write, test, ship, repeat–and most of the work you'll be doing at this level replaces that feedback loop with one that takes weeks, months, and years. These longer timeframes can feel surprisingly demoralizing when you first take on a Staff-plus role. It's normal to end some days as a Staff-plus engineer feeling like you haven't accomplished anything–keep at it!

The impact and the personal growth lives in those longer timeframes, and while everyone I spoke with wished they'd occasionally get more time to code, and admitted worrying some days that they weren't accomplishing much, none of them regretted their transition into their current roles.

Does the title even matter?

If you're safely nestled within the comfortable clutches of the Senior engineer career level[20], you might wonder if you ought to pursue the Staff title. It's a considerable investment of time and energy, along with requiring a good amount of luck. Is that investment worth your time?

The answer is, of course, that it might be! The three consistent advantages that generally come with a Staff-plus title are:

1. allowing you to bypass informal gauges of seniority,
2. facilitating access to "the room,"
3. increase in current and career compensation.

A potential fourth advantage is that some folks find that the title grants more agency to select the projects you work on, but others find that increase in agency is swallowed by a commensurate increase in accountability to the business.

Informal gauges of seniority

When I spoke with Nelson Elhage about whether reaching the Staff level allowed him to take on new work, he answered:

> The question of "allowed" is interesting and might not be quite the right question because there were very few official policies on who got what kind of role. Most things relied on more informal gauges of seniority.

Many technology companies describe themselves as pursuing meritocracy, defined as creating the conditions for talented employees to rise to the top naturally. Given there isn't any widely accepted measure of individual merit, such companies come to rely on what Nelson aptly termed "informal gauges of seniority." While these gauges are believed to evaluate ideas objectively, their sheer informality becomes a broad vector of bias and often conflate confidence with competence.

Freedom from the cycle of re-establishing one's competence came up frequently as a key advantage of the Staff title. These informal gauges weren't mentioned by every Staff-plus engineer I spoke with, but they were routinely mentioned by individuals who didn't conform to their company's stereotype of an experienced technologist.

Keavy McMinn shared,

> *When you have a title, you don't have to spend so much energy putting your credentials on the table. It helps set the context for others. You're more respected from the outset, and that's been really noticeable.*

A Staff-plus title allows you to reinvest the energy you've previously spent on proving yourself into the core work you're evaluated on. If you find that you're not investing much energy into proving yourself, that's great! Perhaps you've been at your current company long enough and proven yourself enough times that it's no longer an issue. If you *do* find your time diverted towards proving and reproving yourself, the title will return a considerable measure of time to you for reinvestment.

Being in the room

Another frequent advantage of a Staff-plus title is "being in the room." Dan Na described this as,

> *I have a seat at the table in higher-level engineering discussions that occur at a level above individual projects and teams. We have recurring staff engineering meetings where we discuss problems that span teams which are both technical and non-technical in nature. As a hypothetical example, I'd feel comfortable surfacing what I perceive as shortcomings in the engineering onboarding process in this type of meeting.*

For any important decision, there's the time leading up to the core decision being made, and then there's everything afterward. In more senior roles, you're often in the right place to provide input when it's relatively cheap to incorporate, where otherwise your feedback might not be incorporated–despite being very valuable–because the related roll out or implementation has advanced too far.

Compensation

Small companies tend to have fairly ad-hoc compensation, and increases come from direct negotiation with your manager. A promotion to a Staff-plus role in such a company might not even come with a corresponding increase in your compensation. However, most companies introduce compensation bands for each role by the time they reach one to two hundred folks. Those compensation bands will generally ensure your compensation increases along with the role.

The highest-paid roles at any company tend to be the executive and senior management roles. As companies grow, they typically create a compensation mapping between management and engineering roles, such that reaching Staff-plus roles (and sometimes this is Sr Staff or Distinguished roles rather than the initial Staff role) will significantly bump your compensation.

Even if your current company doesn't compensate for Staff-plus engineer roles much differently than for Senior engineer roles, *some companies do*[21]. Throughout your career, you can choose to steer towards such companies, and doing so with a Staff-plus title will meaningfully increase your lifetime earnings.

Access to interesting work

Many folks take on Staff-plus roles believing it will give them access to the most visible or exciting work. That's true to some extent, but it depends on the Staff archetypes which are most prevalent at your company. For example, *Solvers* often do get access to the most interesting work. Conversely, a *Tech Lead* would probably be undermining their team if they operated that way.

Among the folks I've spoken with, the most consistently effective way to get access to interesting work is being hired to do it, such as Ritu Vincent who was hired to launch Dropbox's product incubator and Keavy McMinn who was hired to design Fastly's API strategy.

This doesn't always work out. Sometimes the interesting work will be plainly visible but still inaccessible. You'll be too obligated to the business' needs to pursue a project out of personal interest. In earlier roles, you might be able to sneak that sort of project into your backlog, but now you'll have a responsibility to model good behavior. Even in cases where the project is the best thing for the company, you'll often decide to pass the opportunity on to another engineer who would benefit from it more than you would.

Different rather than better

Even though the title does matter, it's not necessarily the case that you ought to pursue the role. Even if you love the privileges and perks of a Staff-plus title, it's important to recognize that they come on the back of a very different job. Michelle Bu captured this in her advice for folks pursuing the Staff title,

> *If you're more focused on hitting Staff than on setting yourself up to do work that energizes you, it's easy to end up stuck in a role you don't want. Being a Staff-plus engineer, especially a broad-scoped Staff-plus engineer, is a very different job than being a Senior engineer. It's important to take a step back and think about whether it's a job you really want.*

The advantages of senior titles are real, and for some folks, those advantages shift their career from one characterized by survival to one with the necessary prerequisites for their success. However, many folks find that their Staff role's heightened expectations eliminate the work that used to excite them. In your career, there are few choices without consequences, and this isn't one of them.

Material but not magic

You'll occasionally meet an engineer who believes that attaining a certain title is the only thing standing between them and an important accomplishment or opportunity. Such folks might express frustrations, such as, "If I just had the Staff title, I could decide the technology stack for our team."

Increased organizational authority does provide new tools for solving problems, but successfully retaining organizational authority in a well-managed organization requires a great deal of nuance and restraint. If you have a problem and believe that your title is the only thing holding you back, I want to reassure you that focusing on developing your approach and skills will be far more impactful than the title. The title will get you over the ledge once you're close, but it'll never do as much work as you'd expect.

The one consistent exception to this rule is that women and minorities often do find they spend significantly less time and energy, proving themselves once they attain a Staff-plus title. The title doesn't unlock new abilities for them, but it does remove some of the weight they'd been carrying with them throughout their career.

Operating at Staff

> One of the best pieces of advice that someone gave me, and that I make sure to pass on to other staff engineers, is that there's a misconception that you become a Staff engineer and then you'll be in control of the work you do, and everyone will listen to you and do what you want them to do. That's absolutely the opposite of what happens! - Katie Sylor-Miller

Many engineers become focused on the Staff-plus career path because the engineering manager path has too many meetings or requires too much collaboration with other coworkers, and yikes, are you going to be surprised if you begin a Staff-plus with that mindset. Although Staff engineer roles are generally positioned as the sequential step beyond Senior engineer, it's genuinely a different role, and you'll increasingly spend your time doing sorts of work that you previously did infrequently or not-at-all.

There is a significant learning curve in Staff-plus roles that initially trip most folks up. Part of the challenge is that much of the work you're doing has a much slower feedback cycle. The delayed feedback can initially feel quite demoralizing as you replace the visceral coding REPL[22] with the uneven progress of mentorship, relationship building, and strategy.

This chapter is about overcoming that learning curve, learning to operate as a Staff engineer, and finding the parts of the role which are personally fulfilling and organizationally transformative.

Topics

In the interviews for this book, as well as my own experience leading and coaching Staff-plus engineers, a handful of topics kept coming up as keystones of personal development. They aren't *everything* you'll do in the role, but they are the places where you're most likely to have an outsized impact or accidentally commit a career-limiting move.

1. **Work on what matters** to make the most of the working hours you have, particularly as you get further along in your career and life's commitments expand.
2. **Write an engineering strategy** to guide your organization's approach to supporting your company's business objectives with its architecture, technology selection, and organizational structure.
3. **Curate technical quality** to maintain the quality of your company's architecture and software as it grows and tacks over time.
4. **Stay aligned with authority** to remain an effective leader over time. Technical leadership roles rely on proxied authority from another (usually, managerial) leader, and continued access to that authority depends on staying aligned, trustworthy, and predictable.
5. **To lead, you have to follow**. Having a vivid sense of how things ought to work is a powerful leadership tool, but it's also essential to learn to blend your vision with the visions from your peers and leadership.
6. **Learn to never be wrong** shift away from being right and towards understanding and communication. Stop spending your social capital repairing relationships frayed by conflict, and learn to collaborate with folks with different priorities and perspectives. This also comes with the added benefit of fewer folks complaining about you to your manager.
7. **Create space for others** so that your team grows stronger than

your contribution.
8. **Build a network of peers** to vet difficult decisions and to give you honest feedback when your role's authority starts to temper feedback.

An astute reader will notice two critical themes discussed in What do Staff engineers actually do? are missing from this topic list: the first is "mentorship and sponsorship," and the second is "being glue." Both concepts are essential to the success of Staff-plus engineers, but ultimately, I think the canonical pieces on these topics already exist, and you're better served by reading those than my watery rehash. For mentorship and sponsorship, spend some time with Lara Hogan's What Does Sponsorship Look Like?, and for being glue, spend time with Tanya Reilly's piece that bore the phrase, Being Glue.

As you deliberately practice in each of these areas, you'll slowly progress from a newly minted Staff engineer to a trusted organizational leader. That said, these won't cover everything you do. At times you'll find your role surprisingly similar to that of an engineering director, and at other times strangely familiar to previous work in your career.

That vast remit is part of what makes describing these roles challenging. If there's a particular topic you're focused on that's missing, check out the Additional resources for learning appendix.

Work on what matters

> *I've taken to using the word "energized" over "impactful." "Impactful" feels company-centric, and while that's important, "energized" is more inwards-looking. Finding energizing work is what has kept me at Stripe for so long, pursuing impactful work. - Michelle Bu*

We all have a finite amount of time to live, and within that mortal countdown, we devote some fraction towards our work. Even for the most career-focused, your life will be filled with many things beyond work: supporting your family, children, exercise, being a mentor and a mentee, hobbies, and so the list goes on. This is the sign of a rich life, but one side-effect is that time to do your work will become increasingly scarce as you get deeper into your career.

If you're continuing to advance in your career, then even as your time available for work shrinks, the expectations around your impact will keep growing. You can try sleeping less or depriving yourself of the non-work activities you need to feel whole, but you'll inevitably find that your work maintains an aloof indifference to your sacrifice rather than rewarding it. Only through pacing your career to your life can you sustain yourself for the long-term.

Indeed, pacing yourself becomes the central challenge of a sustained, successful career: increasingly senior roles require that you accomplish more and more and do it in less and less time. The ledge between these two constraints gets narrower the further you go, but it remains walkable if you take a deliberate approach.

First, a discussion on a few common ways to get tripped up: *snacking*, *preening*, and *chasing ghosts*. Then we'll get into the good stuff: how *do* you work on what really matters?

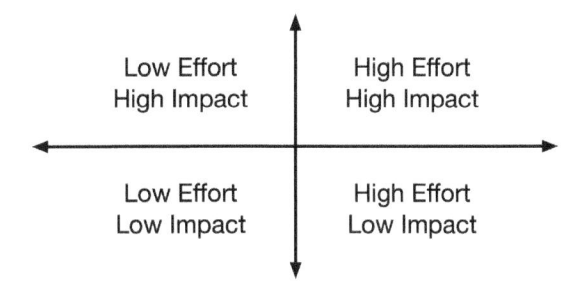

```
     Low Effort    |   High Effort
     High Impact   |   High Impact
    ───────────────┼───────────────
     Low Effort    |   High Effort
     Low Impact    |   Low Impact
```

Quadrants of high and low impact by high and low effort

Avoid snacking

Hunter Walk recommends that folks avoid "snacking"[23] when they prioritize work. If you're in a well-run organization, at some point, you're going to run out of things that are both high-impact and easy. This leaves you with a choice between shifting right to hard and high-impact or shifting down to easy and low-impact. The latter choice–easy and low-impact–is what Walk refers to as *snacking*.

When you're busy, these snacks give a sense of accomplishment that makes them psychologically rewarding. Still, you're unlikely to learn much from doing them, others are likely equally capable of completing them (*and* for some of them, it might be a good development opportunity), and there's a tremendous opportunity cost versus doing something higher impact.

It's ok to spend some of your time on snacks to keep yourself motivated between bigger accomplishments, but you have to keep yourself honest about how much time you're spending on high-impact work versus low-impact work. In senior roles, you're more likely to self-determine your work, and if you're not deliberately tracking your work, it's easy to catch yourself doing little to no high-impact work.

Stop preening

Where "snacking" is the broad category of doing easy and low-impact work, there's a particularly seductive subset of snacking that I call "preening." Preening is doing low-impact, high-visibility work. Many companies conflate high-visibility and high-impact so strongly that they can't distinguish between preening and impact, which is why it's not uncommon to see some companies' senior-most engineers spend the majority of their time doing work that's of dubious value, but that is frequently recognized in company meetings.

If you're taking a short-term look at career growth[24], then optimizing for your current organization's pathologies in evaluating impact is the optimal path: go forth and preen gloriously. However, if you're thinking about developing yourself to succeed as your current role grows in complexity[25] or across multiple organizations, then it's far more important to strike a balance between valued work and self-growth.

This is also an important factor to consider when choosing a company to work at! Dig into what a company values and ensure it aligns with your intended personal growth. If a company's leadership consists entirely of folks who focus their energy on performative urgency or acts of fealty, don't be surprised when your success in the company depends on those activities.

Worse, to be a successful preener requires near invulnerability to criticism of your actual impact, and your true work *will* suffer if your energy is diverted to preening. Typically this means you need to be a vanity hire of a senior leader or to present yourself in the way a company believes leaders look and act. If that isn't you, then your attempt to exchange your good judgment for company success will end up failing anyway: you'll get held accountable for the lack of true impact where others who match the company's expectation of how a leader appears will somehow slip upward.

Stop chasing ghosts

Many folks would assume that companies, rational optimizers that they are, avoid spending much time on low-impact high-effort projects. Unfortunately, that isn't consistently the case. It's surprisingly common for a new senior leader to join a company and immediately drive a strategy shift that fundamentally misunderstands the challenges at hand[26]. The ghosts of their previous situation hold such a firm grasp on their understanding of the new company that they misjudge the familiar as the essential.

As a senior leader, you have to maintain a hold on your ego to avoid investing in meaningless work on a grand scale. This can be surprisingly challenging when during your hiring process, you've been repeatedly told that you've been hired to fix something deeply broken–you're the newly-hired savior. Of course, your instincts are right! Taking the time to understand the status quo before shifting it will always repay diligence with results.

I had a recent discussion with someone who argued that new senior leaders *deliberately* push for major changes even though they suspect the efforts will fail. Such changes make the organization increasingly dependent on the new leader and also ensures anything that *does* go well gets attributed to the new leader directly rather than their team. If this is your approach to leadership, please know that you're awful and take the time to work on yourself until the well-being and success of an entire company matter to you more than being perceived as essential.

Existential issues

Now that you're done snacking, preening, and chasing ghosts, it's time to to start thinking from the other direction: what should you work on? The first place to look for work that matters is exploring whether your company is experiencing an existential risk. Companies operate in an eternal iterative elimination tournament[27], balancing future success against surviving until that future becomes the present. If you're about to lose one of those rounds, then always focus there.

Running out of money, like my experience at Digg[28], can be the most obvious issue, but not every existential issue is financial, like Twitter's fail whale stability challenges[29] or adapting to the shifts caused by the Covid-19 pandemic.

If something dire is happening at your company, then that's the place to be engaged. Nothing else will matter if it doesn't get addressed.

Work where there's room *and* attention

Existential issues are usually *not* the most efficient place to add your efforts, but efficiency isn't a priority when the walls are crashing down around you. You *should* swarm to existential problems, but if a problem isn't existential, then you should be skeptical of adding your efforts where everyone's already focused. Folks often chase leadership's top priority, but with so many folks looking to make their impact there, it's often challenging to have a meaningful impact.

Instead, the most effective places to work are those that matter to your company but still have enough room to actually do work. What are priorities that will become critical in the future, where you can do great work ahead of time? Where are areas that are doing *ok* but could be doing *great* with your support?

Sometimes you'll find work that's *worthy* of attention but which an organization is incapable of paying attention to, usually because its leadership doesn't value that work. In some companies, this is developer tooling work. In others, it's inclusion work. In most companies, it's glue work.

There is almost always a great deal of room to do this sort of work that no one is paying attention to, so you'll be able to make rapid initial progress on it, which *feels* like a good opportunity to invest. At some point, though, you'll find that the work needs support, and it's quite challenging to get support for work that a company is built to ignore or devalue. Your early wins will slowly get eroded by indifference and misalignment, and your initial impact will be reclaimed by the sands of time.

Does this mean you shouldn't do inclusion work? No, that's not the conclusion I want you to take away from this. Sometimes an area that an organization doesn't pay attention to is so important that you're going to want to advocate for it to start paying attention. Teaching a company to value something it doesn't care about is the hardest sort of work you can do, and it often fails, so you should do as little of it as you can, but no less. As a senior leader, you have an ethical obligation that goes beyond maximizing your company-perceived impact, but it's important to recognize what you're up against and time your efforts accordingly.

Foster growth

One area that's often underinvested in (e.g., lots of room to work in) while also being highly leveraged is growing the team around you. *Hiring* has a lot of folks involved in it, usually in terms of optimizing the hiring funnel[30], but onboarding, mentoring, and coaching are wholly neglected at many companies despite being *at least* as impactful as hiring to your company's engineering velocity[31].

If you start dedicating even a couple of hours a week to developing the team around you, it's quite likely that will become your legacy long after your tech specs and pull requests are forgotten.

Edit

A surprising number of projects are one small change away from succeeding, one quick modification away from unlocking a new opportunity, or one conversation away from consensus. I think of making those small changes, quick modifications, and short conversations as *editing* your team's approach.

With your organizational privilege, relationships you've built across the company, and ability to see around corners derived from your experience, you can often shift a project's outcomes by investing the smallest ounce of effort, and this is some of the most valuable work you can do.

It's particularly valuable because it's quick, it's easy, it's highly motivating for both you and the person you help, and it's hugely impactful when done well. (Also, it's highly demotivating when done poorly, so your approach matters!)

Finish things

One special sort of editing is helping finish a project that just can't quite close itself out. Often you'll have a talented engineer earlier in their career who is already doing the work but can't quite create buy-in or figure out how to rescope their project into finishable work. It's surprisingly common that coaching a teammate on how to tweak a project into something finishable and then lending them your privilege to budge the right friction points will transform a six-month slog into a two-week sprint with almost an identical impact.

We only get value from finishing projects[32], and getting a project over the finish line is the magical moment it goes from risk to leverage. Time spent getting work finished is always time well spent.

What only you can

The final category of work that matters is the sort that you're uniquely capable of accomplishing. Sure there's work that you're faster at or better at than some other folks, but much more important is the sort of work that simply won't happen if you don't do it.

This work is an intersection of what you're exceptionally good at and what you genuinely care about. It might be writing your company's technology strategy[33] that folks *will actually follow*, it might be convincing a great candidate to join, it might be changing your CEO's mind on how you pay down tech debt, it might be crafting a discerning API[34].

Whatever it is, things that simply won't happen if you don't do them are your biggest opportunity to work on something that matters, and it's a category that will get both narrower and deeper the further you get into your career.

Why it matters

Suppose you're interviewing for a new role twenty years into your career. Will the folks interviewing you understand your real impact on any of your previous projects or companies? No, I guarantee they won't. Instead, you'll find yourself judged by a series of surprisingly subjective measures: your accumulated prestige, the titles you've had and companies you've worked at, your backchannel reputation, and how you present in your interview process.

You can't escape subjective interview practices, but you can deliberately accumulate expertise from doing valuable work. Indeed, that's the only viable long-term bet on your career: focus on work that matters, do projects that develop you, and steer towards companies that value genuine experience.

Writing engineering strategy

> *I kind of think writing about engineering strategy is hard because good strategy is pretty boring, and it's kind of boring to write about. Also I think when people hear "strategy" they think "innovation" - Camille Fournier*[35]

Few companies understand their engineering strategy and vision. One consequence of this uncertainty is the industry belief that these documents are difficult to write. In some conversations, it can feel like you're talking about something mystical, but these are just mundane documents. The reality is that good engineering strategy is boring and that it's *easier* to write an effective strategy than a bad one.

To write an engineering strategy, write five design documents, and pull the similarities out. That's your engineering strategy. To write an engineering vision, write five engineering strategies, and forecast their implications two years into the future. That's your engineering vision.

If you can't resist the urge to include your most brilliant ideas in the process, then you can include them in your prework. Write all of your best ideas in a giant document, delete it, and never mention any of them again. Now that those ideas are out of your head, your head is cleared for the work ahead.

Durably useful engineering strategy and vision are the output of iterative, bottom-up organizational learning. As such, all learning contributes to your organization's strategy and vision, but your contribution doesn't have to be so abstract. Even if you're not directly responsible for that work, there are practical steps that *you* can take to advance your organization's strategy and vision, starting *right now*.

When and why

Before diving into the recipe for creating effective strategies and visions, a good starting question is, "When and why should I actually create them?" Strategies are tools of proactive alignment that empower teams to move quickly and with confidence. Strategies allow everyone–not just the empowered few–to make quick, confident decisions that might have otherwise cost them a week of discussion. Strategies are also the bricks that narrow your many possible futures down enough that it's possible to write a realistic vision. If you realize that you've rehashed the same discussion three or four times, it's time to write a strategy. When the future's too hazy to identify investments worth making, it's time to write another vision. If neither of those sound like familiar problems – move on to other work for now and return later.

Write five design docs

Design documents describe the decisions and tradeoffs you've made in specific projects. Your company might call them RFCs or tech specs. Stranger names happen, too; Uber bewilderingly called them DUCKS until they later standardized on RFC[36]. A good design document describes a specific problem, surveys possible solutions, and explains the selected approach's details. There are many formats to pick from; a few places to start your thinking are Design Docs, Markdown, and Git[37], Design Docs at Google[38], and Technical Decision-Making and Alignment in a Remote Culture[39].

Whether a given project requires a design document comes down to personal judgment, but I've found a few rules useful. You should write design documents for any project whose capabilities will be used by numerous future projects. You should also write design documents for projects that meaningfully impact your users. You should write a design document for any work taking more than a month of engineering time.

A batch of five design docs is the ideal ingredient for writing an effective strategy because design documents have what bad strategies lack: detailed specifics grounded in reality. It's easy for two well-meaning engineers on the same team to interpret an abstract strategy in different ways, but it's much harder to stay misaligned when you're implementing a specific solution.

A few recommendations as you write:

- **Start from the problem.** The clearer the problem statement, the more obvious the solutions. If solutions aren't obvious, spend more time clarifying the problem. If you're stuck articulating the problem, show what you have to five people and ask them what's missing: fresh eyes always see the truth.
- **Keep the template simple.** Most companies have a design document template, which is a great pattern to follow. However, those templates are often expanded to serve too many goals. Overloaded templates discourage folks from writing design documents in the first place. Prefer minimal design document templates that allow authors to select the most useful sections and only insist on exhaustive details for the riskiest projects.
- **Gather and review together, write alone.** It's very unlikely that you personally have all the relevant context to write the best design document on a given topic. Before getting far into the process, collect input from folks with relevant perspectives, particularly those who will rely on the output of your design document. However, be skeptical of carrying that collaborative process into writing the design document itself. Most folks are better writers than they are editors. This means it's usually harder to edit a group document into clear writing than to identify one author to write a clear document. Gather perspectives widely but write alone. Just be careful not to fall in love with what you've written

until *after* you've reviewed it with others.
- **Prefer good over perfect.** It's better to write a good document and get it in front of others than it is to delay for something marginally better. This is particularly valuable to keep in mind when giving feedback on other folks' designs; it's easy to fall into the trap of expecting their designs to be just as good as your best design. Particularly as you become more senior, it's toxic to push every design to meet the bar of your own best work. Focus on pushing designs to be good, rather than fixating on your own best as the relevant quality bar.

It takes a lot of practice to write great design documents. If you want to improve yours, my best advice is to reread your designs *after* you've finished implementing them and study the places where your implementation deviated from your plan–what caused those deviations? Oh, and of course, just keep writing more of them.

Synthesize those five design docs into a strategy

After your organization has written five design documents, sit down and read them all together. Look for controversial decisions that came up in multiple designs, particularly those that were hard to agree on. A recent example of mine was getting stuck debating whether Redis was appropriate as durable storage or only as a cache. Rather than starting from zero in each design document review, wouldn't it be easier if we reviewed our recent decisions about using Redis, reflected on how we made those decisions and wrote them down as a strategy?

Good strategies guide tradeoffs and explain the rationale behind that guidance. Bad strategies state a policy without explanation, which decouples them from the context they were made. Without context, your strategy rapidly becomes incomprehensible–why did they decide this?–and difficult to adapt as the underlying context shifts. A few interesting strategies to read while thinking about writing your own are A Framework for Responsible Innovation[40] and How Big Technical Changes Happen at Slack[41].

If you're a Good Strategy, Bad Strategy[42] convert–and that book has wholly transformed how I think about strategy–then you'll note this definition of strategy is the "diagnosis" and "guiding policies" sections, deferring "coherent action" to the design documents.

My best advice for writing a strategy document is:

- **Start where you are.** Working on strategy, it's easy to be paralyzed by the inherently vast ambiguity we work in, but you've just got to dive in and start writing. Waiting for missing information doesn't work: every missing document is missing for a good reason. Whatever you write will need to change, and if you write something particularly bad, you'll quickly realize the need to change it. Where you are now is always the best place to start.
- **Write the specifics.** Write until you start to generalize, and then stop writing. If you can't be specific, wait until you've written more design documents. Specific statements create alignment; generic statements create the illusion of alignment.
- **Be opinionated.** Good strategies are opinionated. If they aren't opinionated, then they won't provide any clarity on decision making. However, being opinionated on its own isn't enough. You also need to show your work.
- **Show your work.** In math classes growing up, you had to show your work to get full credit. Here too, you must show the rationale behind your opinions. Showing your work builds confidence in the first version of a document, but even more importantly, by showing your work, you make it possible for others to modify and extend your work as the underlying context shifts.

Some of the best strategies you write may at the time feel too obvious to bother writing. "When should we write design documents?" is a strategy worth writing. "Which databases do we use for which use cases?" is a strategy worth writing. "How should we stage our migration from monolith to services?" is worth writing, too. As we leave behind the idea of strategy as demonstrations of brilliance, we can start to write far more of them, and we can write them more casually. If it ends up not being used, you can always deprecate it later.

Extrapolate five strategies into a vision

As you collect more strategies, it'll become increasingly challenging to reason about how the various strategies interact. Maybe one of your strategies is to Run less software[43] and rely more on cloud solutions, but another one of your strategies is to prefer offloading complexity to the database whenever possible. How do you reconcile those strategies if you identify a database that would allow you to offload a great deal of complexity, but that isn't offered by your cloud vendor?

Take five of your recent strategies, extrapolate how their tradeoffs will play out over the next two to three years. As you edit through the contradictions and weave the threads together, you've written an engineering vision. The final version will give you what Tanya Reilly[44] calls a robust belief in the future[45], which makes it easier to understand how your existing strategies relate to each other and simplifies writing new strategies that stand the test of time.

For a useful vision, a few things to focus on are:

- **Write two to three years out.** Companies, organizations, and technology all change quickly enough that thinking too far into the future is fraught. It also doesn't work if you write a vision that expires in six months–how many strategies would you realistically write within that six-month window? Try to focus on two to three years out; you can expand that horizon a bit if you're a fairly established company.

- **Ground in your business and your users.** Effective visions ground themselves in serving your users and your business. That tight connection keeps the vision aligned with your leadership team's core values–users and business. Bad visions treat technical sophistication as a self-justifying raison d'être–a view that is never shared by your company's leadership.
- **Be optimistic rather than audacious.** Visions should be ambitious, but they shouldn't be audacious. They should be possible, but the best possible version if possible. Do write what you could accomplish if every project is finished on time and without major setbacks. Don't write what you think would be possible with infinite resources.
- **Stay concrete and specific.** Visions get more useful as they get more specific. Generic statements are easy to agree with but don't help reconcile conflicting strategies. Be a bit more detailed than you're comfortable with. Details in visions are often illustrative rather than declarative, giving a taste of the future's flavor rather than offering a binding commitment.
- **Keep it one to two pages long.** The reality is that most people don't read long documents. If you write something five or six pages long, readers will start dropping off without finishing it (or will skim it very rapidly without engaging with the details). Force yourself to write something compact, and reference extra context by linking to other documents for the subset of folks who want the full details.

After you finish writing your vision, the first step folks usually take is sharing it widely across the engineering organization. There is so much work behind the vision–five design docs for each strategy, five strategies for one vision–it's hard *not* to get excited when you're done. So excited that it's easy to get discouraged, then, when the response to your strategy will almost always be muted. There are a few reasons for the muted response. First, the core audience for your vision is folks writing strategies, which is a relatively small cohort. Second, a great vision is usually so *obvious* that it bores more than it excites.

Don't measure vision by the initial excitement it creates. Instead, measure it by reading a design document from two years ago and then one from last week; if there's marked improvement, then your vision is good.

Managing technical quality

> *I feel particularly impactful when I can help improve a proposal that's well-intentioned and solves a real need, but the team that drafted it lacks either experience or context to write a good plan to capture the opportunity. In such cases, having a well-structured plan can help substantially reduce the scope while getting to most of the value, and thus demonstrate impact sooner. - Dmitry Petrashko*

If there's one thing that engineers, engineering managers, and technology executives are likely to agree on, it's that there's a crisis of technical quality. One diagnosis and cure is easy to identify: our engineers aren't prioritizing quality, and we need to hire better engineers or retrain the ones we have. Of course, you should feel free to replace "engineers" with "product managers" or "executives" if that feels more comfortable. It's a compelling narrative with a clear villain, and it conveniently shifts blame away from engineering leadership. Still, like most narratives that move accountability towards the folks with the least power, it's both unhelpful and wrong.

When you accept the premise that low technical quality results from poor decision-making, you start looking for bad judgment, and someone at the company must be the culprit. Is it the previous CTO? Is it that Staff engineer looking at you with a nervous smile? Is it everyone? What if it's none of those folks, and stranger yet isn't even your fault either?

In most cases, low technical quality isn't a crisis; it's the expected, normal state. Engineers generally make reasonable quality decisions when they make them, and successful companies raise their quality bar over time as they scale, pivot, or shift up-market towards enterprise users. At a well-run and successful company, most of your previous technical decisions won't meet your current quality threshold.

Rather than a failure, closing the gap between your current and target technical quality is a routine, essential part of effective engineering leadership.

The problem

As an engineering leadership team, your goal is to maintain an appropriate technical quality level while devoting as much energy as possible towards the core business. You must balance quality across multiple timeframes, and those timeframes generally have conflicting needs. For example, you'll do very different work getting that critical partnership out the door for next week's deadline versus building a platform that supports launching ten times faster next quarter.

Just as your company's technical quality bar will shift over time, your approach to managing technical quality will evolve in tandem:

1. fix the **hot spots** that are causing immediate problems
2. adopt **best practices** that are known to improve quality
3. prioritize **leverage points** that preserve quality as your software changes
4. align **technical vectors** in how your organization changes software
5. **measure technical quality** to guide deeper investment
6. spin up a **technical quality team** to create systems and tools for quality
7. run a **quality program** to measure, track and create accountability

As we dig into this toolkit of approaches, remember to pick the cheapest, most straightforward tool likely to work. Technical quality is a long-term game. There's no such thing as winning, only learning and earning the chance to keep playing.

Ascending the staircase

There's a particular joy in drilling into the challenge at hand until you find a generalized problem worth solving. However, an equally important instinct is solving the current situation quickly and moving on to the next pressing issue.

As you think about the right quality improvements to make for your team and organization, it's generally most effective to start with the lightest weight solutions and only progress towards massive solutions as earlier efforts collapse under the pressure of scale. If you can't get teams to adopt proper code linting, your attempts to roll out a comprehensive quality program are doomed. Although the latter can be more effective at scale, they're much, much harder to execute.

So, do the quick stuff first!

Even if it doesn't work, you'll learn more and more quickly from failing to roll out the easy stuff than failing to roll out the hard stuff. Then you'll get to an improved second iteration sooner. Over time you will move towards comprehensive approaches, but there's no need to rush. Don't abandon the ease, joy, and innocence of early organizations for the perils of enterprise-scale coordination without proper need.

It's convenient to present these phases as a linear staircase to be ascended, but that's rarely how real organizations use them. You're more likely to fix a quality hot spot, roll out a best practice, start running an architecture review, abolish that architecture review, and go back to hot-spotting for a bit. Premature processes add more friction than value and are quick to expose themselves as ineffective. If something isn't working, try for a bit to make it work, and then celebrate its demise.

Hot spots

When confronted by a quality problem, the first instinct is often to identify a process failure that necessarily requires a process solution. If a deployment causes an outage, it's because the author didn't correctly follow the code test process, so now we're going to require tests with every commit – that'll teach those lazy developers!

There's the old joke about Sarbannes-Oxley: it doesn't reduce risk; it just makes it clear who to blame when things go wrong. Unfortunately, that joke applies without humor to how many organizations roll out processes. Accountability has its role, but it's much more important to understand the problem at hand and try to fix it directly than to create process-driven accountability.

Process rollout requires humans to change how they work, which you shouldn't undertake lightly. Rather than reaching for process improvement, start by donning the performance engineer's mindset. Measure the problem at hand, identify where the bulk of the issue occurs, and focus on precisely that area.

The previous example of an untested deploy might benefit from giving direct feedback to the deploying engineer about changing their testing habits. Alternatively, maybe you're better served by acknowledging that your software design is error-prone and adopting the "define errors out of existence" approach described in A Philosophy of Software Design[46].

If you have a development velocity problem, it might be optimizing test runtimes, moving your Docker compile step onto a RAM disk[47], or using the techniques described in Software Design X-Rays[48] to find the specific files to improve.

Systems thinking[49] is the most transformative thinking technique I've encountered in my career. Still, at times it can be a siren beckoning you towards fixing a current system you may be better discarding.

Sure, you can roll out a new training program to teach your team how to write better tests, but alternatively, maybe you can just delete the one test file where 98% of test failures happen. That's the unreasonable effectiveness of prioritizing hot spots and why it should be the first technique you use to improve technical quality.

At some point, you're likely to find that your organization is creating quality problems faster than you're able to fix hot spots, and that's when it's time to move on to adopting best practices.

Best practices

I once worked at a company that didn't have a team planning process. Over time the head of engineering was increasingly frustrated with the inability to project target dates and mandated that we use Scrum[50]). After the mandate, a manager wrote the Scrum process on a wiki. There was an announcement that we were using Scrum. Managers told their teams to use Scrum. Mission accomplished!

Of course, no one started to use Scrum. Everyone kept doing what they'd done before. It's awkward to acknowledge mistakes, so the head of engineering declared adoption a major win, and no one had the heart to say differently.

This sad tale mirrors how many companies try to roll out best practices, and it's one of the reasons why best practices have such a bad reputation. In theory, organizations would benefit from adopting best practices before fixing quality hot spots, but I recommend practices after hot spotting. Adopting best practices requires a level of organizational and leadership maturity that takes some time to develop.

When you're rolling out a new practice, remember that a good process is evolved[51] rather than mandated. Study how other companies adopt similar practices, document your intended approach, experiment with the practice with a few engaged teams, sand down the rough edges, improve the documentation based on the challenges, and only then roll it out further. A rushed process is a failed process.

Equally important is the idea of limiting concurrent process rollouts. If you try to get teams to adopt multiple new practices simultaneously, you're fighting for their attention with yourself. It also makes it harder to attribute impact later if you're considering reverting or modifying one of the new practices. It's a bit draconian, but I've come to believe that you ought to limit yourself to a single best practice rollout at any given time. Channel all your energy towards making one practice a success rather than splitting resources across a handful.

Adopting a single new practice at a time also forces you to think carefully about which to prioritize. Selecting your next process sounds easy, but it's often unclear which best practices are genuinely best practice and which are just familiar or famous. Genuine best practice has to be supported by research, and the best source of research on this topic is Accelerate[52].

While all of Accelerate's recommendations are data-driven and quite good, the handful that I've found most helpful to adopt early are version control, trunk-based development, CI/CD, and production observability (including developers on-call for the systems they write), and working in small, atomic changes. There are many other practices I'd love to advocate for (who hasn't spent a career era advocating for better internal documentation[53]), but I don't trust my intuition like I once did.

The transition from fixing hot spots to adopting best practices comes when you're overwhelmed by too many hot spots to cool. The next transition, from best practices to leverage points, comes when you find yourself wanting to adopt a new best practice before your in-progress best practice is working. Rather than increasing your best practice adoption-in-progress limit[54], move on to the next tool.

Leverage points

In the Hotspotting section, we talked about using the performance engineer's mindset to identify the right problems to fix. Optimization works well for the issues you already have, but it's intentionally inapplicable to the future: the worst sin of performance engineering is applying effort to unproven problems.

However, as you look at how software changes over time, there are a small handful of places where extra investment preserves quality over time, both by preventing gross quality failures and reducing the cost of future quality investments.

I call those quality leverage points, and the three most impactful points are interfaces, stateful systems, and data models.

Interfaces are contracts between systems. Effective interfaces decouple clients from the encapsulated implementation. Durable interfaces expose all the underlying essential complexity and none of the underlying accidental complexity. Delightful interfaces are Eagerly discerning, discerningly eager.

State is the hardest part of any system to change, and that resistance to change makes *stateful systems* another critical leverage point. State gets complex faster than other systems and has an inertia that makes it relatively expensive to improve later. As you incorporate business obligations around security, privacy, and compliance, changing your stateful systems becomes even more challenging.

Data models are the intersection of the interfaces and state, constraining your stateful system's capabilities down to what your application considers legal. A good data model is rigid: it only exposes what it genuinely supports and prevents invalid states' expression. A good data model is tolerant of evolution over time. Effective data models are not even slightly clever.

As you identify these leverage points in your work, take the extra time to approach them deliberately. If it's an interface, integrate half a dozen clients against the mocked implementation. If it's a data model, represent half a dozen real scenarios. If it's stateful, exercise the failure modes, check the consistency behaviors, and establish performance benchmarks resembling your production scenario.

Take everything you've learned, and pull it into a technical specification document that you socialize across your team. Gather industry feedback from peers. Even after you begin implementation, listen to reality's voice and remain open to changes.

One of the hidden powers of investing in leverage points is that you don't need total organizational alignment to do it. To write a technical vision or roll out a best practice, you need that sort of buy-in, which is why I recommend starting with leverage points. However, if you've exhausted the accessible impact from leverage points, it may be time to move on to driving broader organizational alignment.

Technical vectors

Effective organizations marshal the majority of their efforts towards a shared vision. If you plot every technical decision as a vector on a grid, the more those vectors point in the same direction, the more you'll accomplish over time. Conversely, some of the most impressive engineers I've worked with created vectors with an extraordinary magnitude but a misaligned direction. Ultimately those engineers harmed their organizations in their attempts to lead it.

One sure-fire solution to align technical direction is to route all related decisions to the same person with Architect somewhere in their title. This works well but is challenging to scale, and the quality of an architect's decisions degrade the further they get from doing real work on real code in the real process. On the other extreme, you can allow every team to make independent decisions. But an organization that allows any tool is an organization with uniformly unsupported tooling.

Your fundamental tools for aligning technical vectors are:

- **Give direct feedback.** When folks run into misalignment, the first answer is often process change, but instead, start with simply giving direct feedback to the individuals who you believe are misaligned. As much as they're missing your context, you're missing theirs, and a quick conversation can often prevent years of unnecessary process.
- **Refine your engineering strategy** from tech spec, to strategy, to vision.
- **Encapsulate your approach in your workflows and tooling.** Documentation of a clear vision is helpful, but some folks simply won't study your document. Deliberate tools create workflows that nurture habits far better than training and documentation. For example, provisioning a new service might require going to a website that requires you to add a link to a technical spec for that service. Another approach might be blocking deploys to production if the service doesn't have an on-call setup established, with someone currently on-call, and that individual must also have their push notifications enabled.
- **Train new team members during their onboarding.** Changing folks' habits after they've formed is quite challenging, which is frustrating if you're attempting to get folks to adopt new practices. However, if you get folks pointed in the right direction when they join, then that habit-momentum will work in favor of remaining aligned.
- **Use *Conway's Law*.** Conway's Law argues that organizations build software that reflects their structure. If your organization is poorly structured, this will lead to tightly coupled or tangled software. However, it's also a force for quality if your

organization's design is an effective one.
- **Curate technology change** using architecture reviews[55], investment strategies, and a structured process for adopting new tools. Most misalignment comes from missing context, and these are the organizational leverage points to inject context into decision-making. Many organizations start here, but it's the last box of tools that I recommend opening. How can you provide consistent architecture reviews without an articulated vision? Why tell folks your strategy after they've designed something rather than in their onboarding process?

Regardless of the approaches you use to align your technical vectors, this is work that tends to happen over months and years. There's no world where you write the vision document, and the org immediately aligns behind its brilliance. Much more likely is that it gathers dust until you invest in building support.

Most companies can combine the above techniques from hot-spot fixing to vector-alignment into a successful approach for managing technical quality, and hopefully, that's the case for you. However, many find that they're not enough and that you move towards heavier approaches. In that case, the first step is, as always, measurement.

Measure technical quality

The desire to measure in software engineering has generally outpaced our state of measurement. Accelerate[52] identifies metrics to measure velocity, which are powerful for locating process and tooling problems, but these metrics start *after* the code's been merged. How do you measure your codebase's quality such that you can identify gaps, propose a plan of action, and evaluate the impact of your efforts to improve?

There are some process measurements that correlate with effective changes. For example, you could measure the number of files changed in each pull request on the understanding that smaller pull requests are generally higher quality. You could also measure a codebase's lines of code per file, on the assumption that very large files are generally hard to extend. These could both be quite helpful, and I'd even recommend measuring them, but I think they are at best proxy measurements for code quality.

My experience is that it *is* possible to usefully measure code quality, and it comes down to developing an extremely precise definition of quality. The more detailed you can get your definition of quality, the more useful it becomes to measure a codebase, and the more instructive it becomes to folks hoping to improve the quality of the area they're working on. This approach is described in some detail in Building Evolutionary Architectures[56] and Reclaim unreasonable software[57].

Some representative components to consider including in your quality definition:

- What percentage of the code is statically typed?
- How many files have associated tests?
- What is test coverage within your codebase?
- How narrow are the public interfaces across modules?
- What percentage of files use the preferred HTTP library?
- Do endpoints respond to requests within 500ms after a cold start?
- How many functions have dangerous read-after-write behavior? Or perform unnecessary reads against the primary database instance?
- How many endpoints perform all state mutation within a single transaction?
- How many functions acquire low-granularity locks?
- How many hot files exist which are changed in more than half of pull requests?

You're welcome to disagree that some of these properties ought to exist in *your* codebase's definition of quality: your definition should be specific to your codebase and your needs. The important thing is developing a precise, measurable definition. There will be disagreement in the development of that definition, and you will necessarily change the definition over time.

After you've developed the definition, this is an area where instrumentation can be genuinely challenging, and instrumentation is a requirement for useful metrics. Instrumentation complexity is the biggest friction point for adopting these techniques in practice, but if you can push through, you unlock something pretty phenomenal: a real, dynamic quality score that you can track over time and use to create a clarity of alignment in your approach that conceptual alignment cannot.

With quality defined and instrumented, your next step is deciding between investing in a *quality team* or a *quality program*. A dedicated team is easy to coordinate and predictable in its bandwidth and is generally the easier place to start.

Technical quality team

A *technical quality team* is a software engineering team dedicated to creating quality in your codebase. You might call this team Developer Productivity, Developer Tools, or Product Infrastructure. In any case, the team's goal is to create and preserve quality across your company's software.

This is not what's sometimes called a quality assurance team. Although both teams make investments into tests, the technical quality team has a broader remit from workflow to build to test to interface design.

When you're bootstrapping such a team, start with a fixed team size of three to six folks. Having a small team forces you to relentlessly prioritize their roadmap on impact and ensures you'll maintain focus on the achievable. Over time this team will accumulate systems to maintain that require scaling investment, Jenkins clusters are a common example of this, and you'll want to size the team[58] as a function of the broader engineering organization. Rules of thumb are tricky here, but maybe one engineer working on developer tooling for every fifteen product engineers, in addition to your infrastructure engineering investment.

It's rare for these teams to have a product manager, generally one-or-more Staff-plus engineers, and the engineering manager partner to fill that role. Sometimes they employ a Technical Program Manager, but typically that is after they cross into operating a *Quality program* as described in the next section.

When spinning up and operating one of these teams, some fundamentals of success are:

1. **Trust metrics over intuition.** You should have a way to measure every project. Quality is a complex system, the sort of place where your intuition can easily deceive you. Similarly, as you become more senior at your company, your experience will no longer reflect most other folks' experiences. You already know about the rough edges, and you'll be the first person in line to get help if you find a new one, but most other folks don't. Metrics keep you honest.

2. **Keep your intuition fresh.** Code and process change over time, and your intuition is going stale every week you're away from building product features. Most folks find that team embedding and team rotations are the best way to keep your instincts relevant. Others monitor chat for problems, as well as a healthy schedule of 1:1 discussions with product developers. The best

folks do both of those and keep their metrics dashboards handy.

3. **Listen to and learn from your users.** There is a popular idea of "taste level," which implies that some folks simply know what good looks like. There is a huge variance in folks who design effective quality investments, but it isn't an innate skill. The best folks focus on deeply understanding what their users are trying to accomplish *and* prioritize user needs over implementation constraints.

   Adoption and usability of your tools are much more important than raw power. A powerful tool that's difficult to use will get a few power users, but most folks will pass it by. Slow down to get these details right. Hide all the accidental complexity[59]. Watch an engineer try to use your tool for their first time without helping them with it. Improve the gaps. Do that ten more times! If you're not doing user research on your tools, then you are *doomed* as a quality investment team.

4. **Do fewer things, but do them better.** When you're building for the entire engineering organization, anything you do well will accelerate the overall organization. Anything you do poorly, including something almost great with too many rough edges, will drag everyone down. Although it's almost always true that doing the few most important things will contribute more than many mediocre projects, this is even more true in cases where you're trying to roll out tools and workflows to your entire organization (the organizational process-in-progress limits still apply here!).

5. **Don't hoard impact.** There's a fundamental tension between centralized quality teams and the teams that they support. It's often the case that there's a globally optimal approach preferred by the centralized team, which grates heavily on a subset of teams that work on atypical domains or workloads. One repre-

sentative example is a company writing its backend servers in JavaScript and not allowing their machine learning engineers to use the Python ecosystem because they don't want to support two ecosystems. Another case is a company standardized on using REST/HTTP2/JSON for all APIs where a particular team wants to use gRPC instead. There's no perfect answer here, but it's important to establish a thoughtful approach that balances the benefits of exploration against the benefits of standardization[60].

A successful technical quality team using the above approaches will be *unquestionably* more productive than if the same number of engineers were directly doing product engineering work. Indeed, discounted developer productivity (in the spirit of discounted cash flow[61]) is the theoretically correct way to measure such a team's impact. Only theoretically, because such calculations are mostly an evaluation of your self-confidence.

Even if you're quite successful, you'll always have a backlog of high-impact work that you want to take on but don't have the bandwidth to complete. Organizations don't make purely rational team resourcing decisions, and you may find that you lack the bandwidth to complete important projects and likewise can't get approval to hire additional folks onto your team.

It's a good sign when your team has more available high-impact work than you can take on: if you aren't selective about which projects to take on, then you're not thinking broadly enough. This means you shouldn't necessarily try to grow your technical quality team if you have a backlog. However, if you find that there is critical quality work that you can't get to, then it may be time to explore starting a *quality program*.

Quality program

A *quality program* isn't computer code at all, but rather an initiative led by a dedicated team to maintain technical quality across an organization. A quality program takes on the broad remit of achieving the organization's target level of software quality. These are relatively uncommon, but something similar you've probably encountered is an incident program responsible for a company's incident retrospectives and remediations.

The technical components of running a quality program are the sorts of things discussed above, so here we'll focus on managing a program effectively. Your first step is to find a technical program manager who can co-lead the program and operate its mechanics. While you can make considerable progress on an organizational program's informational aspects without a technical program manager; however, it's a trap. You'll be crushed by the coordination overhead of solo-driving a program in a large organization.

Operating organizational programs is a broad topic about which much has been written[62], but the core approach is:

1. **Identify a program sponsor.** You can't change an organization's behavior without an empowered sponsor. Organizations behave the way they do because it's the optimal solution to their current constraints, and you can't shift those constraints without the advocacy of someone powerful.

2. **Generate sustainable, reproducible metrics.** It's common for folks running a program to spend four-plus hours a week maintaining their dataset by hand. This doesn't work. Your data will have holes in it, you won't be able to integrate your data with automation in later steps, and you'll run out of energy to do the work to effect real change; refreshing a metrics dashboard has no inherent value.

3. **Identify program goals for every impacted team and a clear path for them to accomplish those goals.** Your program has to identify specific goals for each impacted team. For example, reducing test flakiness in their tests or closing incident remediations more quickly. However, it's essential that you provide the map to success! So many programs demand participation from other teams without providing clear directions on how they can accomplish their part. The program owner is the subject matter expert, don't offload your strategy to every team to independently reinvent.

4. **Build the tools and documentation to support teams towards their goals.** Once you've identified a clear path for teams to accomplish your program goals, figure out how you can help them make those changes! This might be providing "golden examples" of what things ought to look like, or an example pull request refactoring a challenging section of code into the new pattern. It might be providing a test script to verify the migration worked correctly. It might be auto-generating the conversion commit to test, verify, and merge without having engineers write it themselves. Do as much as you possibly can to avoid every team having to deeply understand the problem space you're attempting to make progress in.

5. **Create a goal dashboard and share it widely.** Once you have your program goals communicated to each team, provide dashboards that help them understand their current state, their goal state, and that give reinforcing feedback on their (hopeful) progress along the way. The best dashboard is going to be both a scorecard for each team's work and also provide breadcrumbs for each team on where to focus their next efforts.

    There are three distinct zoom-levels that your dashboard should support. The fully zoomed-out level helps you evaluate your program's impact. The fully zoomed-in level helps an individual team understand their remaining work. A third level between the two helps organizational leaders hold their teams accountable (and supports your program sponsor in making concrete, specific asks to hold those leaders accountable).

6. **Send programmatic nudges for folks behind on their goals.** Folks are busy. They won't always prioritize your program's goals. Alternatively, they might do an amazing job of making your requested improvements but backtrack later with deprecated practices. Use nudges to direct the attention of teams towards the next work they should take towards your program's goals. Remember, attention is a scarce resource! If you waste folks' time with a nudge email or ping, they won't pay attention to the next one.

7. **Periodically review program status with your sponsor.** Programs are trying to make progress on an organizational priority that doesn't naturally align with the teams' goals. Many teams struggle to break from their local prioritization to accomplish global priorities. This is where it's essential to review your overall progress with your sponsor and point them towards the teams that prioritize program work. Effectively leveraging your sponsor to bridge misaligned prioritization will be essential to your success.

In a lot of ways, a program is just an endless migration, and the techniques that apply to migrations work for programs as well[63].

If you get all of those steps right, you're running a genuinely great program. This might feel like a lot of work, and wow, it is: a lot of programs go wrong. The three leading causes of failed programs are:

1. running it purely from a process perspective and becoming detached from the reality of what you're trying to accomplish,

2. running it purely from a technical perspective and thinking that you can skip the essential steps of advocating for your goal and listening to the folks you're trying to motivate,
3. trying to cover both perspectives as a single person–don't go it alone!

A bad program is a lot like an inefficient non-profit: the goal is right, but few funds reach the intended goal. No matter how you decide to measure technical quality, the most important thing to always remember when running your quality program is that the program isn't the goal. The goal is to create technical quality. Organizational programs are massive and build so much momentum that inertia propels them forward long after they've stopped working. Keep your program lean enough to cancel, and remain self-critical enough to cancel if it ceases driving quality creation.

Start small and add slowly

When you realize your actual technical quality has fallen considerably behind your target technical quality, the natural first reaction is to panic and start rolling out a vast array of techniques and solutions. Dumping all your ingredients into the pot, inevitably, doesn't work well, and worse, you don't even know which parts to keep.

If you find yourself struggling with technical quality–and we all do, frequently–then start with something small, and iterate on it until it works. Then add another technique, and iterate on that too. Slowly build towards something that genuinely works, even if it means weathering accusations of not moving fast enough. When it comes to complex systems and interdependencies, moving quickly is just optics. It's methodical movement that gets the job done.

Stay aligned with authority

> *In my role, we'll often go weeks without being in the same room together, but I still have to operate as if I'm his direct proxy. So I go into a room and think, "What would Matthew do here? What is the question he would want to ask? What guidance has he given on this problem?" Because I can't always run back to him for clarification, it's essential to develop and maintain a deep understanding of his world view. That's essential for me to retain the very deep trust required to be his representative and effectively carry out his strategy and vision. People need to be confident that I'll always give the same answer that Matthew would give if he were there. -Rick Boone*

It's a common misconception that authority makes you powerful. Many folks aspiring towards more senior roles assume they'll finally get to do things their way. They believe that the title inherently creates flexibility and autonomy. They believe that the friction holding them back will burst into a whirl of butterflies that scatter into the wind.

The reality is a bit more nuanced.

Titles come with the sort of power called organizational authority, and that variety of authority is loaned to you by a greater organizational authority. What's bestowed can also be retracted, and retaining organizational authority depends on remaining deeply aligned with the bestowing sponsor, generally your direct manager. To remain effective within a Staff-plus role, you have to learn the art of staying aligned with organizational authority.

Beyond the safety net

Retire your remaining expectations that the company is designed to set you up for success. Now *you* are one of the people responsible for setting the company, your team, and your manager up for success.

Most mature technology companies succeed in creating a predictable promotion pipeline from folks joining early in their careers up through attaining the Senior engineer title. The process of getting a Staff title is generally more complex than preceding titles but usually navigated with the support of your engineering manager. Throughout this pipeline, you may become comfortable with your manager guiding your development and providing a safety net for your continued success. After reaching a Staff role, your safety net will cease to exist, or at best, the safety net will be short enough that you're quite capable of jumping past it and into the awaiting chasm. This will be increasingly true as you go further into Senior Staff and Distinguished engineer roles.

Staff-plus roles are leadership roles, and in leadership roles, the support system that got you here will fade away. Often abruptly, you're now expected to align the pieces around you for your own success.

Serving at the pleasure of the President

When Rick Boone described his role as Strategic Advisor to the Vice-President of Infrastructure at Uber, he compared his role to Hand of the King in *Game of Thrones*, and Leo McGarry from *The West Wing* who frequently remarked, "I serve at the pleasure of the President." In both those examples, authority flows from the tight association with greater authority, and it's a great mental model for operating in a Staff-plus role. This can be a difficult transition from previous roles where your authority primarily accumulated through your personal actions and impact over time.

If you and your manager have worked together for years, then you've already performed a subtle, subterranean sort of alignment over that time. In other cases, a new executive will join who is familiar with supporting these roles and will bring a deliberate map of how they want to work together. However, both of those circumstances are largely out of your control, so it's valuable to develop your own approach to aligning upward with your manager.

To align with your manager, some areas to focus on are:

- **Never surprise your manager.** Nothing destroys trust faster than surprising your manager. Steering a large organization often involves juggling several projects and problems in your head at once, and surprises threaten the juggler's rhythm. Large or frequent surprises also call into question whether a leader is truly taking responsibility for their organization. In general, treat each time you surprise your manager as an incident to be learned from and endeavor to prevent repeats.
- **Don't let your sponsor surprise you.** Most folks have extremely high expectations of their managers, assuming, for example, that they will always remember to relay information relevant to your current work. Managers try to do this, some of them are excellent at it, and others are not particularly good. If your manager isn't great at this, you should certainly give them feedback, but you should also take proactive action to facilitate information flow. This might be weekly email updates[64] or a Slack thread within your team's channel sharing your focuses for the week. During 1:1s, dig for the feedback! Ask if there are other areas you should be focused on and how your current priorities align with your manager's. If you continue to surprise each other, then identify the controls[65] you'll use to partner together.
- **Feed your manager's context.** If the first step is avoiding surprising your manager with your own actions, the next step is to help your manager not get surprised by the wider organization. If teams are frustrated by a new policy or your internal tools aren't

scaling with needs, proactively feed that to your manager. Be clear that you're *not* bringing them a problem to solve, rather conveying information you believe will be useful. Opinions are helpful, but even more helpful is data when you can find it.

Sometimes you'll hear someone disparage a colleague, saying that they're excellent at "managing up." There are certainly destructive ways to manage up where someone controls information to hide problems or misrepresent circumstances, but at its core, managing up is about increasing bandwidth and reducing friction between you and your manager. Cultivating a deliberate partnership with your manager will go far further than practicing disappointment when they don't meet your expectations.

Influencing without too much friction

Part of growing as a leader in developing your own perspective on how the world should work, and you can't reach the Staff-plus level without that perspective. Having a clear sense of how things ought to work sharpens your judgment and enables you to act proactively. As you reach this next step of leadership, you increasingly have to merge your vision with those held by more senior organizational leaders.

Your first approach to solving this problem might be replacing your vision with another leader's vision, and that approach works for some, but for many, it means stepping away from the perspective that facilitated their success as a proactive leader with strong judgment. Instead, I recommend sharpening your awareness of the distinctions between the values that you hold and those that the organization operates under and find a way to advocate for them without getting kicked out of the room[66].

People can only change so quickly, and organizations are made of people. If you're deliberate in your approach, you'll be able to influence your organization's leaders immensely over time, but you'll only get that time if you learn to remain in tight alignment at each step along the way.

To lead, you have to follow

> *It's about taking that global thinking and applying it locally. That means aligning your team's (technical) initiatives/roadmaps to the Engineering-wide technical strategy; and being intentional about when you veer off of that path to serve the needs of your team's immediate stakeholders. That means collaborating with your team's managers in adopting successful practices in hiring, onboarding, and production operations from other teams; and sharing practices from your team that would be beneficial for others. That means taking context from company-wide business/product strategy and translating that to how it impacts your team's immediate projects - Ras Kasa Williams*

Years ago, the company I was working with hired a new Director of Engineering, and the CTO was talking about why the new Director was an amazing hire. The new Director's clinching accomplishment? The best ever explanation of the distinction between leadership and management. This turned out not to be a particularly effective way to evaluate hires, but it is an interesting topic.

Defining leadership and management is such heavily trodden terrain that it's hard to add much to it, but roughly management is a specific profession, and leadership is an approach one can demonstrate within any profession.

The way I think about leadership has evolved a bit over the last few years, though, coming to focus on two specific attributes. First, leaders have a sufficiently refined view of how things *ought to work* such that they can rely on their distinction between how things *are* and how they *ought to be* to identify proactive, congruent actions to narrow that gap. Second, they care enough about the gap to actually attempt those narrowing actions.

If you only see the gap without acting on it, you might be a visionary, but you're inert. If you take action without a clear view of the goal, many will consider you a leader, but your impact will be random, arbitrary, and inefficient. Combining both with some luck is likely to take you a long way in your career, and these are characteristics common in folks I've worked with who successfully navigate the transition into Staff-plus engineering or senior management roles.

But this sort of leadership can only take you so far, and personally, it took me *years* of blundering to understand why my approach to leadership created so much early success for me when first joining a company but slowly eroded how my contribution was received over time. The lesson that I slowly learned was that you couldn't be an effective long-term leader until you learn how to follow.

I think this is the most important lesson I've learned over the past few years: the most effective leaders spend more time following than they do leading. This idea also comes up in the idea of the "the first follower creates a leader[67]," but effective leaders don't split the world into a leader and follower dichotomy, rather they move in and out of leadership and follower roles with the folks around them.

There are many ways to put this approach into practice.

1. Be clear with yourself what your true priorities are, and don't dilute yourself across everything that comes up. If there's something you disagree with but only in a minor way, let others take the lead figuring it out. A helpful question here is, "Will what we do here matter to me in six months?" If it won't, take the opportunity to follow.
2. Give your support quickly to other leaders who are working to make improvements. Even if you disagree with their initial approach, someone trustworthy leading a project will almost always get to a good outcome. If someone trustworthy is leading

a project, and you're still uncomfortable letting them move forward, consider why you lack confidence in your ability to influence them and if you're bad at giving feedback.
3. Make your feedback explicitly non-blocking. This can be classifying a code review comment as an "optional nit," but it can also be writing up detailed feedback but delivering it to someone mentioning that you wanted to share your perspective rather than necessarily change their approach.

If this is something you've struggled with, I'm sympathetic. I've struggled with it too. When you have a strong enough worldview to lead, you'll start to collect others around you who rely on you maintaining that world's physics, and tolerating any deviation from your vision can feel like you're letting them down. But this is the epitome of something that'll get you to one level of success but block the next: continued growth requires learning to incorporate your worldview into the worldviews of those around you, accelerating overall progress around you even if it means tolerating a detour from your vision.

What you can accomplish alone is far from what you can accomplish by creating leaders. To be a great leader, take your time learning to follow.

Learn to never be wrong

> *I present what I think is the best case for us, and people can disagree with that. And, you know, they often do. I'm steering and influencing more than saying, "I've got the authority to just tell you what to do." I've never seen that style work well. - Keavy McMinn*

Most folks have worked with someone who thinks they're never wrong. In each discussion, they lean in, broaden their shoulders and breach their way into the role of the decider. They'll continue debating until their perspective wins the day or time runs out. They are often right, but right in a way that sucks the oxygen out of the room. As their tenure at a company increases, they may fancy that they've become very persuasive, but frequently it's a form of persuasion characterized by the resignation of their peers.

A few of the technical leaders that I've worked with have found a way to never be wrong without dominating the room. To be right while creating space for others. Someone who has always embodied this approach for me is Franklin Hu[68], who I've seen reliably disarm contentious discussions with his commitment to finding the best outcome for everyone, willingness to leave his starting position and the default assumption that there's always an additional piece of context that reconciles seemingly conflicting perspectives into a unified view.

To become a senior technical leader, you must build a deep perspective on technology and architecture. To operate as such a leader, you must then develop an equally deep pragmatism and agnosticism to technical religion to remain skeptical of yourself. This can feel like a paradox, but it's the line you'll need to walk every day.

Listen, clarify and read the room

A lot of times, you'll see engineers go into a discussion confident that their perspective is right and with the goal of getting other folks in the room to agree with their approach. This mentality turns each meeting into a zero-sum debate. Even in the "best case" that their approach is agreed upon, they didn't get to learn from anyone else in the room, and it's unlikely that the rest of the room is leaving energized.

The most effective engineers go into each meeting with the goal of agreeing on the problem at hand, understanding the needs and perspectives within the room, and identifying what needs to happen to align on an approach. They approach each meeting as one round within the broader context of the project and their relationships with the folks in the room. If the room is ready to agree and move forward on a solution, they land the team on that approach. If the room isn't ready, they don't force it to happen.

To get good at this, you need to master three approaches: listen through questions, define the purpose, and know how to read the room.

Listening through questions is a form of active listening with the goal of understanding the rest of the room's perspectives. The act of asking good questions with good intent opens up a conversation, creating space and safety for others to ask their own questions. Good questions are asked with the desire to learn, and they are specific. They sharpen the conversation. They free the answerer from the obligation to defend their position. In a potentially contentious meeting, ask three good questions before you share your perspective, and you'll see the room shift around you.

Good meetings start from a clear purpose and agenda, but many meetings don't meet that definition, particularly ad-hoc discussions. If you ever find yourself in a conversation with an unclear goal, then **define**

the purpose. Take a moment to ask if your understanding of what the group hopes to accomplish is correct. This works best as a statement wrapped in a clarifying question along the lines of, "Just to check, our goal here is to decide whether to postpone launching the project by two weeks?"

Note that defining the purpose can be disruptive if it's used too frequently. Rather than helping to clarify the conversation, in that case, it creates conversational churn. For the most part, try to avoid using it if someone else has already made an attempt. Meetings with multiple failed reframings almost always end with scheduling another meeting.

Finally, in each meeting, you have to **read the room**. Oftentimes folks get frustrated with a conversation and try to force agreement, which creates so much pressure on the discussion that it's unlikely to conclude well. If the folks in the room are too far apart, then identify a subgroup who are able to spend more time digging into it together or identify an appropriate party to escalate to outside of the room. If there's simply too much stuff in the drawer, stop trying to shove it shut.

How to practice

If these behaviors don't come naturally to you, that's okay; the opportunity to practice is all around. Every comment on a document is an opportunity. Every meeting is an opportunity. Every pull request is an opportunity.

Start each week by picking one of these skills you want to explicitly use in the meetings you head into. If you have a particularly difficult meeting come up, spend some time practicing in your head or with a peer how you might use these approaches to facilitate forward progress despite the challenges.

Jerks

The above approach works well most of the time, but not always, and one of the notable exceptions is when you're dealing with a jerk. In this case, a jerk is someone who withholds their consent from the group, isn't willing to compromise, or doesn't listen. This is someone who hasn't learned that their career depends more on being easy to involve than being technically correct.

The two most effective ways to deal with jerks are:

1. including someone they can't be a jerk to in the meeting (like their manager or the CTO)
2. investing heavily into aligning with them before the meeting, so they feel heard and are less likely to derail the discussion

Both of these can feel ridiculous to spend your time on, but they're what tends to work best, especially if it's a jerk you interact with infrequently. If it's someone in an area that you're responsible for or someone you work with frequently, then you have a somewhat different set of obligations. In that case, give them the feedback as kindly as you can while still being honest. Give it a second time. Document both, and if you don't see an improvement, then communicate the concerns to their manager, including the specific documentation, in a face to face or video discussion.

It's also useful to recognize that the authority created by your title shelters you from many of these folks, so whoever you're experiencing is being less of a jerk to you than they are to others. If the behavior feels borderline for you, it's potentially more egregious for others.

How it helps

This approach is powerful because more complex projects get derailed by personal conflict than by technical complexity, and this is a repeatable way to replace tension with partnership. It feels like it's slow because it can take longer to get started, but ultimately it's fast because you're more likely to complete the work without disruption.

In addition, longevity as a senior leader is just as much about maintaining your relationships as it is about standout successes. You'll see a bunch of folks who burn bright for a while but later lack the support to make forward progress. If you want to avoid that fate, learn to never be wrong and never stop practicing.

Create space for others

> *At this point, I spend less time advocating for specific technologies or programs and more time empowering others to advocate for the technologies and programs that they think are important. I also try to be a source of knowledge and support that people can reach out to for feedback, especially on cross-cutting product decisions and on presentation of ideas to the rest of the organization. - Michelle Bu*

One of the best measures of your long-term success as a Staff-plus engineer is that the organization around you increasingly benefits from, **but doesn't rely upon**, your contributions. Because many folks reach their first Staff-plus role by being the "go-to" person for the organization, it can be a difficult transition from essential to adjacent.

This transition requires learning to deliberately create space for the team around you and comes down to actively involving them in discussions, decisions, and ultimately substituting sponsorship for repeating the successes that got you to Staff in the first place.

Discussions

When you're focused on maximizing your personal impact, a good discussion is one that ends quickly with a reasonable answer, alignment among the participants, and positive feelings among the participants. When you start thinking about creating space, the definition of a good discussion expands quite a bit!

This broader definition depends on getting more folks involved and getting to a good set of decisions without much of your own personal contribution. A good discussion is, in this new world, one that it turns out you didn't need to attend. When you make a key contribution, feel good about it, and then think about what needs to happen for someone else to make that contribution next time.

Along with the shift in mindset, there are a few techniques that I've found helpful in creating more space in discussions:

- Shift your contribution towards asking questions. Asking the right questions helps avoid missteps[69], but also makes it easier for more folks to contribute
- If you see someone in the meeting who isn't participating, pull them into the discussion. It works best to pull *exactly one* person at a time into the discussion. It gets confusing when you open it up broadly to everyone or even just try to pull two or three people at once
- Be the one to take notes. This helps destigmatize note-taking as "low status" and also frees up an alternative would-be notetaker to contribute more instead. It also gives you something to focus on other than speaking!
- If you realize someone's missing from the discussion who should be there, be the person to pull them into the next occurrence of the meeting. Talk with the meeting coordinator to let them know why it's valuable to include them

As you follow these more and more faithfully, your speaking in meetings will shrink, and your impact on the organization will grow.

Decisions

For so much of your career, success is making the right decision, and it takes a while to realize that at a certain point making the decisions isn't the work. Ritu Vincent described that transition well,

> *It was also on that project where my manager helped me understand that my first impulse as a tech lead didn't scale. Initially, I was thinking, "I'll break it into twenty pieces, assign out eighteen pieces, and keep the two hardest for myself," and my manager pushed me to delegate the hard pieces to the team to stretch*

and develop them.

On the other hand, it's hard to transfer your judgment to someone else, particularly around complex decisions. Fortunately, it's possible to take an incremental approach to shift increasingly complex and important decisions to your wider team.

- **Write it down.** There's a well-worn model of genius encapsulated in the Feynman algorithm: "1) Write down a problem. 2) Think very hard. 3) Write down the solution." This mystical view of genius is both unapproachable and discouraging. It's also unrealistic, but it's hard for folks to know it's unrealistic if we don't write down our thinking process for others to follow. By writing down the process of finding an answer, as well as the rationale for the answer, folks around us can begin to *learn from* our decisions rather than simply being *directed* by them
- **Circulate early,** and do it before you've crystallized on a decision. Most folks struggle to walk back from a formed opinion, and by gathering feedback early, it's much easier to incorporate feedback and involve folks in the decision-making process so they can see the trajectory of your thinking in addition to the final output
- **Separate style from substance,** and stop giving style feedback on other folks' decisions. If a piece of feedback won't meaningfully change a project's success, then consider not giving it. If it's useful but not critical, potentially make a private suggestion rather than pulling a meeting into your orbit
- **Don't try to show value**[70]. Some senior folks feel like they need to weigh in on everything to justify their seniority. Others require each decision to exactly mirror a similar decision they once made. Both of these center insecurity over impact and prevent others from growing as leaders
- **Change your mind.** One of the biggest signs of respect for your

coworkers is listening to them and then changing your mind afterward. If senior leaders don't change their mind, then soon everyone will correlate bluster with success

Involving folks in decisions you make and sharing your decision-making approach is a valuable component of growing the team around you, but what about making the decisions *theirs*?

Sponsorship

By including folks in your discussions and decisions, you involve them in your work. This is a great way to grow, involve, and learn from those around you, but at some point, you have to take the next step.

Instead of involving them in your work, make the work theirs.

This final step is sponsoring others for the kind of work that got you to a Staff-plus role. When critical work comes to you, your first question should become, "Who could be both successful with and grown by this work?" See if you can get them to lead the work, and then work with them to scaffold the project for their success. What would your approach be? What are some initial concerns they might want to think through? Who are the stakeholders they should discuss the problem with early?

When you identify new critical work, perhaps identifying a gap in your tooling or process, think about who else could be generating that work and then sit down with them to have them put together the proposal you planned to write. Then build support for their proposal just as you would have for your own.

Importantly, when the work becomes theirs, you have to let it be theirs. Councel, give advice, provide context, but ultimately sponsorship includes letting them take an approach that you wouldn't. It might end up going poorly, and they'll learn from that – just like you've learned from your mistakes over your career. It might end up going very well, and then you'll learn something instead.

While sponsorship should become your default approach to problems, it shouldn't be your only tool. Most Staff-plus engineers find it's important to remain directly involved in some projects to retain their context of how their software, tooling, and organization work in practice. If you need a rule of thumb, keep a sponsorship journal and ensure you're sponsoring others at least a few times a month – if you find yourself sponsoring less frequently than that, dig into what's stopping you.

Conversely, if you look back and can't think of anything you've worked on directly in the past few months, that's worth course-correcting too.

What if you don't?

If you've cemented the final cobblestones to a Staff-plus role by becoming the "go-to person" for a key company leader, then you've learned that solving an urgent problem for an organizational leader is one of the surest paths to recognition. If you've become the technical visionary whose ideas saturate the company's architecture roadmap, then you've learned how powerful it feels to operate the gate to your company's technical future.

It's hard to give those up.

However, the best case for this model is a company that thrives temporarily until that individual leaves[71]. The far more common worst case is a company constrained by your personal limitations, and the only company that can tolerate being constrained by you is a company that doesn't grow.

The only way to remain a long-term leader of a genuinely successful company is to continually create space for others to take the recognition, reward, and work that got you to where you're currently sitting. It can be surprisingly uncomfortable, but don't worry: there will always be new work for you anyway.

Build a network of peers

As I talked to more and more Staff-plus engineers about career advice, the most consistent recommendation was to develop a personal network of peers doing similar work. Not *every* person emphasized this approach, but more than half mentioned it, and for those who did, it tended to be their first and strongest recommendation.

Ritu Vincent said,

> *What's been most impactful for me is having a lot of people who I think of as mentors, usually friends, former managers, and folks that I've worked with. I have a decent number of recurring monthly lunches, coffee chats, and dinners with people who've worked with me in the past, know me, and I trust. It's those conversations about career challenges and growth that have gotten me to where I am in my career.*

Keavy McMinn mentioned her network as an important way to get honest feedback,

> *The thing that springs to mind is to find your peers or support network. Just like management, it gets lonely the higher up you go, and it's important to find peers that will still challenge you, and you can brainstorm ideas with. It doesn't even matter if they're in your similar area of work or even are in different companies.*

Nelson Elhage similarly shared,

> *It's also been really valuable for me to cultivate a good personal network of other senior engineers. I chat with them informally about whatever it is that we're working on and thinking about. When you have personal connections, you can get very unvarnished views of the problems people are seeing and the solutions they're considering.*

While it's helpful to know you *should* build a network, some folks struggle to figure out how to do it. Among the various tactics to build your network[72], the two most common strategies are: being easy to find and networking internally.

Be visible

There is so much pent-up demand for community among Staff-plus engineers that the easiest way to build your network is being easy to find as a Staff-plus engineer. One effective approach is contributing to the discussion around Staff-plus engineering itself, like Joy Ebert'z What a Senior Staff Software Engineer Actually Does or Keavy McMinn's Thriving on the Technical Leadership Path[73]. Although there are a good number of folks who've written up their view on the Staff-plus role, each one brings a new, valuable perspective. There's room for your words on the topic.

If writing isn't your jam, there's room for your voice, and speaking at tech conferences is another effective way to become visible in the broader community. Keavy McMinn described her motivation for conference speaking as,

> Mostly, I enjoyed the people I met at conferences. Later the speaker networks led to job opportunities for me.

If those both feel high-stakes, even starting a Twitter account or joining a couple of related Slacks (for example, *#staff-principal-engineering* in the Rands Leadership Slack[74]) can be a good start.

Internal networks, too

Rather than focusing on public speaking and writing, Katie Sylor-Miller's networking advice was to build your internal network within your current company,

> *Networking, networking, networking, networking... You have to be really cognizant of who you're talking to and make sure that you have connections across multiple teams and multiple groups to leverage those networks.*

Although it's easy to think of networking as something that only happens externally, it's often easier to do at the company you're already in, where it happens semi-organically and semi-deliberately over the course of your work. This approach has the added advantage of directly improving your day-to-day work as well. Longer-term, those folks will eventually leave and spread across the industry, bootstrapping your broader network. This works *really* well when you're at a decently large or prestigious company and is a bit less effective as your current company gets smaller or less prestigious.

Ambient networks

Among the folks who didn't mention developing a personal network, most mentioned creating an ambient network of learning based on keeping current with industry books and following industry leaders on social networks, particularly Twitter.

Diana Pojar's comment was

> *I use Twitter extensively, but I'm mostly a consumer and follow many people in tech. I usually follow people that I saw talking at conferences, or I worked with, and I find their content relevant to me. Here's a couple, in no specific order: Camille Fournier[75], Lara Hogan[76], Josh Wills[77], Vicki Boykis[78], David Gasca[79], Julia Grace[80], Holden Karau[81], John Allspaw[82], Charity Majors[83], Theo Schlossnagle[84], Jessica Joy Kerr[85], Sarah Catanzaro[86], Orange Book[87].*

Damian Schenkelman mentioned,

> *I try to follow people on Twitter who I think are doing interest-*

ing things and from who I can learn. There are so many people doing interesting things and so much to learn! Some of the names that come to mind: including [Aphyr[88], Tanya Reilly, and David Fowler[89]].

If the idea of building a network this way feels uncomfortable then building an ambient network can be a good starting step in the right direction. That said, you'll find the personal network more impactful, and finding an authentic way to build one is an important step towards reaching and remaining impactful in senior roles over the long arch of your career.

Quality over quantity

A coworker once told me the story of someone determined to make their name in Business Development, who would fly from SF to NYC with a list of people they wanted to meet. They'd look for tweets and Foursquare check-ins for where those people might be that night, go there, buy a drink, and pretend to serendipitously meet them. On a good night, they'd try to meet six or more new connections this way.

It goes without saying that you shouldn't do that – it's a total violation of boundaries. Further, doing this doesn't even make sense: when it comes to building a network of peers, the volume doesn't matter. Instead, focus on slowly building with folks you genuinely trust, respect, and are inspired by. That's what'll create a truly powerful network to help you solve the hardest problems and trickiest situations that come your way.

Finally, if you've reached this paragraph and really want to build a network but just aren't sure how to get started, I'll share what's worked for me as an introvert who struggled to craft an authentic approach. Find someone you respect and send them a short 1-2 paragraph email or DM with a specific question asking for advice. If they reply, thank them and send another question in six to twelve months. If they subsequently ask you for a favor or question, do what you can to help. If they don't reply, don't worry about it; just move on without comment. This works surprisingly well, and the worst thing that can happen is totally fine: they'll just never reply.

Present to executives

Have you presented to company executives about a key engineering initiative, walking into the room excited and leaving defeated? Maybe you only made it to your second slide before unrelated questions derailed the discussion. Maybe you worked through your entire presentation only to have folks say, "Great job," and leave without any useful debate. Afterward, you're not quite sure what happened, but you know it didn't go well.

Early in your career, you probably won't interact with company executives frequently. Sure, if it's a small enough company, you might, but it isn't the norm. As you get further into your career, though, increasingly, your impact will be constrained by your ability to influence executives effectively. While staying aligned with authority is a prerequisite to influencing executives, there are also some new communication skills for you to develop.

Why this is hard

Everyone has worked with a terrible executive at some point in their career, but most executives aren't awful. Almost all executives are outstanding at *something*; it's just that often that *something* isn't the topic you're communicating about with them. When you combine that lack of familiarity with your domain with limited time for the topic at hand, communication is a challenge.

Those are garden-variety communication challenges, though, and communicating with executives can be unexpectedly difficult for a less apparent reason: the executive has become accustomed to consuming reality preprocessed in a particular way.

Any given executive is almost always uncannily good at one way of consuming information. They feel most comfortable consuming data in that particular way, and the communication systems surrounding them are optimized to communicate with them in that one way. I think of this as preprocessing reality, and preprocessing information the wrong way for a given executive will frequently create miscommunication that neither participant can quite explain.

For example, some executives have an extraordinary talent for pattern matching. Their first instinct in any presentation is to ask a series of detailed, seemingly random questions until they can pattern match against their previous experience. If you try to give a structured, academic presentation to that executive, they will be bored, and you will waste most of your time presenting information they won't consume. Other executives will disregard anything you say that you don't connect to a specific piece of data or dataset. You'll be presenting with confidence, knowing that your data is in the appendix, and they'll be increasingly discrediting your proposal as unsupported.

In most other scenarios, miscommunication creates latency rather than errors. Still, when you're communicating with executives, you'll often not get a second chance to discuss a given topic before the relevant decision is made. Invest ahead of the discussion to avoid lamentations afterward.

How to communicate effectively

The foundation of communicating effectively with executives is to get a clear understanding of why you're communicating with them in the first place. You might be used to communicating with folks to change their mind or inform them about your project, but that's probably not the case here. When you're communicating with an executive, it's almost always one of three things: planning, reporting on status, or resolving misalignment.

Although these are distinct activities, your goal is always to extract as much perspective from the executive as possible. If you go into the meeting to change their mind, you'll probably come across as inflexible. Go into the meeting to understand how you can align with their priorities. You'll come across as strategic and probably leave with enough information to adapt your existing plan to work within the executive's newly articulated focuses or constraints.

The best way to extract their perspective is by writing a structured document. Writing forces you to think comprehensively about your beliefs and data. The structure ensures you focus the reader on what's important. Barbara Minto, whose The Pyramid Principle[90] is the most influential work on effective business communication, is also a big fan of structure:

> *Controlling the sequence in which you present your ideas is the single most important act necessary to clear writing. The clearest sequence is always to give the summarizing idea before you give the individual ideas being summarized. I cannot emphasize this point too much.*

There are many structures that can work, but I'd particularly recommend every document's opening paragraph follow the SCQA format:

- **Situation**: what is the relevant context? *Example*: We've been falling behind our competition in shipping product features for two years. Last year, we doubled our engineering team but shipped fewer features than the year before.
- **Complication:** why is the current situation problematic? *Example*: We plan to double our engineering team again this year, but based on last year's experience, we think that will decrease velocity further while significantly increasing our organizational budget.
- **Question:** what is the core question to address? *Example:* Should we keep moving forward with our plan to double engineering this year?

- **Answer:** what is your best answer to the posed question? Example: We should stop hiring for the next six months and focus on gelling our existing team. Based on progress at that point, we should refresh our hiring plan for the remainder of the year.

In many discussions, a well-structured opening paragraph is enough to spark an important conversation. Although in those cases, you might not discuss the rest of your document, the process of writing the document is still an important step in refining your thinking.

Relatively few folks employ a formal structure for the entirety of their document, but there is at least one popular format that some folks find valuable: Minto's Pyramid Principle from the aforementioned book. Start by brainstorming your proposal into a series of arguments that support your answer. Once you've written them all down, group them into related arguments. Shape those groups into three top-level arguments, with up to three sub-arguments supporting each of those top-level arguments. Recursively apply this approach, ensuring each argument summarizes its at-most-three sub-arguments. Order the arguments within each group by descending importance. At that point, you're done.

Although I personally found SCQA immediately useful, I'll admit that when I first tried to follow the Pyramid Principle, it gave me the same emotional response as staring at Brutalist architecture. It's grown on me with practice, but I'd still recommend most folks start by adopting SCQA as a core practice and only adopt the entirety of the Pyramid Principle if you get feedback that your presentations are hard to follow.

After you've written your structured document, gather feedback on it from your peers and stakeholders. Aligning with stakeholders before your presentation, sometimes called nemawashi[91], is extremely effective at reducing surprises. Some of your peers should have experience presenting to the executives and will have useful feedback on improvements.

For the presentation itself, set a clear agenda, but don't focus on rote conformance. A great meeting with executive leadership is defined by engaged discussion, not addressing every topic on the agenda. Some will consider this a controversial position, preferring to measure every meeting by its action items, but this ignores the often more valuable relationship establishment and development aspects of these meetings.

Mistakes to avoid

Even if you do a great job preparing for your execution presentation, these things sometimes go wrong. There's nothing you can do that will avoid every bad path, but you can avoid most of the anti-patterns that routinely sink these meetings.

Never fight feedback. It's very common for an executive to have a critical piece of feedback but to not quite have the right framing to communicate it within the moment. You want them to deliver the feedback anyway, not hold it back and probably forget to give it later. If you show up as resistant to feedback, then they'll start swallowing their comments, and you'll get relatively little out of the meeting. Focus on gathering feedback; don't worry about whether you agree with it until you have more time afterward. If there's a decision that needs to be made that you disagree with, then you should inject one or two pieces of relevant data that might change their mind, but afterward, let it go. You'll be more effective by reflecting on the feedback and changing their mind later than continuing to push back within the meeting.

Don't evade responsibility or problems. Many folks try to hide issues from their leadership, and this always goes poorly. Successful folks look at informing executives as absolution: once it's on the table, you can move towards solving it rather than hiding it. This is particularly true if an executive sniffs out a problem during a meeting. Lean into the feedback, don't evade it. You will create more credibility by agreeing with their perspective and following up with more data later. You will harm your credibility by arguing with them about it.

Don't present a question without an answer. A frequent piece of advice given to new leaders is to "never bring your manager a problem without a solution." That's not generally great advice, but if you present a problem to an executive without a proposed answer, then in the back of their mind, they're wondering if they need to hire a more senior leader to supplement or replace you. You can't create alignment in the room unless you have a proposal for folks to align behind.

Avoid academic-style presentations. The way you're taught to present about topics in school is more-or-less the entirely wrong approach for presenting to executives. The *Minto Pyramid Principle* will steer you in the right direction if you follow its scripture.

Don't fixate on your preferred outcome. It's very common for folks to get so caught up on the outcome that they want that they spend their energy resisting the clear, unavoidable signs that it isn't going to happen that way. It's very easy to get frustrated about the "wrong" decision getting made, but it's helpful to keep in mind that there is a great deal of context that you're missing. There is no such thing as a permanent decision: almost every decision will be reconsidered multiple times over the next two years.

Presenting to executives can be intimidating, and this might be more advice than helpful. If you want to boil it all down to one concise tip: send an early draft to an executive attending the meeting and ask them what to change. If you listen to and apply that feedback, you'll figure out the other pieces as you go.

Getting the title where you are

The best advice I've heard is that often reaching Staff is a combination of luck, timing, and work. - Bert Fan

Most technology companies have a "career level," which is intended to be the highest level that most folks achieve. Senior engineer is the career level at most companies. While you might get let go for not moving from entry-level engineer to mid-level engineer quickly enough, most companies have no expectation that you'll ever go from Senior to Staff. Six years at mid-level? Ah, that's a problem. Twenty years at Senior? Sure, that's fine.

More than the expectation of progress going away, companies' promotion systems will often impede your further progress once you attain the career level. Sometimes the folks who already have Staff engineer titles are protective of diluting their prestige. In other cases, organizations may be wary of having multiple Staff engineers on a single team due to team health or budgetary concerns. However, I think the strongest source of friction is that the nature of the job changes. A Staff engineer isn't a better Senior engineer, but someone who's moved into fulfilling one of the Staff archetypes.

Even after you've developed the prerequisite skills to become a Staff engineer, there will still be one last hurdle: getting your company to grant you the Staff title. For some, this process is a relative non-event, perhaps taking one or two cycles longer than anticipated but ultimately succeeding, and for others, it may not happen at all at their current company. About two-thirds of the Staff engineers I surveyed attained their title as a promotion at the company they were already working at, and the remaining third changed companies to attain the title.

If pursuing that sort of role *is* your goal, then take the promotion to your career level as an opportunity to reset your approach to navigating your career. From that point onward, there is no standard path to follow. The promotion and performance system will no longer be designed around attaining a timely promotion and may, at times, take on the feel of gatekeeping.

To go further, *you* will have to take more deliberate control of your progression, and this chapter shares the tools that have worked for folks who've made the progression ahead of you.

Finding your trail

If you've been relying on your manager to steer your career up to this point, the transition to a self-directed career can feel rather abrupt. There are many books about managing your software career[92], but most focus from your first job until you reach Senior engineer. Few focus on managing your career beyond the Senior title, which is where this chapter focuses:

- Your **promotion packet** is your foundational tool to demystify the Staff promotion, prioritize the right personal development to ensure you get there and activate your internal sponsors and network in support of your progression
- There is a widespread belief that moving into a Staff-plus role requires successfully completing a **Staff project**. This section discusses the reality that most Staff engineers *do not* have a Staff project but also describes how to approach one if you're at a company that does require them
- A frequent complaint from engineers is that they're not "in the

room" where decisions happen, and they're usually right: there is a room, and they're not in it. What's less frequently acknowledged is that you're probably not in the room for a good reason. This section describes **how to get into the room, and also how to stay there**

- Finally, you won't get promoted if your company's leadership doesn't know who you are. How do you **become visible internally** without hogging all the oxygen?

Apply these techniques consistently, and you'll be on the way towards a Staff title, although even the best-laid plans falter if you're conducting them at the wrong company.

Opportunity is unevenly distributed

One inconvenient reality you'll encounter in pursuit of a Staff role is that opportunity at any given company is unevenly distributed. If your company leadership views infrastructure engineering as inherently "more complex" or "more leveraged" than product engineering, then opportunity will consolidate within infrastructure teams. If you work in an organization that emphasizes shipping features, then it will be easier to be rewarded for fixing an outage you cause than preventing future outages. Your work will be more visible if you work in your company's headquarters than in a distributed office[93].

Many companies believe they have a vested interest in pretending opportunity is evenly distributed, even when it clearly isn't. This makes it hard to have conviction these dynamics exist, but the trends become clear as you collect more data.

Once you recognize these challenges, you have to assess how fixable they are and where you want to prioritize your energy. It's much simpler to align your approach with these unspoken currents rather than reroute the river creating them. If you choose to address the causes of inequality, start by finding a senior sponsor who supports the cause. You can only change a system with sponsorship from within.

Should you try management?

Most folks who reach Staff-plus roles **do not** spend time in engineering management, but some do. It's easy to view this as a critical, life-changing decision, but that's probably overthinking it a bit. If you want to give management a try, you should. Most companies understand that management isn't the right role for everyone and will be glad to let you rotate back into an engineering role.

Those that try management gain a broader perspective that helps them even when they move back into a software engineering role. This was Dan Na's experience,

> *I still enjoy both shipping code and running teams, and I think the ability to do both at a high level is critical for long-term engineering success. Charity Majors has a fantastic blog post on this topic that I recommend reading: "The Engineer/Manager Pendulum[94]". Charity argues that "manager career path vs engineering career path" is a false dichotomy, and taking time to alternate between both roles makes you better at both. This maps to my own experience. I'm a better manager because I know how terrible it is to be an IC on a poorly planned project, and I'm a better IC because I know how and when to sound an alarm when a project is going poorly.*

Ritu Vincent shared a similar perspective,

> *I do pendulum a decent amount because I'm interested in so many things on both sides of the career ladder. I'm interested in growing people, I really like working with recruiting, I'm one of those engineers that actually enjoy interviewing, I like understanding how teams grow. But I also really like writing*

code, and after I spend some time managing, I want to get back into the code and hack around a little bit.

Some folks try management and end up hating it. Joy Ebertz didn't care for engineering management much,

> *I actually managed for about a year and a half in the middle of my time at Box and found that I hated it (you can find more about that in my blog post on that topic[95]). That said, I found that there is actually a lot of overlap between management and staff+ roles in most companies.*

Even though Joy hated her management experience, she felt it might have helped her longer-term career,

> *It's possible that if I hadn't taken a meander through management, I would have gotten to Staff sooner. That said, I don't regret doing it, and I learned a lot about how people think, how organizations are run, and how larger projects are prioritized. All of these have continued to help me do my job on the IC track and likely helped me further get promoted to Senior Staff. While I do think it's distinctly possible that it slowed down when I got to Staff, I'm actually less sure for the next level - I think there's a real chance I would have hung out at Staff longer without it. All of this is to say that even though I didn't take the most direct route, I still learned a lot that has helped me out long term.*

The final caveat I'd give for someone considering this switch is that people management is bigger than simply maximizing your trajectory to a Staff engineer role. You'll have a profound impact on the folks you support as a manager, and if you take it on with the wrong motivations, you'll regret the experience, but not nearly as much as your team will. If you're motivated to help your team grow and succeed, then go ahead and do it; if you're only doing it for yourself, then don't.

A semi-permeable boundary

As a final caveat, Staff-plus titles are leadership positions. It's uniquely challenging to gain a leadership position if the existing leadership team doesn't identify with you as a potential member. What that means is, unfortunately, folks with the privilege of *seeming like* they are already part of the existing leadership team have a much easier time making the transition.

If you read through this chapter and become increasingly frustrated that you're *already* doing everything here, then it's possible that you're experiencing that structural disadvantage. Roughly half the women I spoke with had to change companies to attain the Staff title, whereas promotion friction come up less frequently during discussions with men.

Don't ignore those experiences–they're real and many folks feel stymied by them–but also take hope that there are many successful role models out there regardless of how you identify and how you want to plot your course towards Staff engineer.

Promotion packets

Some folks think of their promotion packet as the capstone of reaching a Staff-plus role, but I've seen many folks succeed by taking the opposite approach: starting to write their first Staff promotion packet long before they think they're likely to be promoted to Staff, much the way they might use a brag document[96]. Used this way, your packet becomes the map to accomplishing your goal.

It's likely your company will have its own format for promotion packets, and *eventually* you'll need to translate your packet into that format before it's submitted to an internal promotion committee or process, but there's no need to rush it. You'll spend more time relying on it as a guide than as a formal artifact for official review, so optimize for the former.

For traversing towards your Staff-plus promotion, a general template format that's useful is:

- What are your Staff projects? What did you do? What was the project's impact (including a well-defined goal[97])? What made this project complex? Keep it very short and then link out to supporting design documents
- What are the high-leverage ways you've improved the organization?
- What is the quantifiable impact of your projects? (Did you increase revenue by $10 million? Did you reduce year-on-year customer support tickets by 20%?)
- Who have you mentored and through what accomplishments?
- What glue work[98] do you do for the organization? What's the impact of that glue work?
- Which teams and leaders are familiar with and advocates for your work? What do they value about your work? One sentence, include data (e.g. survey data) when possible

- Do you have a real or perceived skill or behavior gaps that might hold you back? For each, how would you address the concern? One sentence each

It's useful to spend some time to write out those answers yourself, but getting promoted into a leadership role isn't a solo activity – it's something you can only accomplish with a team of folks supporting you along the way.

The approach that I recommend for iterating on your packet is:

1. **Answer why you're doing this**. Many folks choose not to pursue the Staff level; you should have a reason why this is important to you. If you don't, you're liable to find yourself in a role you don't enjoy.

   Michelle Bu warns, *"My first piece of advice to engineers is that they should avoid pattern matching in ways that lead them towards work they don't enjoy. I'm deeply energized by the work I do, partnering with teams to solve abstract modeling and design problems. It takes a certain amount of fortitude to try again and again after many rounds of feedback. To be honest, it's not for everyone. If you're more focused on hitting Staff than on setting yourself up to do work that energizes you, it's easy to end up stuck in a role you don't want."*

2. **Temper your expectations.** Promotions, especially at this level, are built over quarters, halves, and years. Avoid the expectation of instant results

3. **Bring your manager into the fold.** Bring the *promotion packet* to your next 1:1 with your manager, and tell them that attaining a Staff promotion is a goal of yours. Review the empty packet with them, and ask them what's missing, what to emphasize, and if they'd recommend adding steps to the workflow. Your goal is to ensure they know this is something you're interested in and to solicit their guidance on your approach.

Ritu Vincent suggests, *"People frequently come to me and ask, 'What should I do next to reach Staff?' One of the things that I tell them is to be super open and honest with their manager about what you want from your career. A mistake I made early on in my one-on-ones was telling my manager what I thought they wanted to hear, instead of what I actually felt."*

4. **Write the *promotion packet*.** Sit down for an hour and throw all your ideas together in a first version

5. **Edit the *promotion packet*.** Wait two days, reread your *promotion packet* and edit for content, clarity, and context

6. **Edit the *promotion packet* with peers.** Share your *promotion packet* with several trusted peers to get feedback, preferably peers already in a Staff-plus role. Peers are often better at identifying your strengths and contributions than you are, and they are closer to your work than your manager might be

7. **Edit the *promotion packet* with your manager.** Share your *promotion packet* with your manager and request feedback. Ask for a particular focus on enumerating gaps to address. Ask if you can spend time in the following 1:1 discussing the kinds of projects and opportunities to both address gaps and make the packet stronger

8. **Periodically review the *promotion packet* with your manager.** Continue to review the promotion packet with your manager during your career and performance-oriented 1:1s. Both you and your manager should use it to steer you towards demonstrating the promotion criteria over time. This is particularly important to do if your direct manager changes. Maintaining this sort of document and reviewing it across managers will help mitigate the loss of progress towards your promotion that often occurs after a manager change

If you methodically follow this advice, then you'll put together your first Staff promotion packet long before you're nominated for promotion. From there, you'll use the packet to focus your attention and your partnership with your manager towards that goal. It won't necessarily get you there quickly, and it even might not get you there at your current company, but it will consolidate your energy on the development and work that'll move you towards your goal.

When it finally does come time to write your formal packet, it'll be a matter of editing down what you've collected into the official template rather than an archival process of dusting through years of effort. Hopefully, nothing goes awry in the promotion process[99], and a Staff title follows.

Find your sponsor

> *Having a sponsor was also definitely important. My manager and I had a fantastic relationship, and I also had a great relationship with my skip-level manager. I think that played a big part as well. - Ritu Vincent*

As I've spoken with more folks trying to reach their first Staff-plus role, most folks run into similar challenges. Many have miscalibrated their own impact and simply haven't done the work yet to operate at that level: a Staff engineer isn't just a faster Senior engineer. However, there's a large cohort who have done the work–they're visible across their organization and have pulled together a strong promotion packet–but are still struggling to have that work recognized.

These folks are often frustrated by the distance between their impact and their recognized impact and ask their managers and peers for feedback on closing that gap. They're told to complete a staff project or to create space for others. For folks who haven't done the work yet, this is great advice, but for folks who have these checkboxes are a distraction: what they're really missing is a sponsor willing to push for the recognition of their existing work.

It's common to view promotion systems through the lens of other systems that have evaluated us throughout our lives such as school, but this falsely frames performance evaluation as a solo activity. Whether your company does ad-hoc promotions or uses a calibration process, promotions are a team activity and as Julia Grace, then of Slack, advised me once during a job search, "Don't play team games alone, you'll lose."

Finding your sponsor

The most important member of the team guiding your promotion is you yourself. The second most important person is your organizational sponsor. Lara Hogan has written on sponsorship at length, but roughly this is the person speaking up for your work in forums of influence and when advocating for constrained resources (like the budget for salary increases).

While you'll likely have a variety of sponsors, in the context of getting promoted—especially to a Staff-plus role—this almost always needs to be your direct manager. They'll be the person to take your drafted promotion packet and turn it into the company's format. They'll be the person to advocate for your promotion during a calibration meeting as others drill into your qualifications. They'll also be the person who has to have an honest conversation with you about the gaps you still have before you're a strong promotion candidate.

While you'll always need your direct manager engaged as your sponsor, you may need additional sponsorship. If your manager has never promoted someone to a Staff-plus role before, they're likely going to get surprised or make a misstep along the way. Invest in establishing a relationship further along your management chain. You don't need to spend much time with your skip-level manager, but if they aren't familiar enough with your work's impact to remember it in a meeting two months from now, you're unlikely to get promoted into a Staff role.

Activating your sponsor

The first step of activating your sponsors is explicitly sharing your goals. "I'm looking to be recognized as a Staff engineer" is a great start. Ritu Vincent mentioned this as her top advice for folks seeking Staff-plus roles,

> *People frequently come to me and ask, "What should I do next to reach Staff?" One of the things that I tell them is to be super open and honest with your manager about what you want from your career. A mistake I made early on in my one-on-ones was*

telling my manager what I thought they wanted to hear, instead of what I actually felt.

Once they've identified their sponsors, many folks see their work as complete: it's up to the sponsor to do the heavy lifting. This usually fails! Sponsors are folks with more organizational capital than bandwidth to deploy that capital, and they'll help you most when you align the pieces for them. Ask your sponsor how you can support their sponsorship. Owning your career isn't only about asking for things. It *is* about that, but it's much more about facilitating those things happening.

Reviewing your promotion packet collaboratively with your sponsors is a great way to facilitate this conversation. Focus on asking for what the gaps are in a way that doesn't prompt your sponsor to make up an answer. Most folks forget they can answer questions with, "I don't know," and instead make up unhelpful answers if you push them to answer questions they're uncertain about. If you keep getting answers like, "Work on larger, high impact technical projects," then you're asking in the wrong way, the wrong questions, or the wrong person.

One starting prompt is, "If I don't get promoted this cycle, what are some of the likely causes?" Another question worth asking is, "What's the most effective thing I can do to make myself a stronger candidate?" That said, the best questions are very specific and do a lot of the work for the answerer. Think about how hard it is to answer those questions compared to a question like, "This quarter I completed the API refactor, which I thought would demonstrate Staff-level work, but the schedule slipped a lot, and it ended up frustrating our product managers because their work got dropped. How could I have handled this project more effectively?" The latter question is much easier to give a useful answer to, even if the answerer isn't too familiar with the details of the project.

Finally, remember that activating your sponsor isn't a transactional thing to do once before your promotion. Build a relationship over time, and put in the work to help them when they need your support. Stay aligned with their initiatives. Suppose they need folks to join a working group, volunteer, and put in the work. These folks have a lot of people asking them for things, and they are pretty cognizant of folks who show up right before promotion time. I once had a colleague who rarely visited the office but *always* visited the office the week before promotion decisions were made. People noticed.

What if it doesn't work?

If you find yourself in a situation where you and your manager don't work together well, which isn't quite the same thing as *liking* each other, then you're not going to get promoted into a leadership role. Your manager has too direct an influence on your impact and your perceived impact for that to happen. Similarly, you might have an amazing relationship with your manager, who then leaves the company. You're hardly *doomed*, but your promotion clock will likely get reset as you build a relationship with your new manager. (Sometimes, this works out the other way, with your new manager working hard to prove themselves to you by advocating on your behalf.)

You'll cheat yourself if you immediately try to switch teams or companies after running into friction with your manager. Companies generally don't allow transfers unless your manager approves it, so you may burn a bridge to nowhere that you're standing on. More importantly, you'll lose the opportunity to develop your skill of working with folks you don't immediately click with: it's not a fun skill to develop, but leadership *always* involves influencing and building relationships with those with conflicting goals and styles.

If you've spent six months proactively trying to make the relationship work, then it probably is time to explore moving teams and to perhaps consider switching companies. This is one of many cases where it's extremely helpful to have developed your relationship with your skip-level manager, who can help you find a new team, even if you and your manager aren't working together effectively.

Staff projects

> *There isn't an explicit expectation, nor is it listed anywhere as a formal requirement, but it is understood that you'll complete a Staff Project to get promoted. I can't think of any Staff promotion that didn't include a really strong project, typically a multi-person project where the engineer was the Tech Lead. - Ritu Vincent*

A popular recurring idea around reaching a Staff-plus role is that first, you need to successfully complete a "Staff project." This is a project that is considered complex and important enough that the person who completes it has proven themselves as a Staff engineer. However popular this idea is, if you're pursuing a Staff-plus role, it's important to pierce the mythology of these projects and focus on the experiences of folks who've walked the path before you.

The short answer on Staff projects is that most engineers don't complete one as part of reaching a Staff role, although a large minority do complete one, particularly folks who attain the role via promotion at a company they've grown up in. For the folks who don't complete one, typically, it's either because they accumulated a track record of success over a longer period without a single capstone or because they switched companies to reach the title.

We'll dig into a few different angles on staff projects:

1. Folks who didn't complete Staff projects
2. Folks who did complete Staff projects, including where they don't end up working as planned
3. Identifying and approaching your Staff project

Into the messy details, we go.

No Staff project required

When I asked folks whether they had a Staff project, some of the answers were quite concise:

- Joy Ebertz, *"I actually didn't really have a Staff Project."*
- Diana Pojar, *"No, I did not have an assigned 'Staff Project,' and that is not something that is part of the promotion process at Slack."*

Some folks were even skeptical of the Staff project concept overall. Nelson Elhage said,

> *I'm instinctively a little bit wary of this sort of idea of a staff project, in part because one of the archetypes of Staff engineers that I've seen are people who don't necessarily run grand projects themselves or do big things. But just are sort of incredibly effective gurus and routers who make the whole engineering organization run better.*

There are also folks like Dan Na or Damian Schenkelman who took a detour through engineering management to reach the role. Damian describes bypassing the Staff project,

> *I did not. Because of how I grew at Auth0, I kind of "skipped that part". As a Director at a startup, I got the opportunity to technically lead a lot of big, critical initiatives, but there was no specific/explicit "staff/principal project."*

From these stories, it's clear that anyone who tells you that you *must* complete a Staff project to reach a Staff-plus title is wrong: there are many avenues to reach Staff-plus titles without doing a Staff project, with a stint in engineering management prominent among them.

Staff project required

However, it's also true that many companies require, or informally enforce, Staff projects for internal promotions, and consequently, many folks do take on a Staff project as part of their role transition.

Ritu Vincent describes her experience at Dropbox,

> *I definitely had a Staff Project. Back in the day, Dropbox was initially a consumer product that people downloaded and installed on their machines. When we launched Dropbox for Business, there was a request for both your personal and work Dropbox accounts to work simultaneously, including being able to switch across them without needing to log out and log back in. The initial implementation was written under immense time pressure, and it ran multiple Dropbox processes. One for your personal account and another for business. My Staff project was to make it so a single Dropbox process could run with multiple users logged in. The hard part was that the project stretched from the kernel all the way to the user interface. I had to understand every single layer of the Dropbox system. Initially, we thought it would take six months, and it ended up taking eighteen months. It took up most of the Desktop Client team's resources for quite a while.*

Ras Kasa Williams joined an inflight project that he later became the lead on, which served as his Staff project:

> *I joined Mailchimp as a Senior engineer. I was immediately added to a project team (which included an Engineering Director and two Principal engineers) meant to build out Mailchimp's first internal, self-service analytics platform. A key aspect of this project was being effective and executing at a high level. For better, or for worse, having two other Principal engineers meant expectations for me likely weren't that high. But I was able to jump in immediately and start contributing to core aspects of the project with very little hand-holding from them; by the end, I was one of the key contributors on the team.*

> *I would ultimately be formally installed as a tech lead to help continue shepherding that project work as it was absorbed into my current engineering group, Data Services.*

Few companies write down their Staff project requirements. They're more frequently the sort of "soft gate" that's brought up during a promotion meeting, sometimes to the surprise of both the manager and the would-be Staff engineer. The most reliable technique for uncovering these requirements is your "sure thing" promotion not getting approved, but that isn't much fun. Almost as reliable and much less frustrating is relying on the strategy of maintaining and getting feedback on your promotion packet well in advance of your promotion attempt.

Why you should do a Staff project

Sometimes it's hard to determine the precise line between gatekeeping and evaluation, and the premise of a Staff project exists in that hazy realm. Taking on a project of immense scope, navigating that ambiguity, and delivering it successfully is an effective way to distinguish folks who've reached Staff-plus impact, but it's also clear that many folks attain Staff-plus roles without completing such a project.

My advice is that although you can attain a Staff-plus role without completing a Staff project, they're a particularly valuable opportunity to develop yourself as an engineer. You will *personally* be stretched and grown by this kind of project in a way that you won't be by other varieties of Staff level work.

Keavy McMinn describes how her Staff project helped her,

> *I've never heard it given a name, but I understand the idea. I did lead and architect that type of project - solving gnarly engineering problems, with large impact for the company - a few times, but unfortunately, they didn't lead to me being pro-*

moted. They did lead to my career progression though. Those projects gave me the experience, knowledge, and confidence to position myself differently. Even to give public conference talks or know that "I've done X and could do X again."

Although each of these projects is different, there are a few typical characteristics that capture why they're so effective at stretching you as an engineer:

- **Complex and ambiguous** - early in your career, you're given well-defined problems, but as you get deeper into it, you'll increasingly encounter poorly defined or undefined problems, and Staff projects will generally start with a poorly scoped but complex and *important* problem. Your project might start with only the assertion that your company's aging monolith is crippling product development. From that broad, unclear (and potentially wrong) statement, you'll have to identify a concrete approach that works.
- **Numerous and divided stakeholders** - the easiest projects start with organizational alignment around both the problem and the solution, but your Staff project might likely start with neither. It might be an area which management views as an existential risk, but many engineers feel it is good enough. It might be an area that everyone agrees is a problem, but with strong factional disagreement about approach, for example, disagreement between pursuing a service strategy or reinvesting in your existing monolith.
- **Named bet where failure matters** - it's going to be a project important enough that senior leadership talks about it at all-organization or all-company meetings. This means folks will be watching your work closely, and any failures will be very visible. Success will be highly visible, as well!

If you meet these, it's probably a staff project. These can be pretty nerve-wracking, which is also why they're so effective at developing you.

Getting access to Staff projects

While deciding that you want to take on a Staff project is the first step, you still need to get *access* to these projects, which depends on your management chain trusting you enough to bet on your success.

This comes down to three factors.

1. First is learning to stay aligned with your leadership team, some strategies for which are described in Getting in the room and Staying aligned with authority.
2. Second, you need to be known to have the technical aptitude for the problem at hand, which requires Being Visible.
3. Third, is less in your control, which is your company having a pressing need to solve a Staff-level problem, which can require some patience.

Should you pursue a Staff project?

In summary, if you're looking to get promoted within your current company and haven't previously held a Staff or management title before, then you'll likely need to pursue a Staff project to establish yourself at that level. In other cases, you likely won't.

In any case, it's worth keeping in mind that whether or not these projects are required, they are also some of the most challenging work you can find and are the sort of work that will stretch and develop you into a better engineer. In the short-term pursuit of the title, it may well be optimal to avoid these projects, but in the long-term pursuit of self-growth, they're irreplaceable.

Get in the room, and stay there

One of the most common frustrations I've heard from engineers is that they're not in the room where important decisions are being made. They don't understand the company's decisions and have important context that seems to be missing or ignored. Staff-plus engineers frequently cite access to "the room" as a major benefit of their level, and titles do increase the likelihood that you'll be involved in decisions that impact you.

However, it's important to remember there's no single "room" to enter. Getting into the right room isn't a one-time challenge to be faced. Entering rooms will be an ongoing, iterative career challenge. That means it's worth getting good at!

Early in your career, it might be a sprint pre planning meeting with your tech lead and product manager. Later it might be a quarterly planning meeting, an architecture review, the performance calibration, the engineering leadership team, or the executive team. There will always be another room to enter. To reach senior levels, you have to become effective at not only *entering* but also *staying* in these rooms of power.

Getting in the room

To get into the room, you need:

- **To bring something useful to the room...** This could be details on a critical project, context from a critical team, subject matter expertise related to the room's purpose, experience running a similar project or team at a previous company, a relationship with a key relevant customer, or something else entirely.
- **...that the room doesn't already have.** It's not enough to have something useful to bring to the room. It also needs to be a perspective that isn't already present within the room. Small groups

function better than larger ones, so operating forums generally sacrifice redundancy and representation for efficiency. To be included in those rooms, you'll need to bring something distinct from the current membership.

- **A sponsor in the room.** These rooms have limited slots and have to function well as a group. To get into the room, you'll need someone to sponsor your membership. Your sponsor is allocating their social capital towards your inclusion, and their peers will judge them based on your actions within the room. These rooms often have a mix of seniority levels, so it's often the case that your sponsor's manager is in the room evaluating *them* based on their decision to sponsor *you*.
- **Your sponsor needs to know you want to be there.** Your sponsor is probably in many different rooms and probably daydreams of leaving most of those meetings behind them. They won't necessarily assume you want to be in any particular meeting, and in fact might assume you don't want to be there at all. Make sure that they know if you want to be included.

How you bring something useful to the room is going to be context-specific to you and the room you're trying to enter: there isn't any single pattern to follow. Whether someone with similar context is already in the room is also unique to your circumstances, and at some points in time, the only options are to wait or look for another room to enter.

On the other side of things, sometimes the easiest way to increase your value to the room is by decreasing the cost of including you. Some of the approaches that work well are:

- **Stay aligned with your manager.** Folks evaluate leaders on how aligned their teams are with their announced approach. If they've proclaimed a shift to continuous deployment, but their team is chanting for release trains, then folks get skeptical about who is leading who. You'll be much more likely to be sponsored into the room if you're highly aligned with your sponsor. If you're *particularly* aligned, they're more likely to yield their own seat to you and stop attending.

- **Optimize for the group.** One of Stripe's old operating principles was "Optimize for Stripe," and that mentality of optimizing widely for others builds trust and confidence in your judgment.
- **Speak clearly and concisely.** Learn to speak concisely: as you develop an economy of speech, you'll be able to contribute more ideas with less time. Learn to speak clearly: if folks don't understand your proposal, then it doesn't matter how good it is. Keep in mind that it's your obligation to be understood, not the obligation of everyone else to understand you.
- **Be low friction.** It's easy to fall into the trap of viewing each discussion as the last opportunity to stop an impending disaster. With that mindset, each discussion is a near-emergency, and emotions run high. Those sorts of discussions usually spend their time draining frustration rather than making forward progress. If you're known as someone who can navigate difficult conversations effectively, you're much more likely to be involved.
- **Come prepared.** Some companies infantilize their engineers, accepting that even very senior engineers won't read the agenda, do the pre-reads or prepare for the discussion. There's a considerable gap between what's tolerated and what's rewarded, and you'll stand out if you take the time to organize your thoughts before each meeting. Equally important is following up on what you committed to.
- **Focus and be present.** Once you've entered the room, be sure to show up and engage. Be attentive and engaged. Whatever else you want to be doing, it will wait.
- **Volunteer for low-status tasks.** If someone needs to take notes, raise your hand. If someone needs to follow up on action items,

be available. Prioritize being useful, especially when it isn't the most exciting work.

To get into the room, you have to work both the numerator and denominator: keep developing a unique and useful perspective while also becoming more effective at delivering that perspective within the constraints of a meeting.

Staying in the room

Getting into the room is your first hurdle, but the second hurdle is staying in the room. Most important is to keep doing the things that got you into the room: bring important context into the room, present a polished version of yourself, be concise, be flexible.

There are a few patterns that will consistently get you kicked out of the room:

- **Misunderstanding the room's purpose.** Each room has its own purpose[100], and you'll create friction if you attempt to use a room against the existing group's intent. It's very common for the external perception of a given room's function ("they make all the decisions in the leadership team meeting") to be rather far from how the room thinks of its role ("we don't make decisions, just surface problems to discuss"). Take the time to understand how the room operates and integrate into it with respect for that intention.
- **Being dogmatic.** As rooms get more senior, they have to discuss very sensitive topics (compensation, layoffs, promotions, acquisitions, etc), and they have a fixed amount of time to work together each week. If you're dogmatic, you will create friction that slows down discussion and impedes the group's ability to make progress.
- **Withholding consent.** Effective groups are formed from indi-

viduals who are willing to disagree and commit[101]. You can often force a group towards your perspective by withholding your consent until thinking moves your way, but the group's pace will slow to a halt, and you'll likely get removed from it.
- **Sucking the oxygen out of the room.** There are brainstorm discussions where every idea is welcome, and there are moments when you've shifted into operating mode to unblock project execution, and you have to read the room on which is happening. Usually, this comes from an urge to show value, but remember that you're in the room because of what got you into the room, not in the hopes that entering the room will magically transform you into someone entirely new.
- **Embarrassing your sponsor.** Remember that you got into a room because someone in the room advocated for your inclusion.
- **Being flakey or not showing up regularly.** There are only so many slots, and the person running the meeting will prioritize them on people who show up.

That said, I think it's easy to get caught up worrying too much about staying in the room. Sometimes you're better off thinking about whether the room's a valuable place to invest your time.

Exiting the room

It's important to remember that while there are infinite rooms to be in, there's no room where the work actually happens. You'll be most impactful if you're selective on which rooms you stay in. While I've met many folks who resent not being allowed entry into some room they're fixated on, I've never met anyone who regrets leaving a room too soon. If any given room doesn't feel useful, exit the room. While exiting, sponsor someone else into the opportunity you're leaving behind.

Being visible

> When folks, particularly women and non-binary people, come to me for advice, I think they expect me to talk about how to grow as a technical leader, and are surprised when I say "You've probably already got the technical chops, what you need to do is work on your reputation at the company." For better or for worse, you can't get to Staff without a good reputation. - Katie Sylor-Miller

Bert Fan's best advice for those trying to reach a Staff-plus role was, "Often reaching Staff is a combination of luck, timing, and work." Timing is a particular sort of luck, so you can simplify this even further down to just luck and work.

If you're fortunate, then you won't have to pursue a deliberate path to a Staff-plus role. You're already working on your company's top priorities, have a well-positioned manager who cares about supporting your career and are working from your company's headquarters office. If you're starting with none of those things, getting promoted will be quite a challenge, but don't count yourself out: it's easy to underestimate your own role in getting lucky.

One of the most effective ways to get luckier is to be more visible within your organization. There are, of course, very quick, very negative ways to increase your visibility, so I'll refine the statement a bit. Your goal is to be known for good things while minimizing the organizational bandwidth you consume to do so.

Why visibility matters

Katie Sylor-Miller describes visibility as a critical piece of getting promoted to Staff,

> Something I haven't talked about enough is communication and transparency. A big part of being promoted to Staff is mak-

ing sure that your work is visible, that people know your name and you have a good reputation.

Staff-plus roles are *leadership* roles, and by recognizing you with such a position, the company is bringing you into its leadership team. The existing members of that team want to be comfortable that they're expanding their ranks with folks they believe in, and they can't believe in you if they don't know you.

If you're operating without much visibility within your company, this may likely come across as cliquey or gatekeeping behavior. Conversely, if you are well-known internally, this may feel like the necessary cost for maintaining a consistent set of expectations and criteria for folks taking on leadership roles – how could you maintain consistency if you are unfamiliar with their work?

It's interesting to briefly reflect on how inclusive organizations mitigate the negative gatekeeping aspects of validating folks as appropriate additions to their leadership team. The answer is that they design mechanisms to ensure the *full* swath of potential leaders get exposure to the folks who will evaluate them for leadership roles. Conversely, less inclusive organizations inadvertently center access on folks who most aggressively self-advertise.

Internal visibility

The single best way to create internal visibility is to work on the things that matter to your company and company leadership. This path is also the most aligned with how a well-managed company will evaluate your contribution.

Sometimes that isn't enough, though, and some other strategies are:

- Write and distribute more long-lived documents, like architec-

ture docs or technical specification
- Lead (and, to a lesser extent, participate in) company forums like architecture reviews, company all hands, and learning circles
- Be a cheerleader for your team's and peers' work on Slack
- You can also cheerlead via email instead of Slack
- Share weekly notes of your work to your team and stakeholders in a way that other folks can get access to your notes if they're interested
- Contribute to your company's blog
- Attend, or potentially even host, office hours for your team or org

Find the right mix of activities that leverage your strengths, aren't already overburdened with volume, and feel authentic to you. If you've never communicated about your work, it may feel awkward to self-promote. You never want to wholly lose that sense of awkwardness–restraint helps–but you will have to get comfortable with some of it.

Executive visibility

To be promoted to a leadership role, the most important kind of internal visibility is executive visibility. Using the promotion packet, you will create visibility with your manager, but it's helpful to go further. It's particularly valuable to find opportunities to build a relationship with your manager's manager, but all positive, visibility at that layer will be helpful to you.

These are the folks who tend to be in the room that approves promotions into Staff-plus roles, and they rarely support folks whose work they don't know.

External visibility

It's helpful to complement your internal visibility work with external visibility work. There are many successful Staff-plus engineers with no external presence, but many find external visibility contributes to their career.

Compared to an exclusively internal focus, one advantage of building an external presence is that there's a lot more room to create a niche and name for yourself. Internal efforts often end up competing for attention with your peers in a way that external efforts simply don't.

In terms of how to create this sort of visibility for yourself and your work, it could be giving a conference talk like Keavy McMinn or Dan Na, going on a podcast like Michelle Bu, turning a problem into a website and book like Katie Sylor-Miller's *ohshitgit*[102], or creating a mailing list like Stephen Whitworth's *High Growth Engineering*[103].

Should *you* focus on visibility?

You can always have more visibility within your organization, but at some point, increasing your visibility is likely reducing the opportunities for others to create visibility for themselves. Internal visibility is not strictly zero-sum, but it's constrained by the attention of the folks you want to see your work.

My advice would be to use the promotion packet exercise to identify if the lack of visibility is likely to hold you back in the promotion process. If so, work to clear that threshold, but not much further. Visibility is a transient currency. Learning and developing yourself is a permanent one; focus on the latter once you've done the minimum to clear the former's cliff.

Deciding to switch companies

> *I was hired at Fastly as a Principal engineer. So, to be honest, for me, the biggest factor was changing companies. The type of work I was doing didn't dramatically change, but changing companies was the thing that ultimately enabled me to get the title. - Keavy McMinn*

My father was a professor of economics. After he completed his Ph.D. in his late twenties, he started teaching at one university, got tenure at that university, and walked out forty-some years later into retirement. Working in technology, that sounds like a fairytale.

There are very few software companies with a forty-year track record, and even fewer folks whose forty-year career consisted of one employer. There used to be a meme that many engineers spent either one or four years at each company to maximize their equity grants and then bounced on to the next. If that ever happened, it certainly isn't common behavior for folks who aspire towards or reach Staff-plus roles.

Instead, generally, those folks stay and are rewarded for staying at a given company as long as the circumstances support their success. If those circumstances change, they tend to either leave shortly thereafter or spend a while burning out and then leave after exhausting their emotional reservoir.

It takes years to build the visibility and social credibility to get promoted from a Senior engineer role to a Staff-plus role, which makes it very difficult to walk away if you feel like you're *just* one hump away from the promotion. Leaving, it can feel like, means starting over from scratch.

Then again, as described by Keavy McMinn, it's common for folks to attain their first Staff-plus title by joining a new company. Even with all your internal credibility, sometimes leaving is the most effective path forward.

What's the right decision for you?

Before going further, I want to recognize two very different job-switching experiences: one of privileged flexibility and another of rigid constraints. Your residency might depend on a work-sponsored visa. You might be supporting an extended family. You might be constrained to a geographical area with few employers. This advice focuses on the former circumstances, which are more common circumstances for someone who's deep enough into a technology career to pursue a Staff role. You should absolutely discount it to the extent this doesn't reflect your circumstances.

Why leaving works

The company that knows your strengths the best is your current company, and they are the company most likely to give you a Staff-plus role. However, actually awarding the role depends on so many circumstantial factors that this isn't how it works out in practice.

If your current team is very senior, it may be hard to justify your impact at the Staff engineer level because it's being attributed to your peers. Your manager might have a limited budget that doesn't have room for another Staff engineer. You might lack an internal sponsor. There simply might not be the need for an additional Staff engineer at your company. Any of these can mean that while you ought to be promoted, you won't be at your current company.

Conversely, when you interview for new roles, you can keep interviewing until you find a company that's able to grant the title. You can also deliberately choose to interview at earlier stage companies who are likely to value your experience more highly. The interview process also brings an automatic sponsor with it–the hiring manager–whose incentives will never be more aligned with yours than in the interview process.

Technical interviews are an inconsistent and unreliable predictor of success, which is bad for the industry and bad for companies, but works in your favor if you're set on attaining a Staff-plus role and are willing to conduct a broad search. Interviewing creates the opportunity to play "bias arbitrage," finding a company that disproportionately values *you*. That might be a company that values folks with conference speaking visibility, your experience designing APIs, or your Ph.D. thesis on compilers.

Similarly, sometimes you'll get into a rut at a company where your reputation is preventing forward progress. Perhaps you're tagged as "difficult" after flagging inclusion issues. Maybe you embarrassed an influential Director at lunch, and they're blocking your promotion. A new company lets you leave that baggage behind.

Yeah, of course, it's always an open question whether you can *really* leave anything behind you in the tech industry. It can feel a bit cliquey at times. If you've worked in tech hubs, at larger companies, and for more than ten years, then you almost certainly have mutual connections with the folks interviewing you.

If you have a bad run at a company, maybe your manager was a bully, or maybe you were going through a challenging period in your own life, it can feel like a cloud poisoning your future prospects. That said, much like the interview process in general, references and backchannel reference checks are deeply random. If you need any further evidence of that, look to the serial harassers who continue to get hired job after job at prominent companies.

Things to try before leaving

If you're planning to leave due to a lack of interest, excitement, support, or opportunity, it's worthwhile to at least explore the internal waters first. This lets you carry your internal network with you while still getting many of the advantages of switching companies. Depending on your company's size and growth rate, this might not be an option for you, but there are some folks who switch roles every two-to-three years within the same parent company and find that an effective way to remain engaged and learning.

On the other hand, if you're considering leaving due to burnout or exhaustion, it's sometimes possible to negotiate a paid or unpaid sabbatical where you can take a few months recharging yourself, often in conjunction with switching internal roles. This is more common at larger companies. (In case you were wondering, no, your coworkers taking parental leave are not "on sabbatical" or "on vacation.")

Leaving without a job

Speaking of burnout, if you're *particularly* burned out, it's worth considering leaving your job without another job lined up. There's a fairly simple checklist to determine if this is a good option for you:

- Does your visa support this?
- Are you financially secure for at least a year without working?
- Do you work in a high-density job market remotely, or are you flexible on where your next job is?
- Do you interview well?
- Could you articulate a coherent narrative to someone asking you

why you left without a job lined up?
- Are there folks who can provide positive references on your work?

If all of those are true, I don't know anyone who *regrets* taking a sabbatical. However, bear in mind that it's only the folks who took six-month-plus sabbaticals who felt reborn by the experience. Folks taking shorter stints have appreciated them but often come back only partially restored. If you do take a sabbatical, I highly recommend flushing out your experiences into writing. Even if you don't share what you've written, it'll help process the experiences.

Taking the plunge

If you're almost at the Staff promotion in your current company, there is absolutely another company out there that will give you the Staff title. Whether or not you'll enjoy working there or be supported after getting there, that's a lot harder to predetermine. If your internal reputation is damaged or if you've been repeatedly on the cusp of promotion but a victim to a moving criteria line, then you should seriously consider switching roles if the title is important to you. At some point, you have to hear what your current company is telling you.

Conversely, if you're happy in your current role outside of the title, consider if you can be more intentional about pursuing your promotion rather than leaving. Many folks hit a rut in their promotion path to Staff-plus, and using techniques like the promotion packet can help you get unstuck. If you've used all the approaches, taken your self-development seriously, and still can't get there–it's probably time to leave.

That said, it's easy to overthink these things. Few folks tell their decade-past story of staying at or leaving some job.

Finding the right company

There are only a few magic spells to attain a Staff-plus role: negotiate for the title while switching roles or find a supportive environment to "bake in place" while building your internal credibility with an empowered sponsor who'll advocate for you. The most important reagent in both spells is picking the right company to perform them at.

The good news is you're applying to a new company is that while you might invest *weeks* of energy into determining if you can get a Staff role there, you won't need to invest *years*. On the other hand, if you're looking for a company to join and grow within, you're embarking on a years-long journey into an unknown organization. This is a daunting decision to make, and picking the right company for *you* will have a considerable impact on whether you attain a Staff-plus role.

Find a place that disproportionately values you

If career velocity is your aim, then join a company that, for whatever reason, disproportionately values what you're good at. For example, Fastly valued Keavy's API design experience, and Stripe valued Dmitry's work on compilers. If there's a gap matching your particular shape that's limiting their success, your impact on the company will be uniquely high.

Well-run organizations value you for what you're good at. Less well-run companies value you for your identity. For example, a culture that views aggression as leadership would indeed promote and center the most aggressive folks, but to their culture's and team's detriment. Sometimes you'll find a company that net values you appropriately because it values your incidentals without valuing the contributions that you consider to be valuable; that seems like it'll work out, but generally speaking, it's a recipe for frustration.

Meritocrats and Proceduralists

When you're trying to identify a company to make the Staff transition to, there are a number of company values to consider in your decision. One that's particularly important is understanding if the company's leadership fundamentally subscribes to an exception-heavy "meritocratic" view of the world or a consistency-heavy "proceduralist" view. Few companies exist exclusively at one end of this continuum, but most slant heavily in one direction.

Of course, folks won't describe themselves in these terms. The first style would have called themselves a meritocracy a few years ago. Now that the term has fallen out of favor, they'd avoid it, but their core beliefs remain intact. This style is particularly common in Silicon Valley, is heavily exception-driven, and consolidates its efforts feting a small cadre of treasured individuals. Generally, in these companies, you're going to be very successful if you pattern match with whatever they believe high potential looks like. You're likely in for a rough ride if you don't.

Another style of company you'll find out there believes that consistency drives fairness. They're the sort that work the policy rather than the exceptions[104]: they design the clock, set it in motion, watch it tick, and make occasional repairs. These companies tend to be more structure-driven and less intuition-driven, which can create wider access to opportunity for more folks, but they can also be rigid bureaucracies who look smugly on while their machinery grinds an individual down.

Inevitably, both meritocrats and proceduralists view their world-view as a moral position and depending on who you are and who the company's leadership is, you'll have a radically different experience.

Some ways to explore during your interview process to help distinguish these mindsets:

- Companies with rigid compensation bands and who *actually stick to them* tend to be run by Proceduralists. Those that willingly eschew their bands are Meritocrats.
- Companies that create one-off roles for individuals to get them on board tend to be run by Meritocrats. Those that hire to their planned roles are Proceduralists.
- Companies with ad-hoc or unstructured interview processes looking to get your "feel," particularly for senior roles, tend to be run by Meritocrats. More structure means Proceduralists.
- Companies that perform ad-hoc conjurations of new, rubric-less interviews tend to be run by Meritocrats. Those that evaluate you rigidly, even if they don't let you shine, tend to be Proceduralists.

Neither Meritocratic nor Proceduralist companies have inherently better odds of propelling you into a Staff-plus role. Rather it'll depend on your identity and the identities of folks in a company's leadership roles. Depending on how those pieces align, you can estimate the level of support and friction you'll encounter pursuing a Staff-plus role.

Archetypes

Most companies only hire one or two of the Staff archetypes, even though they all use the same titles to describe the role they're hiring for. If you're trying to figure out a given company's preferences, it's most effective to reach out to some of their existing Staff-plus engineers and get a sense of the work they do. Most companies don't deliberately think about the sort of Staff engineers they support, so asking directly rarely works as well as it should.

Sufficiently large companies end up with at least some folks operating in each of the archetypes, but it takes a long time until that's the case, usually *after* their engineering organization has scaled to *thousands* of engineers.

Growth

If you've exclusively worked at fast-growing, successful startups, then it might not cross your mind that there can be a lack of room for additional folks operating in Staff-plus engineering roles, but it's surprisingly common for slower-growing companies to simply not have the work or the budget for more folks in leadership roles. This is also a common constraint for companies that haven't reached product-market fit–there are limited leadership slots when a company needs to remain highly aligned while frequently changing–with potential exceptions for those that happen to be selling a developer-centric or technical infrastructure product of some sort.

If you join a fast-growing company, new Staff opportunities will organically open up. In slower-growing companies, you may need to wait for someone to vacate their current role before another becomes available. That's not to say that you should necessarily join a fast-growing company if you don't want to–they're often stressful and run on perpetually out-of-date processes–just another factor to consider.

Sponsorship

Getting a Staff-plus offer at a new company requires someone inside that company who believes in you and is willing to push through a fair amount of organizational friction to get you the title. Getting promoted to Staff-plus requires a manager and management chain who believe in you and their willingness to push through *even more* friction to get you the title. Without an empowered leader within a company who's willing to invest their organizational capital in you, you can't get a leadership role.

When looking for a company to pursue a Staff-plus role at, a big part of the equation is identifying a company where you'll have an effective sponsor. Interviewing outside of your current company is often effective at finding you a sponsor: your would-be hiring manager tends to have well-aligned incentives to extend you a Staff offer. Equally important, your time investment is high but still *relatively* low compared to working at a company for two years to realize you're never going to reach your goal.

The easiest sponsors to find are folks who you've worked with before. The flying wedge[105] pattern of one senior leader joining a company and then bringing on their previous coworkers is a well-known and justifiably-despised pattern that relies on this built-in referrer-as-sponsor, but it doesn't have to be toxic if done sparingly.

This is also where having an external presence and network can greatly aid your search. Folks who've seen your presentations, read your blog posts, or nodded in agreement at your tweets are more likely to become your proactive sponsor in the interview process and later during promotion discussions.

Durability

Particularly if you're earlier in your career and pursuing a promotion into a Staff role, it's important to consider the company's durability: will the company even exist five years from now when you're hoping your work will culminate in a Staff-plus promotion?

Somewhat more subtly, you also have to consider the longevity of your would-be Staff sponsor. There are some wonderful engineering leaders creating pockets of equitable access to Staff-plus roles, but those pockets can quickly turn into a Values Oasis[106] that can't sustain itself once the sponsoring leader departs the company or changes roles.

Derisk durability by ensuring you join companies with business models that actually work and work for leaders who are values-aligned with their organization's senior-most leadership (that way, even if they leave, you're still aligned with potential sponsors).

Pace

Throughout a forty-year career, there are times when you're rested and looking for a challenging, enveloping role. There are going to be other times when you're drained and worn out. You will harm yourself by accepting a role that demands more pace from you than you're able to presently sustain. When taking on a technical leadership role, it's particularly important to make sure that the company's pace expectations align with what you're able to provide because you'll be evaluated in part on being a role model for the company's pace.

And everything else, too

Job searches for leadership roles are much slower than the typical software search, taking months rather than weeks, and trying to rush it rarely works out. As you evaluate whether a company might be an effective place to reach a Staff-plus role, you also have to assess it on everything else that you'd look into in a typical process.

Dig into your whisper network for toxic issues and individuals. Make sure the mission is something you can stay supportive of and engaged with for years. Search for the folks you'll be able to learn from during your work. If you find that these Staff criteria are pulling you towards a company that you otherwise have concerns about, the good money is that you'll regret that decision.

Interviewing for Staff-plus roles

When you decide to interview for a Senior engineer role, you roughly know what to expect. You'll refresh your resume[107], work through *Cracking the Coding Interview*[108], and do some research on the company to prepare questions. When you go into the interview, you know it's going to be five-ish interviews composed of a few programming exercises, something about technical architecture, and some cultural, behavioral, or career questions.

It would be amazing if you could start a Staff-plus interview process with similarly clear expectations, but most companies struggle with their Staff-plus interview loops. It might be the same exact interview you'd get for a Senior engineer role. It might be an engineering manager loop with a programming question added. It might be something else entirely.

Getting comfortable navigating ambiguity is a core part of the Staff-plus role, so a particularly optimistic person might view the state of Staff-plus interviewing as a good opportunity to demonstrate your skills. If you're less optimistic, you might find it a bit frustrating, but a bit of preparation can go a long way in making these interviews more predictable.

Draw your lines

The engineering leadership phase of your career may last twenty years, but if you think of that in terms of roles, how you spend that time will likely come down to four or five pivotal decisions. Each of those decisions is a scarce resource, and you should allocate them deliberately. Before jumping into an interview process, spend some time refining your criteria for the kinds of processes you're willing to participate in, as well as reflecting on the right company for you.

There are certain signals you'll get during an interview loop that indicate that the company doesn't quite know how to interview Staff-plus engineers. Because most companies have mediocre Staff-plus interview processes, you shouldn't automatically opt-out of poorly run processes, but you should consider which of those signals represent a line you're unwilling to cross.

One line that many folks in Staff-plus roles draw is they're unwilling to practice interview programming. This often means they are slower or make more mistakes in the sort of algorithmic questions that many companies use to evaluate early career candidates. Folks who don't practice take that stance because they've decided that a company who cares about fast programming is likely to misuse its Staff-plus engineer. Is that a line *you* want to draw? Maybe, decide for yourself.

Debug the process

After you've drawn your lines, next, you'll need to figure out the actual interview process used at the company you're interviewing with. It might feel like asking these questions could push the company to reconsider your candidacy, but it's *always* reasonable to ask the recruiting team and hiring manager for more details about your interview process. At the Staff-plus level, it's almost a point of concern if you *don't* ask for more details. Companies want you to succeed, and understanding the process is an essential part of preparation.

The three most important things to understand before you start interviewing are:

1. What are the interview formats, including what are they evaluating for?
2. Do any of the interviews require specific preparation?
3. Who are the interviewers?

Once you've answered those, then it's just a matter of preparation. Take notes about how you want to approach the different kinds of questions. Prepare materials for any presentation interviews. *Briefly* research the interviewers to tailor questions to their background.

This is also a moment to debug if you're in the right process. If your interview panel is composed primarily of early-career and mid-level engineers, it will rarely generate a Staff-plus offer; the panel will be ill-equipped to evaluate your strengths, and folks are often resistant to offers more senior than their own. If there are no deep-dives into your previous accomplishments and no presentation opportunities, it's similarly hard to demonstrate the expertise to support a Staff-plus offer.

If it's the wrong loop, but you're exceptionally good at whatever the loop does measure, then you'll potentially get a Staff-plus offer anyway. However, if you're less confident in those incidental measures, then raise your concerns politely and constructively, perhaps pointing the recruiter to resources around designing Staff-plus interview loops. Don't allow momentum to pull you into a process that doesn't support your goals.

It's particularly valuable to understand when leveling happens within the company's progress. Some companies advertise roles with level-specific titles, which lets you apply directly to the level you think is appropriate. If you're hoping for a Senior engineer role, then apply for the Staff engineer job posting. However, many companies use those as provisional titles and finalize them later; other companies are quite rigid. The only way to know is to ask.

It may feel very unnatural to take more control over your interview process, and in theory, you might miss out on some opportunities this way, but that's a good outcome: your goal is to find the best available leadership opportunity, not the first available opportunity.

Finish well

Even if you skate through the interview process, always negotiate the details, and remember to finish well. Brief your references on the role's details. Send follow-up emails to interviewers. Accept the offered sell chats and bring thoughtful questions into them. In this case, the last mile is the easiest as long as you take the time to walk it.

Negotiating your offer

Back in 2012, Patrick McKenzie wrote Salary Negotiation[109], which has since become the defacto guide to negotiating salaries for software engineers. It's a great piece and a good primer on how you'd negotiate any offer, including a Staff-plus offer: if you haven't thought about this topic much before, start there.

For much of your career, the offer you get is generated in a relatively formulaic way. Maybe they have a compensation calculator, or maybe they base it off your previous compensation, but it's the company's system driving the numbers. However, there is a threshold where offer negotiations shift, and companies are willing to engage in a bespoke offer rather than a system-driven offer, but you're expected to somehow intuit that you've crossed the threshold–no one will ever tell you.

This sort of bespoke offer *starts* with more flexibility around compensation, and in particular more flexibility around the equity component of your offer. That said, it's more than just the raw compensation. It's also about other aspects of the offer that the company doesn't generally have flexibility around but is willing to make private exceptions around for senior leaders.

For example:

- Their standard contract might give them three months to exercise vested equity after leaving, but they might be willing to extend a Distinguished engineer's exercise window to five years.
- They might not operationally be prepared to support early exercise for everyone but might be willing to make an exception to close a Sr Staff engineer offer.
- They might be willing to offer a deferred compensation plan to support a tax-advantaged payout schedule (this is mostly a thing at public companies).
- They may be open to additional vacation days if they're using

metered, as opposed to unlimited, vacation.
- They may support flexibility around work-from-home, working hours, or incorporating in a state or country they don't currently support employing folks in.

It can be hard to know if a given role at a given company is over the threshold, and it's hard to ask the other Staff-plus folks already at the company because it's likely they didn't negotiate these aspects (perhaps because they were promoted from within and never given the opportunity). As a rule of thumb, if a company has more than twenty and fewer than five hundred employees, it's pretty unlikely they are going to do much custom work for you unless you're coming into a quasi-executive role–they simply don't have the operational ability to do so. However, if a company has thousands of folks but only a dozen at your level, it's fairly likely they're open to negotiating bespoke terms.

It's important to be strategic about what you negotiate for. If you hold firm on First Class flights for all your business travel, you *might* get it, but it'll probably also send a message about your priorities that the company doesn't like.

Whatever you attempt to negotiate, take the time to frame your request in a narrative of why it's important for you. For example, I worked with one senior candidate who framed their request for an extended exercise window in the context of having just bought a house and recently exercising their previous company's equity after leaving. That's a lot more palatable than just asking for more cash compensation. The right narrative gets the negotiation done and does it without generating a negative signal about your motivations.

Stories

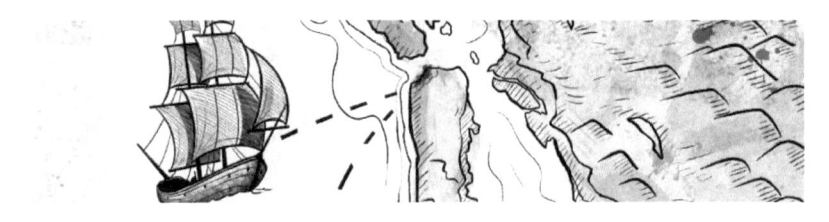

It didn't take me long to realize after publishing my first book that I wasn't the sort of person who enjoyed reading reviews of my work. At best, I felt good about myself for a moment, but often I just felt sad. During that window when I was still reading reviews, and I read one commenting that it was too Silicon Valley-centric for most folks to benefit.

That line stuck with me as I started to brainstorm what eventually became this book, and I wanted to avoid centering my own experiences to the exclusion of all others. Even more importantly, it's clear to me that my career is built on a particular set of perspectives, luck, and privilege, and I wanted this book to be a useful guide for folks who experience the industry differently.

All of that is to say that the best parts of this book rest heavily on the candid and insightful interviews from industry practitioners, and I'm grateful to be able to include those interviews in this final, following chapter. Even if you didn't get much from the book thus far, I hope you'll find something unique in these career stories.

Michelle Bu - Payments Products Tech Lead at Stripe

This story was recorded in April, 2020. Learn more about Michelle on her blog[110], Twitter[111], and Linkedin[112].

Tell us a little about your current role at Stripe: what's your title and generally what sort of work do you and your team do?

I'm the Payments Products Tech Lead at Stripe, working directly with our Chief Product Officer. I support critical initiatives and work on mitigating urgent problems across the organization. I typically spend 80% of my time on one or two large cross-organizational design projects. I spend the remaining 20% reviewing and supporting technical and product design (in particular, API design) across the organization.

Sample of a "top 3" document I keep evergreen:

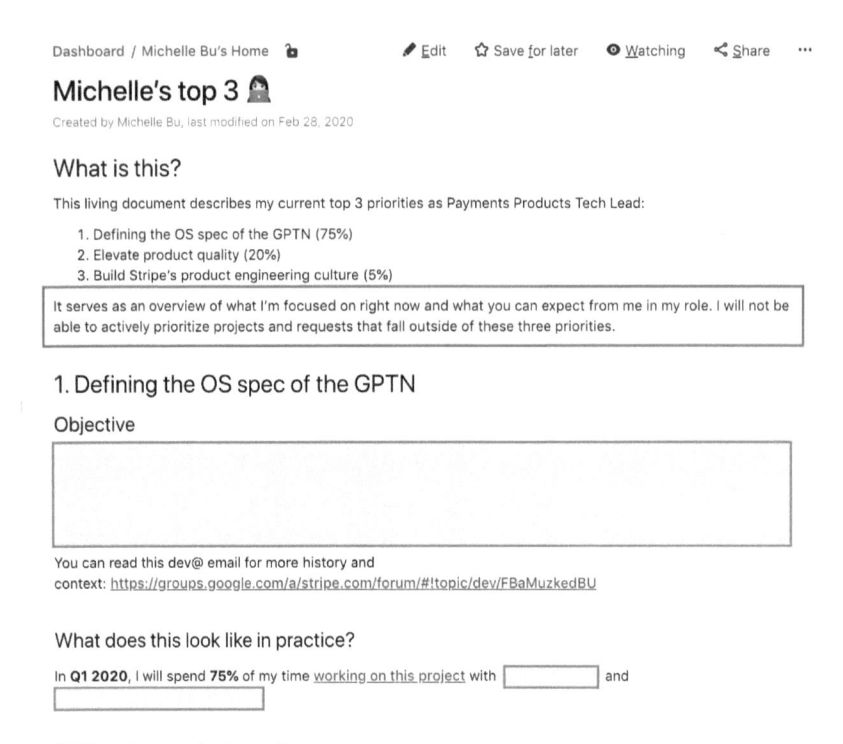

Dashboard / Michelle Bu's Home   Edit   Save for later   Watching   Share   ...

Michelle's top 3 🔒

Created by Michelle Bu, last modified on Feb 28, 2020

What is this?

This living document describes my current top 3 priorities as Payments Products Tech Lead:

1. Defining the OS spec of the GPTN (75%)
2. Elevate product quality (20%)
3. Build Stripe's product engineering culture (5%)

> It serves as an overview of what I'm focused on right now and what you can expect from me in my role. I will not be able to actively prioritize projects and requests that fall outside of these three priorities.

1. Defining the OS spec of the GPTN

Objective

You can read this dev@ email for more history and context: https://groups.google.com/a/stripe.com/forum/#!topic/dev/FBaMuzkedBU

What does this look like in practice?

In **Q1 2020**, I will spend **75%** of my time working on this project with [   ] and [   ]

2. Elevate product quality

I manage two engineers who embed into high priority areas. This both helps me scale my impact and also gives these engineers the chance to dip into many areas of Stripe. Right now, one is working on the core payments APIs and the other is focused on improving integration experience. I'm still evaluated on the IC ladder—the plan is to never have more than a few reports at a time.

What does a "normal" Staff-plus engineer do at your company? Does your role look that way or does it differ?

Most engineers in Staff-plus roles at Stripe work on specific teams. There are some Staff-plus Engineers who also have a Tech Lead title, and take on broader projects across a particular product area or technical domain.

There are two kinds of Staff-plus Engineers at Stripe: those whose scope is deep and those whose scope is broad.

Broad-scoped engineers create impact by working on vague, cross-organizational projects. They tend to accumulate a lot of context across many different domains and play a support role in many projects across the org. This shape of Staff-plus Engineer is most common on our product engineering teams.

Deep-scoped engineers tend to be subject-matter experts in a specific domain. They lead ambitious multi-year projects. This shape of Staff-plus Engineer can generally be found on our product infrastructure and systems teams.

Where do you feel most impactful as a Staff-plus engineer?

This has changed over time for me as I've moved into my current Payment Products Tech Lead role. (For some context, Payments Products is made up of over 20 teams. We're responsible for most of our user-facing APIs and UI libraries.)

I've taken to using the word "energized" over "impactful." "Impactful" feels company-centric, and while that's important, "energized" is more inwards-looking. Finding *energizing* work is what has kept me at Stripe for so long, pursuing impactful work.

When I worked directly on a team, I felt most energized when I was able to directly interact with users, whether it was helping users on the #stripe IRC channel or designing and shipping an API that users can integrate seamlessly.

In my current role, I feel energized when someone I've sponsored sends an announcement that they've shipped their work, or when I see that I've helped shape or shift an engineering team's model of an important topic. It's these teams, not me, who are doing the hard work day-to-day of building and supporting their technology. I measure my impact based on their progress and more importantly, the directionality of that progress and the alignment of their work to the company's goals.

One concrete example from recent memory is when another staff-plus engineer and I categorized the shapes of APIs we commonly see: labeling some as flows, some as engines, some as configs, etc. The intent of this work was to build up a shared mental model and vocabulary for categorizing existing APIs and for discussing and designing new ones. Folks started to organically use these categories after seeing them once! It's in these moments that I feel like I'm creating leverage and scaling my own impact by disseminating useful mental models and ideas.

I spend time on several of our review forums like API Review, but often these sorts of forums work more like code review. They happen so late in the design process that they tend to do a better job of preventing bad outcomes than of partnering with teams to steer great outcomes. I feel more impactful when I'm able to give engineers on product teams the tools to design great APIs.

Can you think of anything you've done as a Staff-plus engineer that you weren't able to do or wouldn't have done before reaching that title?

I've been at Stripe for a long time (since 2013!). While I've always had some amount of clout because of my tenure, my role of Payment Products Tech Lead (and the fact that I report directly to the CPO) has definitely changed how people interact with me. I'm definitely feeling lonelier at work now (and am actively working on adapting to this new normal).

One thing that's taken some getting used to is that now folks expect me to have an opinion about whatever we're discussing! That didn't happen as often when I was a staff-level engineer working directly on a team. I remember being in a meeting shortly after my role change where I was a bit quieter than usual because I was a little tired. I later heard that the presenters were worried that I hadn't liked their proposal because I didn't say anything. This was the first time that I realized people *looked to me* to have an opinion and to support their ideas! I've been careful since then to always stay engaged during meetings and to give feedback, even if it is just to explicitly say that I haven't fully formed any opinions yet.

It's a bit disorienting that some folks take my opinions more seriously and are nicer to me than when I wasn't in such a visible role. Previously, there were cases where people weren't collaborative or would dismiss my opinions. I think it was a good thing to have experienced that. I was confident enough (and trusted enough by the organization) to give them strong feedback on their collaboration so that I could ensure things like this weren't happening to others like me. I now worry that I'm losing visibility into where these interactions are happening.

How do you maintain empathy for other engineers' development experiences as you spend less time programming?

I've only had one year in my new role, so I don't feel too disconnected yet. Maybe this is something that will change over time. I was previously tech lead for a smaller area. In that role, I wrote a small amount of software and contributed to some of my teams' "run rotations," where we triaged incoming requests and fixed urgent bugs.

To maintain context in my new role, I spend a good amount of time in one-on-ones with engineers and PMs working directly on execution. This week alone, I had 12 30-minute 1-1s. I also follow every incident that's reported at Stripe. (We have a Slack group you can join to be automatically invited to Slack rooms for each incident!) The hum of incidents is particularly useful to tune into. By reading through the details of each incident, I'm able to estimate the distance between the reality of our systems and the idealized architecture / product that I spend my days thinking about. I want to know the shapes of issues that engineers are running into, the pits of failure they're falling into, and how the developer environment was or wasn't supporting them in getting out of those pits. I see myself as an advocate of engineers to leadership, so it's important for me to deeply understand our present reality.

Do you spend time advocating for technology, process or architectural change?

At this point I spend less time advocating for *specific* technologies or programs and more time empowering others to advocate for the technologies and programs that they think are important. I also try to be a source of knowledge and support that people can reach out to for feedback, especially on cross-cutting product decisions and on presentation of ideas to the rest of the organization.

I do work on projects where I'm explicitly thinking about idealized architecture and interfaces. However, at the end of the day, migration to any idealized state is going to be done by individual teams, so they *need* to feel a sense of ownership and empowerment. I spend a lot of time having direct conversations with the engineers and PMs who are actually making day-to-day decisions. The ideal outcome is that we're able to get directionally aligned, and they're then able to advocate for our north star within their teams and make good local decisions.

It's a lot harder to do this for the project I'm working on right now because it involves defining the idealized architecture and interfaces for many, many teams—essentially every team working in payments! I haven't yet figured out a scalable way to bring everyone along. Even writing documents (the most scalable way of distributing information!) is hard because different teams are (by definition) coming at the interface from a different angle and so very different framings of the problem and solution will resonate with each team. Our current approach is treating reviews of our documents like user testing: watching as individuals on teams read the documents, seeing where their cursor goes, what they're reacting to, etc. That's worked pretty well so far!

Designing the Payment Intents API[113], a rethinking of our beloved Charges API for the changing payments space, was a similarly cross-cutting project that I worked on previously. It took two years for the vision to fully land with everyone in the company. Even with that organizational buy-in, we still haven't realized the full potential of its original idealized design. This is not a bug, though! We focused on delivering incremental value to users while proving out the design. I expect any sufficiently-ambitious design project to continue even when I am no longer on the team. An important part of making this work was writing *everything* down.

We created a canonical document that defines our idealized abstractions. Even today, folks working on that team use these abstractions as a north star:

🖼 Payment abstractions overview

Michelle B   This document is an overview of the core payment abstractions defined by the Payment Flows team. These abstractions purposefully ignore current Stripe abstractions and constraints, but do consider network, regulatory, and payment method realities. Understanding these concepts is critical to understanding our incremental phases & proposed flows, which you can find at the end of this document.

               Note that all object, parameter, and enum names in this document are internal names, not the final user-facing API names — we're more than happy to discuss naming possibilities!

If two people asked the same question, we immediately added it to a FAQ that we kept. We took everyone's feedback and questions very seriously and put the burden of proof on ourselves. Finally, we worked to be fully transparent in our work, even creating a decision log that anyone at the company could use to follow our progress. Each entry in the decision log concisely describes a product or technical decision, documents who was involved in the decision, and links to detailed supporting technical design documents that generally contain the full problem statement and evaluation of alternatives.

⚖ Payment Flows decisions

go/payment-flows-decisions
Instructions
• 🗳 Decisions Template

Historical decision logs
Looking for a decision? Try these docs.

2019	⚖ gavel: 2019 Payment Flows Decisions
2018	⚖ gavel: 2018 Payment Flows Decisions

2020-03-25
One PaymentIntent never results in more than one successful payment
Elaborated in: Decision: One PaymentIntent never results in more than one successful payment

One PaymentIntent never results in more than one successful payment. Additionally, one PaymentIntent only attempts to move funds with one payment instrument at a time.

PaymentIntents are the pay-in mechanism of Stripe to collect a single payment from a single payment instrument.

The linked document elaborates on edge cases like multicapture, split tender, and PaymentIntents that kick off Subscriptions.

@Ellen S @Maddie S @Michelle B @Dan W @Kelvin L

In general, I've found that for ambitious design projects, being extremely transparent but also explicit about whether or not you're ready for feedback has landed well with folks who care about the topic. Here's some wording you can find at the top of the (public) notes docs for some projects I've led:

> Feedback and contributions[0] are **welcome and encouraged** on items in "Things we shipped last week." Items in "Things we're working on this week" are rough WIPs — feel free to leave comments (especially if you have context that the DRIs are missing), but **please be mindful** that documents and prototypes are still undergoing active iteration and that DRIs are still forming their own ideas and opinions in these areas.
>
> [0] Yes, please make PRs for small things!

> Please note that we're not yet ready for feedback on these ideas, as our thoughts are still early! 😊

Is sponsoring other engineers an important aspect of your role?

Yes, and it's one of my favorite parts of the role! I care a lot about the people I work with—they're the main reason I feel energized to go to work.

A big part of sponsorship for me is creating the space for ICs to do the impactful work that they care about. I'm lucky that in my current role I don't have to spend time actively proving that I'm competent, so I can spend a good chunk of time in support roles for projects and elevating others. I rarely feel like I have to "claim credit" for work or have my name explicitly mentioned on a byline for a project I helped with (though it's always a nice feeling when it happens). For more open-ended projects, it's sometimes useful for me to lend my name to the project. For example, I recently kicked off a product quality mentorship program where I play more of a facilitator role, selecting mentees, pairing them with mentors, and occasionally reviewing their work. I'm not doing *nearly* as much as the mentors in the program are, but we were able to get this org-wide program off the ground because I sponsored it.

Day to day, I find that I can be helpful as a "rubber duck" for folks who want advice on how to navigate a complex project or resolve a technical disagreement. I find this work—helping others make progress without getting directly involved—particularly rewarding.

Finally, I always keep in mind a list of folks who are amazing at what they do and advocate for them as *visible* opportunities that align with their interests become available. There's a balance here, though. I've learned that it's sometimes difficult for folks to say no to me. Recently, I asked an engineer on a team I work with to send an email about some good work she had done. She told me after she sent the email that she originally didn't want to do it, but she also didn't want to say no to me. She then showed me the relevant entry in her "no log":[114]

| feb 21 | the not-shipped email | yes - I wrote the email | Well, I dunno, I guess I want to do the right thing for Michelle. It was something that I uniquely would have to do. I would have been OK with it not being done, but it was important to Michelle, and it's important to me to do things that are important to people who are important to me (I lost my words here). Is this even glue? |
| | | | Now that it was sent: I don't regret it because people said such nice things |

Stripe is the first company you've worked full time at, and you're still at Stripe. What was your path to the Staff level?

I joined Stripe right out of college. I actually had a slower growth curve when I joined than the other engineers in my cohort. My trajectory over my first four years was slow compared to other ambitious new college graduates. I think this was partially because I hadn't been coding for that long (I took my first programming class in 2011 and joined Stripe in 2013), and partially because my first large project at Stripe was a 1.5-year rewrite project that was ultimately canceled.

When Stripe first introduced levels, I had been at the company for two and a half years and was leveled as an L2, a level that we expect a recent college graduate to reach in 6-18 months. I was honestly pretty disappointed, since my peers were already reaching "senior engineer" levels. At that point I'd already done a lot of impactful work, spun up most of the new product engineers who joined, and consistently jumped in to help during incidents. I worked so hard and on so many impactful things, even outside of my main projects! What else would they want me to do? Should I *not* help others out?

In retrospect, L2 was 100% fair based on the ladder. I worked hard and stayed late because I was naturally a bit slower than others in writing good code due to my lack of experience. I didn't yet have a good foundation for software development, mostly because I just didn't have enough practice yet! The impactful work I did was valuable, but also not something that I uniquely could have done. I was, at the time, solidly a high-performing L2.

In those early days, I spent a lot more time learning about the product and about the payments domain than I did writing code. I spent a lot of time helping our users (developers) with their integrations on IRC. I did smaller tasks (bug fixes, small features, bandages to paper cuts) that weren't technically challenging but were important to those users. This sort of work doesn't always map to growing as an engineer (though I did fine-tune my debugging skills—I'm a pretty great debugger now). I also built up relationships with other teams and other engineers by being overly helpful on Slack and on tickets and by helping teams navigate to the best solutions for our users. I helped spin up most of the new product engineers that joined in my first two years. Over time, I started having a reputation for caring deeply about our users and for being a fountain of knowledge about the product. ("Users first" is still my favorite Stripe operating principle.)

Later on I realized that during that time, while I wasn't efficiently mapping towards growing on the technical side of being a software engineer, I was actually learning critical skills that allowed me to move very quickly from senior to Staff, and from Staff to my current role (together, this only took 3 years!). In fact, I'm pretty sure it's the relationships I built during those first few years that made a canceled 1.5-year technical project not feel like too much of a setback to my career.

I slowly and deliberately built out my technical foundation when I worked on the first versions of Stripe Radar[115] and Stripe Elements[116]. I strongly believe that long as I'm being thoughtful about my technical gaps, about filling in those gaps for the projects I'm working on, and about challenging myself with projects that take me outside of my technical comfort zone, I can build up and practice my technical skills organically. The softer skills, the connections across the company, the user focus, understanding the product deeply—these are the skills that took much longer to learn and ultimately helped me accelerate my path to Staff after I built my technical foundation.

Did you have a Staff Project?

I've worked very broadly on just about every component of Stripe's product. Over time, the projects that I've worked on have generally spun off into their own dedicated teams, and two in particular that I worked on while I was a senior engineer might qualify as Staff projects: Stripe Radar[115] and Stripe Elements[116].

With Radar, we built a brand new product from scratch, making thoughtful tradeoffs about what to build and what we could safely descope in order to get something out to users as soon as possible. When we launched in October 2016, it was one of the smoothest product launches we'd ever had. It's since become a very successful product.

With Stripe Elements, I built out the infrastructure, designed the initial Card Elements API from scratch, and shipped to production in under 3 months. This was only possible because we did extensive dogfooding. While building Elements, I created three tiny e-commerce stores with different design frameworks and designs (of varying quality) to test the limits of its customization APIs. Since then, dozens of engineers have successfully developed in the codebase, it's the home of the new Stripe Checkout, and most importantly, we've had very few regrets about its original API design. Breaking API changes are always to be expected as an API product expands and we learn more about how developers use them in practice. We did a good job validating our initial API design to avoid these breaking changes while still shipping rapidly.

In making sure new engineers could onboard onto a pretty complex product that involved a ton of IFRAME-shenanigans, I wrote a lot of documentation. I found that telling a story worked well for teaching folks why things needed to be the way they were:

🏝 Stripe.js mini-map

This walkthrough of Stripe.js is intended to help you formulate a "mini-map" of the world of Stripe.js 🗺.

There are two high-level flows Stripe.js enables today:
1. **Collecting customer data with Elements, Stripe's pre-built UI components.**
2. **Making API requests of various types (PaymentIntent confirmation, Token creation, etc).** For simplicity, we will focus on Token creation in this document, because other API requests generally work the same way.

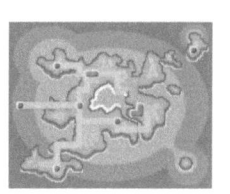

In the following sections, we'll be digging into these two flows in order to gain a full understanding of how (and why) things work.

⌁ ▼ What the user sees

NB. "User" in this context refers to Stripe's user — the "merchant." We'll refer to Stripe's user's user as the "customer."↑

In this document, we'll define the various components of a Stripe.js feature.

Overview

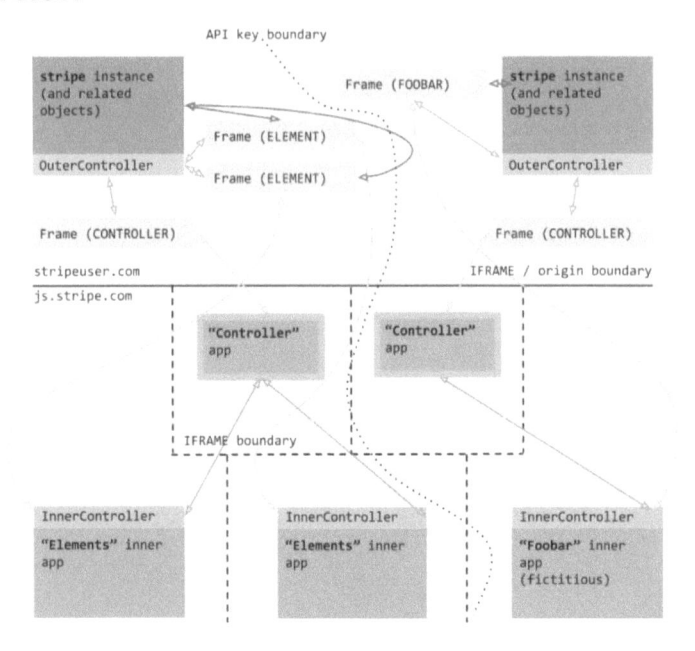

```
                        API key boundary
  ┌──────────────┐                          ┌──────────────┐
  │stripe instance│      Frame (FOOBAR)     │stripe instance│
  │(and related   │                         │(and related   │
  │objects)       │                         │objects)       │
  ├──────────────┤      Frame (ELEMENT)     ├──────────────┤
  │OuterController│                         │OuterController│
  └──────────────┘      Frame (ELEMENT)     └──────────────┘

    Frame (CONTROLLER)                        Frame (CONTROLLER)

  stripeuser.com                            IFRAME / origin boundary
  ─────────────────────────────────────────────────────────────
  js.stripe.com
                  ┌──────────┐   ┌──────────┐
                  │"Controller│   │"Controller│
                  │ app       │   │ app       │
                  └──────────┘   └──────────┘

                       IFRAME boundary

  ┌──────────────┐  ┌──────────────┐  ┌──────────────┐
  │InnerController│  │InnerController│  │InnerController│
  │"Elements" inner│ │"Elements" inner│ │"Foobar" inner │
  │ app           │  │ app           │  │ app           │
  │               │  │               │  │ (fictitious)  │
  └──────────────┘  └──────────────┘  └──────────────┘
```

"Outer" objects

Outer objects **expose user-facing APIs**. For example, Stripe Elements is exposed via `Stripe#elements()` and the `Elements` and `StripeElement` objects.

Looking back now, the product architecture has generally held up since launch for both projects. At the time, in addition to implementing these products, I had to wait for a while after they launched for the product choices to prove themselves out with our users and for the technical choices to prove themselves out with engineers internally as they ramped up.

I think that's an important criteria for Staff-plus Engineers in product:

not to just build something that ships, but for it to roll out smoothly and continue to succeed and grow over time with as few regrettable choices as possible. There will always be corners cut and features descoped during product development, especially for new products. A Staff product engineer makes those product and technical choices deliberately, taking on various different user personas to make the best choice possible and documenting rough edges thoroughly for future engineers.

Did you have to put together a promotion packet?

When I was promoted to Staff, I was fortunate to have a manager who was extremely engaged in supporting my promotion. To be honest, at the time I didn't really understand how to write my self-reviews the right way. I wrote self-reflective development plans for what I wanted to learn over the next year instead of documenting the impact and scope of my work. My manager actually did most of the work by writing out my impact in his review.

There were a couple of other things that helped me. First, I worked with the same manager for much of that time. If you change managers then your manager loses context and that pushes the work of creating continuity onto you. Second, my manager was managing a relatively small team and was able to spend a lot of time keeping track of and understanding the details of what I was working on. If I'd been reporting to a manager supporting say, 10+ engineers, I likely would have had to put a lot more work into my own promotion packet.

What two or three factors were most important for you to reach the Staff level?

Thinking back, a potentially-surprising important factor for me was (and is) my imposter syndrome. It made me extraordinarily open to feedback; to learning and growing and to taking responsibility for anything remotely related to my work. It made me proactively seek out feedback on everything from the validity of my comments on PRs to how I ran a particular meeting. If something was broken (whether it was technical or organizational), I felt unsettled and was deeply, intrinsically motivated to go learn about it and to fix it. No part of Stripe's product was "not my problem." This developed into two superpowers that are perhaps even more important to have as a Staff-plus Engineer than technical superpowers are:

1. Truly listening to and empathizing with others.
2. A deep care for solving all types of problems.

Of course, imposter syndrome is a double-edged sword. It often makes me scared and self-conscious—early on I constantly felt like I would get fired for not being fast or effective enough. I grew more secure about my own strengths over time, but to be frank, this took a *lot* of time and positive reinforcement from my managers and from leaders at the company.

Is it harder to reach Staff-plus roles when working in product engineering rather than in infrastructure engineering?

I do think that is the case. I also think it's a bit easier at Stripe, where the core product is infrastructure. This means there are many opportunities within product engineering to work on projects that need to consider scale, robustness, migration path, and well-designed interfaces.

It can definitely be tricky to reach Staff if you're on a team that mostly builds UI, because UI products are by nature more temporary and allow for more iteration and experimentation. To reach the Staff level of impact as an engineer on a UI team, you need to be able to create leverage. You could do this by building well-designed component libraries, experimentation frameworks, etc.

Another aspect of building leverage as a product engineer is creating processes and systems to manage "product debt." Folks often talk about "technical debt," but equally important is the "product debt" caused by supporting old versions of your product, and much of the difficulty of product engineering at scale is related to managing product debt and product drift (that is, products that need to interoperate with each other moving in different directions) over time. I believe that a company's accumulation of product debt does create Staff-complexity roles within product engineering at a certain scale.

Can you remember any piece of advice on reaching Staff that was particularly helpful for you?

I haven't gotten much *generically* useful advice. There was good situation-specific advice that I got along the way, but those pieces of advice are always tied to the situations at hand.

The most useful general learning for me was becoming comfortable with uncertainty. Sustained success in senior roles depends on your ability to adapt and grow as the needs of the organization change.

Advice for someone who wants to become a Staff-plus engineer?

Some caveats:

- I think I've been particularly lucky with the managers I've had.
- My interests have always been aligned with what was most important for the company. (At this point it's a bit unclear to me if my personal interests (i.e., developer products, mentorship) were aligned, or if over time I'd aligned myself to what was important for the company. I *feel* like it's the former, but in either case, I feel like I've always been really interested in my work.)

I'm probably one of the most visible product engineers at the company, so engineers will sometimes see what I'm doing and try to pattern match on that to become a Staff-plus Engineer. That feels great, and I'm lucky to be able to be a role model for others like me.

That said, my first piece of advice to engineers is that they should avoid pattern matching in ways that lead them towards work they don't enjoy. I'm deeply energized by the work I do, partnering with teams to solve abstract modeling and design problems. It takes a certain amount of fortitude to try again and again after many rounds of feedback, and to be honest, it's not for everyone. If you're more focused on hitting Staff than on setting yourself up to do work that energizes you, it's easy to end up stuck in a role you don't want. Being a Staff-plus Engineer, especially a broad-scoped Staff-plus Engineer, is a very different job than being a Senior Engineer.

Instead, pursue work that you find energizing, even if on paper it doesn't seem like it'd get you to a Staff-plus. A big component of being successful as a Staff-plus Engineer is being able to identify and scope net-new impactful work and to convince others of its value and impact. If the work you're doing energizes you, it's actually much easier to achieve this because you'll enjoy thinking deeply about your work a lot more!

What about advice for someone who has just started as a Staff-plus engineer?

Your job as a Staff-plus Engineer is specific to your team and organization, and it's important to avoid taking advice that doesn't apply to your situation. For example, when I moved into my current role, many of the other Staff-plus Engineers were focused on writing personal charters describing what they want to accomplish over the next 1-2 years. That approach likely works well for deep-scoped engineers, but it hasn't been as helpful for me as a broad-scoped engineer who needs to respond quickly to organizational changes and shifts to product strategy.

Did you ever consider engineering management?

I do manage two engineers right now. That said, I don't do a lot of the things that a traditional manager would do. I'm not involved in recruiting like a hiring manager would be, and I don't experience the same sort of performance management situations that other managers would because the engineers who are selected for my team are already high performers.

I care a LOT about Stripe: when I see something out of place I feel antsy and want to fix it. In some organizations I think that could have led me towards engineering management rather than my current role, and I'm grateful that management wasn't the only path that was available to me. My strengths and interests lie in product engineering and API design and execution, and I'm able to use these strengths every day in my role.

What are some resources (books, blogs, people, etc) you've learned from?

I love reading fiction and I learn a lot about the world from great literature. I don't like reading non-fiction business or technical books nearly as much. When it comes to learning about topics more directly relevant to my job, I treasure my peer relationships. My peers give me valuable in-the-moment feedback and help me tease out the answers that were in my head all along.

Stripe also has a program called "Leadership In Practice" which is taken by all managers and some senior engineers. That program included a class on adaptive leadership[117] which was particularly helpful. I've since applied the frameworks I learned to many situations.

I've never been a person who looks to a single mentor for advice. Instead, I follow what I used to call a "Frankenstein," build-your-own-mentor approach, similar to what Lara Hogan wrote about in her post on building a manager voltron[118]. Programs that match me up with a single mentor have never quite felt natural to me. I tend to be intentional about the particular topic or area I want to grow in, and will gravitate towards individuals who excel in that area, even if they're not my "official" mentor.

I spend most of my time on hard, specific questions that don't have an easy, generic answer. Figuring out the right approach requires a lot of situational context that someone outside the situation won't have much insight into.

Some non-fiction that I've read recently and enjoyed:

- Draft No. 4, John McPhee[119]: I spend most of my time writing at work, and experience writer's block quite a bit. But it's super important to power through that, because a good piece of written communication is the most effective means of broadcasting ideas and scaling yourself.
- Creativity Inc., Ed Catmull[120]: The tone of this book definitely made me raise my eyebrows, but there's a LOT to learn here about how to foster a creative working environment at scale. This is something I think about a lot as we grow our product organization and our product engineering function.
- Impro, Keith Johnstone[121]: I see my superpower (especially as the company grows) as being able to learn and adapt quickly, so I love reading books about different forms of learning and teaching. This book is about learning how to act/improvise, and pushes on conventional metaphors and narratives about education.

Ras Kasa Williams - Staff Engineer at Mailchimp

This story was recorded in July, 2020. Learn more about Kasa on Linkedin[122].

Tell us a little about your current role: where do you work, your title and generally the sort of work that you and your team do.

I'm a Staff Engineer at Mailchimp, working in the Data Services engineering group. Data Services can be seen as the home of data engineering within the company. Our group builds systems that primarily support our data science and analyst teams (i.e. product analysts, finance analysts, marketing analysts, etc.).

I have been serving as one of the tech leads in this group where I focused on building scalable data processing pipelines that power our internal analytics platform and supporting the advancement of critical business intelligence initiatives. I have been performing a significant portion of the Eng Manager responsibilities for the team as well (although I wasn't formally the Eng Manager). After almost 2 years in this role, I am actively transitioning it to another engineer.

What does a "normal" Staff-plus engineer do at your company? Does your role look that way or does it differ?

At Mailchimp, once you become a Staff Engineer, you're a member of "Engineering Leadership". Since a formal engineering ladder was implemented only a couple years ago, the answer to *"What does it mean to be a Staff Engineer?"* or *"What does it mean to be a member of Engineering Leadership?"* will likely vary.

In my view, it's about thinking globally. That means partnering with other members of that cohort to understand the company–wide business / product strategy and distill that into an Engineering–wide technical strategy that seeks to enable execution for Product, Marketing, and our peers across other functions. That means partnering to improve on processes like hiring, onboarding, cross-team communication, and production operations. That means partnering to grow the entire department's technical and social skills.

It's about taking that global thinking and applying it locally. That means aligning your team's (technical) initiatives / roadmaps to the Engineering-wide technical strategy; and being intentional about when you veer off of that path to serve the needs of your team's immediate stakeholders. That means collaborating with your team's managers in adopting successful practices in hiring, onboarding, and production operations from other teams; and sharing practices from your team that would be beneficial for others. That means taking context from company-wide business / product strategy and translating that to how it impacts your team's immediate projects. That means being intentional about creating opportunities for your team's individual contributors to grow their skills, get visibility, and access to others across the company.

Of course, I don't get it right all the time. But it's been a successful mode of operation for me.

How do you spend your time day-to-day?

As mentioned before, I have been serving as one of the tech leads in Data Services (and performing a lot of the Eng Manager responsibilities).

As tech lead, I was responsible for defining, and accountable for execution of, my team's technical strategy and approach. I worked to underpin this strategy in its value to our internal customers (or the business) and effectively communicate that across the company when needed. A couple of times a year I reflected on what progress was made, and if anything had changed within the business that required adjustments to this strategy. I still contributed code regularly—certainly less than the rest of the engineers on my team; but it was important that I sustained "hand to keyboard" work to ensure that my technical strategy (and other macro-level decision-making) was informed by the on-the-ground experiences of the rest of my team. A focus for me was growing and developing the other engineers on the team as a result of the technical direction I set. More concretely: I worked to help my teammates (via mentoring or coaching) understand how to approach technical decision-making and how it should be underpinned by the customer / business problem it's solving and the value it's providing; I worked to help them understand how to drive engineering projects from problem statement to production release / long-term operations; I worked to help them understand the proper communication practices for different audiences (i.e. engineering peers, vs. engineering management, vs. non-technical stakeholders, etc.). In aggregate, I worked to help them get to a level of self-sufficiency where they can operate and communicate in a way that aligns with my technical strategy, direction, and approach without me having to be in the room or in the conversation.

Our group doesn't have product managers. But those needs around things like understanding internal customer needs and stakeholder management still exist. The recently hired Eng Manager for my team is accountable for this; but we shared a lot of the responsibility here. I did a fair amount of chatting with internal customers, answering quick one-off questions, understanding needs for new pieces of work (i.e. new datasets), recommending paths forward, setting expectations around when we'd be able to execute on the new piece of work, etc.

Our group doesn't have project managers either. But, again, those needs exist. I believe in empowering each team member to own the project management responsibilities for their assigned project (i.e. status updates to stakeholders, etc.). I did a fair amount of coaching on project management tactics like proactively communicating risks / blockers so that I can help unblock them and how to continuously deliver incremental value to maintain momentum.

I spent a good amount of time building passive internal customer and business context. I'd occasionally read merged pull requests for repos that I didn't maintain; I'd read tech specs and proposals that are shared publicly; I'd occasionally attend various internal presentations from the data science and analyst teams where they presented projects they completed or ideas they're exploring. All of these are small tactics, but they aided in my situational awareness and was one key input into my team's quarterly planning activities.

As a tech lead, I was a member of the Eng Tech Lead Cohort. It's a formal group of all of the tech leads across the Engineering department meant to share context, talk through ideas, and help advance the Engineering-wide technical roadmap. There's some ad hoc conversations and work that may come out of this group from time to time. There's also a recurring call for all Staff, Senior Staff, and Principal Engineers meant as a space to surface and discuss problems, assign owners and actions items when needed, and generally build community with each other. We have a close partnership with Google; they serve as our cloud provider. Occasionally, I'd spend time talking with our assigned partner team about challenges we're running into, plans we have, proper approaches to solutions, formal training that would be helpful, etc.

As I'm transitioning out of the tech lead role, there will definitely be a change in how I spend my time day-to-day. But I'm honestly not sure what that will look like.

Where do you feel most impactful as a Staff-plus engineer?

It's always a rewarding feeling if I can end the work day and feel like I've helped my peers get unblocked and maintain momentum.

That can mean helping one of my Data Services team members think through options for solving a complex technical problem and trade-offs like providing immediate value versus being sustainable long-term. Or helping them think through how to deeply investigate a new technology and if it can be applicable to solving one of our top 3 problems.

That can mean helping a peer on another team think through their deliverables over the past quarter, whether those deliverables provided real business / customer value, and how to build a narrative around that impact to make the case for promotion.

That can mean identifying that a short-term piece of "org work" is at a standstill because consensus wasn't achieved, encouraging an involved peer to take ownership of making a decision (with proper feedback from interested parties), and drive it to completion.

This is a feeling I've always felt throughout my career; I enjoy the success of my peers as much as I do my own. But taking on the tech lead role certainly elevated the importance of doing it. It morphed from something I just liked doing, to something that I liked and was also important for the health of the team I was responsible for.

Can you think of anything you've done as a Staff-plus engineer that you weren't able to or wouldn't have done before reaching that title?

As mentioned before, once you become a Staff Engineer at Mailchimp, you're a member of Eng Leadership.

It's noticeable that Staff+ Engineers generally have more agency and ownership of their time. They encounter less resistance when they make time for work outside of their primary responsibilities. This has certainly been my personal experience.

I've also had a lot more organic opportunities to coach, mentor, and generally support more peers outside my team. It was something I was certainly doing before being promoted to Staff Engineer; but it noticeably increased. It's definitely a rewarding part of my work day, so I welcome it.

Often industry peers tend to make the case that titles don't matter. But I disagree 100% with this statement; my personal experiences and observations across the companies that I've worked at have shown me otherwise.

There is a popular idea that becoming a Staff engineer requires completing a "Staff Project." Did you have a Staff Project, and if so what was it?

In some sense, I guess.

I joined Mailchimp as a Senior Engineer. I was immediately added to a project team (which included an Engineering Director and two Principal Engineers) meant to build out Mailchimp's first internal, self-service analytics platform.

A key aspect of this project was **being effective and executing at a high level**. For better, or for worse, having two other Principal Engineers meant expectations for me likely weren't that high. But I was able to jump in immediately and start contributing to core aspects of the project with very little hand-holding from them; by the end, I was one of the key contributors on the team. I would ultimately be formally installed as a tech lead to help continue shepherding that project work as it was absorbed into my current engineering group, Data Services.

Another key aspect of this project was a lot of **visibility across the company**. The project team's work was categorized as a company-level initiative. This meant a lot of executive-level visibility; and, of course, the associated pressures of that. But the overall project team was able to sustain good momentum throughout and ultimately succeed in building out an initial iteration of the analytics platform. Also, my manager and the team's Principal Engineers were intentional about creating opportunities for me to present the work of the project team; I ended up presenting at an Engineering All

Hands, a company-wide All Hands, and co-delivering a tech talk at an Engineering recruiting event. Because of the visibility of the project and general culture at Mailchimp, I was able to collaborate with engineers at all levels in the company and engage with analysts from other departments in a very short time after joining—which is something most folks take a year or so to have the opportunity to do.

So, it was a combination of doing good work and being really effective alongside more senior engineers; and those senior engineers (and others) being intentional about giving me visibility and access across the company even though they were the technical leaders on the project.

Important note: The promotion didn't come until I had also served some meaningful time as tech lead and delivered a lot of value there. But this project was definitely the firestarter.

Can you remember any piece of advice on reaching Staff that was particularly helpful for you?

First was from my manager, Marc Hedlund[123]. He told me to write my performance review in the third person. The idea being that you're more likely to praise others, and be less critical, when giving them a review. It's pretty simple, but has been super useful to me. Oddly enough, it's played a part in helping me understand how to build a coherent narrative around the work I do and the value it provides to the business.

Second was from Dan McKinely[124], one of the senior engineers on the "Staff project" I talked about. He provided direct feedback on my strengths and weaknesses when I asked for them. He noted that my strength around building relationships across the company is an important skill to have since the people / social aspects of engineering don't go away; in fact, they are key to getting anything done.

Third was from Coda Hale[125], the other senior engineer on the "Staff project" I talked about. He talked about scaling your impact. Specifically:

> *first, effectively setting technical direction for other engineers; second, mentoring them and developing their talent as a consequence of the work you're structuring for them.*

This advice is core to how I think about my role as tech lead; like, really being intentional about creating opportunities for the team to extend, flex their skills, and learn a lot.

What about a piece of advice for someone who has just started as a Staff engineer?

Don't think you're going to solve ALL of the Engineering department's problems; from what I've seen, it'll get exhausting and you'll get jaded pretty quickly. Slowly build up to those things. Hopefully, you were promoted because you were already operating at the Staff level; so you shouldn't have to do anything dramatically different. Continue to do the great work that got you to this title. Once you feel like you're settling into things, extend from there.

Communication and building narratives are key. Make sure to write ... A LOT. When thinking through problems or ideas, write it down (even if you don't intend to share them). Usually when I can't capture a problem statement or idea in a coherent, concise paragraph it means I need to do more research and / or I'll have a rough time trying to convince others it's a worthwhile investment. Also, the written word allows you to scale your ideas and discussion around them more effectively; much easier than scheduling a meeting with every possible person to pitch the idea.

Try to make your managers' job easier. Don't just bring them problems; also bring them (multiple if possible) recommendations / suggestions for solutions to that problem and ask for their feedback. This way, the manager doesn't have to do all the work of solving the problem for you (they likely have enough on their plates) and they have an opportunity to draw from their experiences to help you rule in / out your suggestions. Funny enough, it's probably much easier for someone to provide feedback on why your solution is bad than it is to come up with a fleshed out solution on their own.

Start thinking intentionally about creating opportunities for other engineers you work directly with to grow their skills and get access and visibility to others in the company that they usually wouldn't.

Build relationships early. It can help in situations where you need to spend some social / political capital to take a stance on something. If the first time you engage with someone is when, as an example, you're fighting for opposing solutions to a hiring problem, you're already starting from a deficit with that person. To be clear, you should never look to "people please". But your working relationship and ability to collaborate productively on future endeavors with a specific person can be significantly easier if a relationship was built up beforehand.

Frankly speaking, trying to apply all of this is a lot; and it's just one person's opinion. Treat it like a restaurant menu; choose what resonates with you and try to apply it. Then, pay it forward by sharing your experience with the next person trying to make it to Staff.

Did you ever consider engineering management, and if so how did you decide to pursue the staff engineer path?

I get asked this regularly.

I do have a goal of being a CTO; but that's more of a directional thing to ensure I don't get complacent about my career progression. In the context of Mailchimp, getting promoted to Principal Engineer would satisfy that goal for me. I've been able to deliver real, tangible business value at my current level; so I think I could continue that and continue to feel rewarded by sticking with the individual contributor track.

Also, I had been fulfilling a lot of the responsibilities of an Eng Manager for my team (without formally being the Eng Manager). So, a lot of the things I would have wanted to start doing if I switched to management, I was able to put in practice and get that experience. So, I'm sure that satisfied any itch I had for the time being.

What are some resources (books, blogs, people, etc) you've learned from? Who are your role models in the field?

Verbal communication about technology with various technical and non-technical audiences is a skill. It's one that I try to cultivate and hone everyday. One person that I watch for a visual on how to do it right is Kelsey Hightower[126]. Another is my college professor for a couple of my Software Engineering courses. He rarely ever came to class; but when he did I usually learned more about software development than I have in any other academic setting. They both know how to explain things well and tailor it to the audience.

There are a couple blogs that I've come across that have helped me hone, and fine tune, how I develop a technical approach and strategy. The first is *"Delivering on an architecture strategy" from Pete Hodgson*[127] that presents a framework for achieving a sustainable balance between feature delivery and foundational architectural work. The second is *"Stepping Stones not Milestones" from James Cowling*[128] which is about delivering real value with big architectural initiatives.

Keavy McMinn - Senior Principal Engineer at Fastly

This story was recorded in March, 2020. Learn more about Keavy on her blog[129], Twitter[130], and Linkedin[131].

Tell us a little about your current role: your title, the company you work at, and generally what sort of work does your team do?

I'm a senior principal engineer at Fastly[132]. Fastly is an edge cloud platform that provides services like a CDN. I work in OCTO, the Office of the CTO, which is composed of about ten principal or distinguished engineers who report directly to the CTO. Each member of OCTO tends to have their own focus, and mine is being the API Lead.

What does a Staff-plus engineer do at your company? How do you spend your time?

There are several quite different types of principal and distinguished engineers in OCTO. There are also principal engineers that work within engineering teams directly, rather than within OCTO. In the OCTO group, some work on internet standards or academic research, some do deep technical research and prototyping, some help incubate a team building something completely new. I'm closely involved with the broader engineering organization in my API Lead role.

We all work on different things, but we have a common goal of taking a holistic, long-term and system-wide view on things. We also try to find and help with the sort of things across engineering that might get overlooked or fall between the cracks. Our CTO supports our work, but doesn't identify the projects to work on, that's up to us.

I've never thought about my time in terms of percentages. Some of my work goes in phases, with more of one thing this week, more of that the next. A massive amount of my time is spent doing written work, research, and talking to people. I'll have regular meetings with the teams and managers that build APIs. I'll spend time breaking a long-term strategy into little chunks, doing research, and writing a proposal on that. Then I'll have to market that proposal around the company. Less on writing code lately, but in other phases I'll build demos or tooling to support the wider work. That coding work is still really enjoyable.

Where do you feel most impactful as a Staff-plus engineer? What's something you've done as a Staff-plus engineer that you wouldn't have done earlier in your career?

As a regular engineer, it can be hard to carve out time. You have to work more within the constraints and cadence of regularly scheduled projects. As a principal, you have the trust, the time and the space to try something out.

When you have a title, you don't have to spend so much energy putting your credentials on the table. It helps set the context for others. You're more respected from the outset, and that's been really noticeable. You also get access to executives, so you get information earlier and might have a seat at the table to influence things.

Do you spend time advocating for technology, practice, process or architectural change?

I was hired specifically to set the direction for strategy for the API. Part of that is steering the technical direction and choices we make. I approach it as a collaborative exercise. You know I'll do the grind work of doing the research, I analyse all the information, present tradeoffs, and make a recommendation. I'll take in all the organizational and engineering group context.

I present what I think is the best case for us, and people can disagree with that. And, you know, they often do. I'm steering and influencing more than saying, "I've got the authority to just tell you what to do." I've never seen that style work well.

For controversial decisions, I'll meet up with representatives from different, relevant groups. I'll meet with a group of engineers, tell them what I'm going to recommend, and ask "What do y'all think about that? What am I missing?" I'll also meet with the management and product side, and maybe legal, docs, security or different people depending on the project. I've also done it the opposite direction of just presenting the thing first, and then having calls to get feedback instead of just waiting for people to leave a comment in the document.

What's something you've advocated for?

One of the things that I've been advocating hard for in my current job is design documents for API changes. So before anybody writes any code, when the cost of making changes is low, they write down the user workflows and what would an interface look like that could enable those workflows. Sometimes it turns out that a seemingly simple thing is really difficult, particularly when the group isn't used to flexing those muscles.

My approach to advocacy is to remind ourselves what the pain points are that everyone felt that led us to trying to make a change. We're not trying to be perfect for sake of theory, code beauty, or a lofty concern. I bring it back to "These are the pain points that everybody said they felt, and this is an approach that you know ultimately is going to help with that."

I help get other people to care about the same things, like I'm going to start pairing with more engineers on API reviews. While I do the reviews, I try to help teach others what I'm looking at, and be encouraging through the processes and conversations.

How have you sponsored other engineers? Is sponsoring other engineers an important aspect of your role?

This hasn't been as much of a focus for me in my current role. At GitHub I was conscious that I had privileges from my seniority and tenure, and sponsored an engineer there. I would give him more and more challenging things to work on, encouraged him to question anything that was unclear or curious to him about my work, and advocated for further responsibility and recognition for him.

How did you build organizational trust?

At Fastly, I was given trust from the beginning. When I joined, I was hired to come in and work on specific things. I remember asking, "Is there a time scale for this?" and for their notions about strategy, and being told explicitly that they wanted *me* to figure it out and tell *them*. So definitely a lot of trust and responsibility.

There are pros and cons of when you build that trust instead of being hired with it. As you build up trust, you simultaneously build up a lot of context, which is how it worked for me at GitHub. Although, I find in my current job that it was actually really useful to come in without context and be a set of fresh eyes. That makes it easy to question when folks think, "Oh, well, maybe we've just always done it this way." It can be liberating not to be tied to the past.

There is a popular idea that becoming a Staff engineer requires completing a "Staff Project." Did you have a "Staff Project," and if so what was it?

I've never heard it given a name, but I understand the idea. I did lead and architect that type of project - solving gnarly engineering problems, with large impact for the company - a few times, but unfortunately they didn't lead to me being promoted. They did lead to my career progression though. Those projects gave me the experience, knowledge and confidence to position myself differently. Even to give public conference talks or know that "I've done X and could do X again."

Were public speaking or public visibility important to reaching your current level?

Yeah, I think it's been a huge factor for my career development in general. I don't think it's necessary, but I think it can definitely be helpful, it's been helpful for me. My very first conference talk I was asked to do - because the organizers thought I had an interesting perspective to share, coming from an art background. It was terrifying, and initially I wanted to say no. But my mother persuaded me to say yes. So public speaking was a slightly more accidental than deliberate strategy to start with.

Mostly, I enjoyed the people I met at conferences. Later the speaker networks led to job opportunities for me.

How did you first get a Staff or Principal title? What factors contributed most in you reaching that title?

I was hired at Fastly as a Principal Engineer. So, to be honest, for me the biggest factor was changing companies. The type of work I was doing didn't dramatically change, but changing companies was the thing that ultimately enabled me to get the title.

There was someone that was a strong advocate for hiring me specifically, and I'm sure that helped. They weren't someone I'd directly worked with before, but they were familiar with my work.

Has working remotely impacted your career trajectory?

Not that I'm aware of. I've always been a remote employee and I'm sure it's been a factor in being able to have serendipitous conversations but I've just been doing it so long. You make a deliberate effort to have the conversations and build relationships. Also, my companies have been largely distributed. I can imagine it being more of a potential issue if being remote is the minority, or the company doesn't fully embrace being distributed.

Did you get any advice on reaching Staff that was particularly helpful for you?

Not really, I got some bad advice. It's such a cliche, but the "This is great. Now you have to prove it again." There's some advice that pushes people more in the sort of hero direction, like saying that you need to invent something unusual or magical to qualify. There are so many different directions one can make it. Engineering ladders often contribute to these beliefs.

What about a piece of advice for someone who has just started as a Staff engineer?

The thing that springs to mind is to find your peers or support network. Just like management, it gets lonely the higher up you go and it's important to find peers that will still challenge you and you can brainstorm ideas with. It doesn't even matter if they're in your similar area of work or even are in different companies.

Did you ever consider engineering management, and if so how did you decide to pursue the staff engineer path?

I tried it once and didn't have a good experience. I realized it's just not where my passions lie. I have too much respect for engineering management to do it for anything other than the right reason. The right reason is to support other people.

What are some resources (books, blogs, people, etc) you've learned from? Who are your role models in the field?

Conferences have been a resource for me, as well as getting to work with mature, low-ego, wonderful engineering leaders and engineers. Chad Fowler, and his book The Passionate Programmer[133], is at top of that list. Dave Thomas is another one of those people whose workshops I used to go to when I was first learning Ruby and his book The Pragmatic Programmer[134] is another great one.

Bert Fan - Senior Staff Engineer at Slack

This story was recorded in May, 2020. Learn more about Bert on his blog[135], Twitter[136], and Linkedin[137].

Tell us a little about your current role: where do you work, your title and generally the sort of work do you and your team do.

I'm a Senior Staff Engineer on the Platform team at Slack. I was lucky enough to join Slack shortly after we launched the Slack App Directory[138] so I've had the opportunity to help evolve the Slack Platform into what it is today.

It's hard to generalize the work that I do but the goal is always the same: enable developers to build on top of Slack to make our customers' working lives simpler, more pleasant, and more productive. Examples of this include building new platform features, improving API performance, writing documentation, and working with partners, internal integrators, and third-party developers to ensure that they can build impactful software.

What does a "normal" Staff-plus engineer do at your company? Does your role look that way or does it differ?

The work that Staff-plus engineers at Slack do is incredibly varied depending on which part of the company you're in, the composition and size of your team, and what the business needs from you. Staff-plus engineers are often the tech leads of projects, which means that they help write the tech spec, get feedback from various stakeholders, work closely with design and product to decide what to build, and lead the technical implementation for the project. They also mentor other engineers, improve our interview process and engineering culture, develop engineering processes and tools, and provide technical direction for refactors and tech debt. Staff-plus is all about enabling other people to do better work - to be a force multiplier.

My role includes all the things that I've mentioned but I tend to focus less on specific pieces of technology and more on what the technology is enabling. So I might spend time prototyping concepts that will almost certainly be thrown away or gathering usage metrics around a particular user flow to better understand how to improve the system. I will often build apps on top of the Slack Platform to keep myself honest about what the developer experience is actually like and actively try to build on other people's platforms to see what works and what doesn't. A lot less of the code that I write makes it into production than other engineers at the company and I'm completely fine with that.

Can you think of anything you've done as a Staff-plus engineer that you weren't able to or wouldn't have done before reaching that title?

I've done a lot of experimentation with various product ideas in the last year, some of which have evolved into actual features of our Platform. Part of the reason I was given the opportunity to do that is that I've established trust through other projects that I've successfully shipped, but having a Staff-plus title seems to bestow a little more flexibility in what I choose to work on.

For better or worse, I'm also in a lot of strategy and planning meetings I was never in before. If you've ever wanted to know how the sausage was made from a leadership angle, maybe consider if you actually want to know how the sausage is made.

How do you keep in touch with how things really work as you spend less time on hands-on development?

The best way I've found is to have regular 1:1s with engineers across the company and spend a lot of time listening. You can learn a lot about the current state of engineering if you take the time to develop relationships where engineers feel like they can be honest with you. As a Staff-plus engineer, you have no real influence over how much money someone makes or their next promotion, so engineers can be more candid with you if you make yourself accessible to them.

What two or three factors were most important in you reaching Staff? How have the companies you joined, your location, or your education impacted your path?

I come from a fairly privileged background - I graduated from college with a computer science degree and no debt or student loans and part of what that bought me was the flexibility to leave a job without worrying how I was going to make rent or if I was going to find a new one. And I leveraged that flexibility into becoming pickier and more strategic about the places that I wanted to work.

I acknowledge that most people don't have that option but for me I thought it was important to work on things that I felt were meaningful - things that I personally used that I thought were having a positive impact on the world. And I believe those choices have paid dividends because companies like that attract like-minded folks who will go on to other companies that hopefully are aligned in the same way. This is not a meritocracy and your professional network is important. I've gotten jobs because I've applied on the company's website like everybody else but I've also gotten jobs because I've awkwardly e-mailed a manager there that I haven't talked to in years but that I respect and know that they respect me as an engineer. We work in an industry where there are a lot of options of how to spend your time and if you're lucky enough to be in a position where you have the flexibility and privilege to choose, you're doing yourself a disservice by not regularly evaluating what you work on.

Maybe at one point you'll become the kind of engineer that when you announce on Twitter that you're starting a new job, people who you've worked with before will create a calendar reminder for four years in the future when you're fully vested so they they have the highest likelihood of poaching you, but until then, you're going to have to write awkward e-mails to people that you would like to work with again.

Can you remember any piece of advice on reaching Staff that was particularly helpful for you?

The best advice I've heard is that often reaching Staff is a combination of luck, timing, and work. Here's a path of events that I've observed and personally experienced:

1. Develop a relationship with your manager where they implicitly trust you and you implicitly trust them. Be honest and direct with them about what you want. Developing this trust will require you successfully delivering on the things they ask you to work on.
2. Because your manager trusts you, when they hear about projects that will have a significant impact for the company, they will advocate for you to lead those projects. Alternatively, you'll have to find or create a project yourself and advocate for it to happen. This is much harder but still plausible.
3. Deliver the project successfully.
4. The project has a significant impact on the company.
5. Because you successfully delivered a project that had a significant impact on the company, it's easy to advocate for your promotion to Staff, which your manager is happy to do.

Hopefully you can see where luck and timing can affect this simple plan - what if you don't get along with your manager? What if your manager leaves the company or gets promoted? What if you're in an area of a company that gets no interesting projects? What if the project is doomed to fail? What if the project succeeds but has no impact?

These are all possible and there's no generic piece of advice that I can give to overcome any of them except that sometimes you're never going to get promoted and you should probably be honest with yourself and identify when you're in that situation. In that case, sometimes the only way to get promoted would be to leave the company and do something else. You may boomerang back into the company at a higher level than you left at later in your career, but much like a failed relationship that you revisit, do you still want to be there or is there too much baggage to ever make it work?

What about a piece of advice for someone who has just started as a Staff engineer?

It's kind of a running joke in engineering but a lot of people get into this profession because they don't like talking to people but to be effective at your job as a Staff Engineer, you're likely going to spend a lot of your time talking to people. I think you can progress early in your career by focusing on just writing better and better code but at some point you should probably shift to focusing on working better with other people. Trusting other people and giving them the freedom to make technical decisions (even ones that you disagree with!), understanding other people's motivations, learning to give difficult feedback, knowing when to pick your battles - these are all useful skills to have.

If you haven't already, try to become the engineer that people want to work with. There are a handful of engineers at every company who, if you ever left your job, you would try to circumvent a non-solicitation agreement to work with again. Become one of those engineers for other people and it'll unlock a lot of doors for you in your career.

Did you ever consider engineering management, and if so how did you decide to pursue the staff engineer path?

Early in my career, I once told my manager I was concerned that I would have to go into management at some point and they said something like, "Don't worry about that! At this company we have two different tracks, the management track and the IC (individual contributor) track, and there are equivalent roles in the IC track for the highest management positions, so you'll never have to switch to management in order to move up in the company." While technically true, the omission that seems obvious to me now is that at a lot of companies, the management track is a lot less vague than the engineering track.

The higher up you climb in the engineering ladder, the less examples you'll have of what to emulate and the examples seem more and more unattainable. When you start to dig into it, you may realize that someone had gotten the title when their company was acquired or they were the author of a programming language or framework or they unlocked tens of millions of dollars in revenue for the company.

A lot of my colleagues have gone into management for various reasons and I suspect one of those reasons may be the more obvious, reliable progression that I've described. But I believe strongly that that shouldn't be your primary motivating factor. If you have open calendars, take a look at your manager's schedule and the number of 1:1s they conduct a week. Is that a schedule that you would enjoy? The desire to write code isn't black and white since there are tech lead manager positions where you write code and Staff-plus engineer roles where you never write a line of production code and spend the majority of your day in Google Docs or Dropbox Paper. But in my career, I've never had to lay someone off or deny them a promotion or write performance reviews - I know which side of the coin I'd rather be on.

Katie Sylor-Miller - Frontend Architect at Etsy

This story was recorded in August, 2020. Learn more about Katie on her website[139], Linkedin[140], and Twitter[141].

Tell us a little about your current role: your title, the company you work at, and generally what sort of work does your team do?

I work at Etsy, which is the world's leading online marketplace for sellers of handmade goods. We let sellers put their items up for sale and sell them to folks all around the world. We really focus on providing people with unique, special or handmade goods that are an alternative to kind of the facelessness of big box stores.

I'm currently on the Frontend Systems team, which is a product infrastructure team that's responsible for our frontend architecture - including our PHP view rendering framework, although I'm not super actively participating in the work that the team is doing right now. For the last several months I've been focusing on web performance - functioning in an advisory capacity for all things performance - improving our monitoring and reporting systems, identifying areas for improvement, and being available to product teams for help with performance related questions.

Web Performance is something that I think many companies either ignore or don't focus on. When I started at Etsy, we had a great performance culture thanks to folks like Lara Hogan, but due to organizational changes a few years ago, we no longer had a web performance team, and I think that as an organization, we rested on our laurels and deprioritized web performance. Now, we're bringing it back to the forefront because there have been a lot of changes in the industry around how "good" performance is defined and measured, particularly for SEO. Google is really pushing for web performance being a criteria that companies focus on as part of their search ranking. So it's very much a top of mind area, especially for retailers.

What does a "normal" Staff-plus engineer do at your company? Does your role look that way or does it differ?

The interesting thing to me about how we think about the role of a "staff engineer" is that we take two different ways that a person can be senior and we put all of those people into one bucket called staff engineer. But really, there are two different buckets.

Someone can become really senior in their role by being an expert in a particular subject area, by really taking on the role of tech lead, where they are driving their team or org's technical approach and roadmap. Then there's this other way to be a senior engineer, which are the folks who broaden their scope of work and their focus such that they're thinking about problems that are cross cutting, they're driving the creation of systems and practices that operate across multiple teams. That second bucket is what I think of as an architect. It's not that you aren't a subject matter expert, but it's just that the scope of influence that you have is greater than operating as a tech lead for a particular team.

At Etsy we have a few levels of seniority: Senior Engineer I and II, then Staff I and II, then Senior Staff which is considered equivalent to a Director level role. I'm technically a Staff Engineer II, and that's how I think of myself, but my specific role is as the frontend architect. That means instead of being responsible for just what my team is doing, I'm responsible for looking at what all of Etsy is doing in the frontend space. What does the future look like? What are the problems we need to solve? How are we going to get there? I think about all that, and advocate for the technical approaches that will get us there at the company level.

In your role as an architect, do you spend much time doing software development?

Yeah, it's funny. I'm a frontend architect, but by far the main thing I've been writing lately is SQL, because I'm doing a lot of data analysis. I've been looking at our performance metrics to figure out where the areas for improvement are, and what would be the most impactful issues to fix to improve performance and business metrics. I will write little bits of JS or PHP here and there, but it's mostly to help unblock teams or to run small performance-related experiments, or if there is something important that needs to be done but other folks don't have time for.

I've definitely found that I'm moving slower, and it's taking me longer to actually find the dedicated focus time to write code as my calendar fills up with meetings. So I don't think you want me to write much code anymore! I'm much more focused on identifying areas for opportunity and then trying to sell that as work that my team or other teams should be doing.

How do you spend your time day-to-day?

I would say 50% meetings, and the rest of the time it varies pretty widely from day to day. Sometimes I spend the other 50% writing docs, sometimes I'm in SQL doing a lot of data analysis, sometimes I'm in Slack talking to people across multiple teams and roles. At times my meeting load will spike a bit as projects come into my lap where I'm reaching out to other teams to learn more about what they're working on, or trying to influence them to make changes. It varies pretty widely.

I've found that folks in these roles often struggle to quantify their work, have you found any useful ways to measure your impact?

I'm glad to hear that because it is something that I really, really struggle with. I always have a bunch of different projects and discussions happening at any given time, and I have a bad tendency to get caught up in the newest thing or let my focus wander, so I have to be really thoughtful and cognizant about how I organize my work and my notes. I'm always looking at everything that I could potentially be doing and picking what is the most impactful or the most important thing for me to do that day, and that can be really hard.

I didn't realize, until I moved into the architect role, how much I relied on sprints and JIRA boards and the ritual of completing a ticket and moving it to the "done" column as a way to check in with myself and know that I am accomplishing the things that I need to accomplish. Now that I don't have that kind of team context to help me organize my day, I've had to rely much more on my own to-do lists and I'm still working to improve my systems for that.

One thing that has definitely been helpful is making sure that I'm keeping track of all of the different tasks I complete every day - logging meetings, emails, Slack discussions, etc. Then, when I have my official quarterly goals check-in with my manager, I review all of my notes and realize, wow, I helped engineers fix performance issues on six different experiments, or I influenced this team to take a better direction with their new feature, or I gave that engineer feedback that helped them. These are all little things that in the moment don't feel like much, but taken together show real impact.

Where do you feel most impactful as a Staff-plus engineer?

What I absolutely love to do the most is to identify a new or unique problem that hasn't been tackled before, come up with a wild idea to solve the problem, and then my brilliant coworkers take that idea and really run with it to build something awesome. It starts with taking in a ton of input from the work folks are doing - seeing that this team has a problem doing x, and another team has a problem doing y. Then you mix all that input up with your experience and what's happening in the industry as a whole and let it sit in your brain for a while, until finally it all clicks and you realize that the deeper cause underlying both problems is z, so you come up with a plan to fix that problem which is really hard to fix.

An example of this process from before I moved into the Architect role was when my team owned our Design System components. Making changes or fixing issues with our shared components was really difficult because we didn't have a single source of truth for the markup and the templates for each component. Rather than everyone in the company reusing the same template file, folks were copying and pasting the HTML into a bunch of different places. So when we had to make changes to a component, it was hard to find all the places to update because the pieces of the component were spread out and managed in different places - sometimes in JavaScript, sometimes in Mustache, sometimes in PHP logic.

So I had this wild idea: what if we extended our custom PHP framework to enable reusable template blocks in mustache that represented all of our components, and we were able to easily compose them together the way that you would in a React application. I went out and made a proof of concept and wrote up a proposal for the project and brought that to the team. Then the team really took the ball and ran with it, they built the infrastructure to support this component system and it turned out far better and more robust than anything I could have done on my own.

The part that I really enjoyed was identifying the problem and thinking creatively about how we can solve it, then shopping the proposal around and getting other people engaged with the work to execute it.

Can people doing frontend work create leverage for a company similarly to folks in developer productivity or infrastructure roles?

Yes, most definitely. I personally only know a handful of other Frontend-specific staff engineers, and I think that frontend as a skillset is not valued in the industry as much as I think that it should be. I'm very lucky that I got my foot in the door at a place like Etsy, which tends to hire "full stack" engineers, by having computer science fundamentals in my background - I went to school for Computer Science, and I have experience working in and understanding the whole stack. But really, my passion and my focus has always been the frontend because it's what's in front of your users. I'd love to see more companies value the frontend, because I believe we bring valuable skills and a unique way of thinking to the table.

As far as becoming a staff engineer, I think that the qualities of a good Staff Engineer transcend what stack you're working in. Ultimately, staff engineers need to be able to think about engineering decisions as a series of tradeoffs, and articulating those tradeoffs is a skill that you can have from any perspective within the stack.

I also think that Staff Engineers should have a broad understanding of all of the adjacent fields of work to their own specialty. For me, working in the frontend, I put a lot of time and effort into understanding marketing, business goals, user experience, visual design, the view and business logic layers on the server, how we ship code to the browser, how browsers take all that code and turn it into a website, and then how users interact with it. Having expertise in all of these different areas makes it easier for me to see the broader impact of my technical decisions and understand those tradeoffs better.

Having empathy for your users, in particular, is an important skill for all types of engineers to develop, and I think it can be undervalued in many infrastructure or developer support orgs that don't understand that yes, they actually do have users! I work in Frontend Infrastructure, and we really try to see ourselves as product engineers - it's just that the products we're building are systems for other engineers to use. So we have customers. We have users. When we think about the API for the systems that we build, we're designing our APIs for users, and we need to understand our users - aka product engineers - to do that well.

So I personally think that frontend-leaning folks make great Staff Engineers, because they're so used to constantly thinking about users and how users are going to interact with what they build. User empathy is a superpower that frontend people bring to the table.

How do you maintain empathy and awareness of the realities of developing at your company when you do less development yourself?

Networking, networking, networking, networking. One-on-ones are particularly important because I'm a full-time remote. Obviously, everyone's remote right now, but as a remote on a not-completely-distributed team, you have to be really cognizant of who you're talking to, and make sure that you have connections across multiple teams and multiple groups to leverage those networks.

At Etsy, we are really lucky that we have a few different Employee Resource Groups for folks to connect across the company. I'm fairly active in the ERG for marginalized gender identities in tech (MAGIC), and it's great because there are folks who are part of that community who work in every single department in engineering. The same is true with the community of remote employees. I make time to mentor more junior folks, have regular 1:1's, and participate in Slack discussions to foster and grow these connections, because it helps so much to have a finger on the pulse of what's happening broadly in the org. I also try to make sure that I'm talking to engineers throughout product engineering in particular, because product engineers are our customer base.

Something I'm working on getting better about is connecting a lot more with managers. For a long time I've had really good networks inside the Individual Contributor track and I've been working a lot in the last few months on broadening the reach of my network to include more engineering managers. A lot of times the work that I do requires "influence without authority", I'm not making the decisions myself, but trying to influence the decisions that others are making, and a lot of times, managers are the ones who make the final decisions on things.

How have you sponsored other engineers? Is sponsoring other engineers an important aspect of your role?

I was very lucky to work with Lara Hogan for a few years at Etsy and she's talked a ton about sponsorship and as a woman in tech I've benefited from and seen the value of sponsorship myself. I definitely put a lot of time and energy into that.

About a year and a half ago, my colleague Andy Yaco-Mink, another Staff Engineer, and I noticed there wasn't really a good method of communication for product teams to share what they are working on with each other, or to connect with teams working on product infrastructure. To try and fix that, we proposed and started up a monthly meeting that we call the Product Engineering Confab. It's an open forum for folks to bring up questions, share their work, celebrate wins, and for us folks in infra to share what we're working on.

Something that I don't think we fully anticipated is that it's also been a really great way to create opportunities for sponsorship . Every month Andy and I have to figure out what folks are doing that would be interesting to share more broadly. What are experiments that have run that have gotten interesting results? Who's out there doing cool stuff that should be shared? Then we'll reach out to engineers on those teams and say, "You should come and talk about what you've been working on at the confab!" It's really easy. It's five minutes. It's super informal, but it's a good way to get public speaking experience.

Since then, we've had a couple of folks who've come and spoken at the meeting, and then went on to speak at company all-hands meetings or local meetups. At least one person ended up giving an expanded version of their talk at a big conference. We've also heard from folks that giving a talk at the confab was something they used as evidence of leadership in their promotion packet, which is an amazing feeling!

You first got the title Staff engineer at your current company. What was the process of getting promoted to Staff?

I was hired as a Senior Engineer because at the time we didn't hire into the Staff title, although we've since changed that policy. I was working in the industry for almost ten years before I joined Etsy, but largely at smaller and lesser known companies. I'd been serving as a frontend tech lead for more than five years before I came to Etsy. Because of that, I was already extremely comfortable in the role of being a mentor and a leader. I'd already spent a lot of time working closely with management, product and design, as well as figuring out roadmaps and execution. Altogether, I felt like I had the tech lead role down pat.

But, when I came to Etsy the scope was much bigger than what I'd seen previously. The engineering department was many magnitudes bigger than any engineering department I'd worked at before. I had a lot to learn about operating at a really big scale and how that's very different than when you're at a smaller company. I learned to be more cognizant of looking at data: I had to go out and teach myself basic statistics to understand the experimentation framework.

From the beginning, though, I was always looking around for places we could improve. I came in and said, "Oh hey, we're not doing this thing. We should be doing this thing." For example, I noticed that folks had been writing the design system JavaScript components any old way, so I said "Let's come up with a framework and a standard boilerplate for that." It was such a small thing and it felt obvious to me, but it was a big improvement in our practices. I think a lot of what gets someone to Staff is noticing problems and acting on solving them proactively, instead of letting them go.

Altogether, I had been at Etsy for a little less than two years when the promotion to Staff came. My manager at the time was brand new and didn't know my track record, so we worked really closely and collaboratively on putting together my packet. I've heard experiences on both ends of the spectrum of manager-driven versus IC-driven, and I'm glad that I ended up being a big part of the promotion process. Especially being a remote, I think that unless you're proactive a lot of your work can go unnoticed because it happens over Slack, in pull requests or documents, and not out in the open where managers tend to operate. You're always going to be your best advocate, but that's even more true as a remote. You have to put a lot of effort into making sure your accomplishments are out there and they're known.

What two or three factors were most important in you reaching Staff? How have the companies you joined, your location, or your education impacted your path?

I've discussed a few things in this vein already: creativity, proactiveness, empathy, etc. Something I haven't talked about enough is communication and transparency. A big part of being promoted to Staff is making sure that your work is visible, that people know your name and you have a good reputation.

I'm lucky to be on a team that builds frontend infrastructure because we naturally write a lot of emails to everyone in engineering about the work we do, so we get a lot of visibility. But a bigger part of being in infrastructure is customer service - helping folks who come into your Slack channel with questions or issues to be solved. I worked in the service industry for several years before going back to school to finish my degree in computer science, and I always try to model the lessons I learned about customer service from that experience in every interaction I have with folks at work: be available, be humble, and focus on really hearing and understanding people's needs. When you truly care about helping our colleagues it shows.

Do you think some companies are particularly good at growing Staff engineers?

To be perfectly honest, I don't really know how Staff engineering works at companies other than Etsy, so I am totally biased! I think Etsy is good at growing Staff Engineers because we have a strong internal culture that values technical excellence combined with a culture of blamelessness and a desire to do good in the larger world. I think that leads to really smart and kind people working at Etsy, and that combination of intelligence and humbleness makes folks great staff engineers. This kind of environment feeds on itself, creating good role models and people who want to emulate those role models in order to get promoted. So I think that on the whole, we have a great cohort of folks who work or have worked at Etsy and model good practices for Staff Engineers.

I think it's important to remember, though, that there are lots of smaller and less-well-known companies with amazing people who do Staff engineering type work, but aren't called staff engineers, they're acknowledged as technical-track leaders in other ways. In many companies people who are strong technical leads become managers, and might not even have the idea of something like a Staff engineer role. It's easy in a big name company to get stuck on this title of Staff as the end-all be-all, but remember that there are as many different ways of growing your career.

Can you remember any piece of advice on reaching Staff that was particularly helpful for you?

One of the best pieces of advice that someone gave me, and that I make sure to pass on to other staff engineers, is that there's a misconception that you become a Staff Engineer and then you'll be in control of the work you do, and everyone will listen to you and do what you want them to do. That's absolutely the opposite of what happens! You have this really tangible goal of getting a promotion for so long, and then you become a Staff Engineer, and all of a sudden, everything is vague and ambiguous. You transition from solving somewhat clear-cut problems, to being responsible for finding the right problems, and then figuring out how to convince people that it's important to solve them. You are going to be challenged in a completely different way than you have been in your career thus far.

What's your advice to people pursuing a Staff role?

I was nominated for the Staff Engineer promotion twice before I got promoted; the third time was the charm. I think what finally pushed it forward for me was that I had a good sponsor in my Director. So my advice is to make sure that you develop your network and start meeting with your Director or your VP, because those are the people who are in the room making the decision about whether you're getting promoted or not. It's not your peers and it's not really your manager, it's this other group of people, so you want them to know your name and your work. During that promotion discussion, you want them to think, "Oh, she sent that engineering-wide email about this project." or "I see him in Slack answering people's questions all the time." or "They spoke at that conference, didn't they?"

When folks, particularly women and non-binary people, come to me for advice, I think they expect me to talk about how to grow as a technical leader, and are surprised when I say "You've probably already got the technical chops, what you need to do is work on your reputation at the company." For better or for worse, you can't get to Staff without a good reputation. I think people want or expect it to be a meritocracy, when it's really not. There are so many factors that go into getting a Staff-level role.

Advice for navigating uncertainty and ambiguity that comes with more senior roles?

It's important to develop a lot of self-knowledge to see when you're pursuing something because it's what you want and not because it's going to be beneficial for the organization. That can be really hard to do. You have to be ready to kill your darlings, pivot, and try something new. If an approach you're taking doesn't work, don't try to force it.

I also really love Dan Na's talk about pushing through friction[142], because that's something you experience constantly when you're growing as a technical leader. I think about this concept of "influence without authority" a lot, because when you're a Staff Engineer then your job is to figure out what the team or organization needs to do, align the organization around that goal, and figure out how to get people to do that when you have no authority over staffing or final decision making. It takes a lot of tenacity and you have to flex a whole bunch of quote-unquote non technical skills to push things forward.

What are some resources (books, blogs, people, etc) you've learned from? Who are your role models in the field?

A lot of names that I've already said, especially Lara Hogan[143], Dan Na[144]. I just love everything that Julia Evans[145] does and I am really lucky that I got to collaborate with her on a project. Ryn Daniels[146] who used to work at Etsy blogs a lot on career progression. Tanya Reilly[147] is a big inspiration to me as another badass working Mom who is also a respected technical leader. In the frontend space, Nicole Sullivan[148], Jen Simmons[149], and Ethan Marcotte[150] are huge inspirations to me to name just a few. I really enjoyed reading Camille Fournier's The Manager's Path[151]. I've never done the management track so it was a bit of a black box and anything that gives you insight into the world of management is helpful because as a Staff Engineer you're almost like a manager without the people aspect.

Ritu Vincent - Staff Engineer at Dropbox

This story was recorded in March, 2020. Learn more about Ritu on her Linkedin[152].

Tell us a little about your current role: your title, the company you work at, and generally what sort of work does your team do?

I'm a Staff Engineer at Dropbox. I actually was a Staff Engineer at Dropbox, left to join a different startup, and then recently came back to Dropbox just a few months ago. I came back because a really interesting opportunity opened up within Dropbox to launch an internal incubator. We're working to foster innovation within the company. Dropbox has become a strong brand in the file sync space, but there's beginning to be a lot of competition there now, so we need to do more and branch out into new products. The incubator works directly with the CEO, and is a very small team.

I'd been at Dropbox long enough that I built really close bonds with a lot of people here, so when folks pitched me this role it sounded really fun. I'd also been a manager for a couple of years and was getting a little itchy to code again. Putting those together led me back to Dropbox.

There are two parts to the incubator.

The first is a more classic incubator where engineers across the company can pitch ideas and get funding to join the program, and try to show product-market fit or other forms of progress to continue getting funded every few months. The goal is for successful projects to graduate into their own lines of business, although we're still early.

The second part is engineers who are permanently part of the incubator, and are always generating ideas from within the incubator and operating with a lot of autonomy. I'm one of the two engineers on that permanent "scouting" team, and we're planning on growing over the next year. It's very different from anything I've done before, which is why I wanted to sign up for it. It's a huge paradigm shift for me. Honestly, the first few months have been a combination of really fun and really frustrating because it's harder to measure obvious impact when your primary goal is to very quickly try out a ton of new ideas, many of which will not go anywhere. I've had to learn to think of impact in longer timescales - not in terms of what I'm shipping today, but what I could influence the company to ship in the future,

What does a Staff-plus engineer do at your company?

I'd say there are two different profiles of Staff Engineer at Dropbox. One is a tech lead who does a lot of coordination, designs work for their team, and spends time driving projects. The other is more of a specialist.

The tech lead was definitely my profile when I initially became Staff where I took a team of about eight engineers and drove an eighteen month project. That project had a lot of dependencies, a lot of gnarly parts. I had to control the communication around the project, as well as figure out how to allocate pieces of the project to the team in a way that both helped them grow and got the project done.

The specialist is deeply specialized in a particular area, for example Guido van Rossum[153], the creator of Python. Specialists would take on really complex projects and execute it themselves, often projects that no one else could take on effectively. There were fewer specialists than tech leads.

Were the specialists predominantly external hires?

There were some specialists that came in from industry, like Guido and a lot of very experienced folks on the ML team, but a lot of specialists ended up being homegrown. That might be related to rolling out titles relatively late at Dropbox, which gave folks longer to develop deep context in our technology.

How do you spend your time day-to-day?

In my current role within the incubator I'm spending all day prototyping, but in my previous tech lead role I did a lot of different things.

I was coding, but I wasn't coding very much, maybe 20% of my time. I was the tech lead for the desktop client area, and spent a lot of time coordinating and providing guidance on projects. I also spent a lot of time partnering with recruiting, which was something that I did because I was interested in it, not because it was required.

For example, I worked on designing specialty interview loops, moderating debriefs and candidate screening. I also did a lot of work on diversity initiatives. That's one of the reasons that I've tried engineering management multiple times during my career, because I enjoy participating in organizational growth.

Where do you feel most impactful as a Staff-plus engineer?

One of the things that I'm really proud of having worked on was a big revamp of our engineering levels. Back in 2017, I was one of the few individual contributors selected to work on an engineer levels refresh, most everyone else was a director or manager. I'm proud because the new ladder impacted every person at Dropbox working in Engineering, Product and Design.

It was also just really interesting to think deeply about how company growth changed roles and responsibilities. We were starting to bring in people from a lot of different backgrounds, and we wanted to be able to reward everyone in a healthy way. That was very different from my normal day-to-day responsibilities and pushed me outside of my comfort zone pretty significantly.

I'm also proud of my Staff Project, which was very technically complex. That project also gave me a chance to help a lot of people on the team grow. Years later, I've had engineers who left the company email me and say how much more confident they are or how much they learned because of that project.

It was also on that project where my manager helped me understand that my first impulse as a tech lead didn't scale. Initially I was thinking, "I'll break it into twenty pieces, assign out eighteen pieces, and keep the two hardest for myself," and my manager pushed me to delegate the hard pieces to the team to stretch and develop them.

Do you spend time advocating for technology, practice, process or architectural change?

As a tech lead I spent a lot of time advocating for change. I would jump into a lot of different architecture and technical discussions, even in areas that weren't directly within my area of expertise, because people seemed to trust my intuition. I know tons of engineers who have amazing technical intuition and don't have the Staff Engineer title, but the title does formalize having that intuition.

I do prefer for the team that's going to own a project to make the final decisions about it. In cases where I have a very clear "right decision" in my head, I'll try to lead the team towards that decision rather than going in and saying "this is the right decision."

How have you sponsored other engineers? Is sponsoring other engineers an important aspect of your role?

I definitely think of myself as a sponsor. Execution is one of the most rewarding parts of my job–I love building stuff–but I've always loved helping people grow. I feel really proud when I see somebody who I informally mentored or helped on a project go on to do something great.

As a Staff Engineer, and especially as a woman who is a Staff Engineer, I feel like a lot of people look up to me. There seem to be a lot more role models on the manager career path, so I try to make being a role model part of my responsibilities, instead of just keeping my head down coding. I mean, I could just keep my head down coding and that would be great, but I want to help other people, especially people with imposter syndrome.

I often get people coming to me and saying, "I don't know how to make the next step." or "I don't know how to become a staff engineer, so I'm going to go be a manager instead." I want to try to help them figure out their path. As a Staff Engineer, I think being visible and available for people to ask these sorts of questions is an important part of the role.

What's something you've done as a Staff-plus engineer that you weren't able to or wouldn't have done earlier in your career?

There wasn't anything I wasn't able to do without the title, but the title did give me confidence. In addition to the title, the other thing that gave me confidence was realizing that everyone else is also struggling with imposter syndrome. The latter I learned in a pivotal conversation with someone who I thought was the most confident engineer I'd ever worked with, and when I talked with him about it he said, "I question every single thing I do. I go home and agonize over what I said earlier that day, and whether it was silly."

It was really that conversation in combination with the title that pushed me to believe in myself as a Staff Engineer. Together they gave me the confidence to ask for the harder projects, or to ask my manager to give me more projects to work on.

What was your proces of getting promoted to Staff engineer at Dropbox?

They rolled out external titles a while after I joined Dropbox. In the first review season with titles, they gave the Staff title to a very small number of engineers. They were really still calibrating the titles at that point. It was in the second review season that I got my Staff title.

By the second season, I'd been a Tech Lead for a while and my manager and I both felt that I had clearly been executing at the Staff level. We did go over the new career level definitions to identify any gaps before the review cycle, but overall it went pretty smoothly.

What two or three factors were most important in you reaching Staff?

One of the big factors for me was definitely visibility. Part of that came from doing so many things outside of normal engineering responsibilities.

For example, I helped recruiting with running the intern program one summer. During the program I worked with a ton of intern mentors across different teams, and since Dropbox tended to have very large intern classes, that ended up meaning that I gained visibility across pretty much the entire company. The hiring work helped too. If you're moderating dozens of hiring debriefs every month, and driving hiring and calibration conversations, then you'll get to interact with everyone in engineering. I also helped with onboarding, giving a core engineering presentation to incoming new hires.

Having a sponsor was also definitely important. My manager and I had a fantastic relationship, and I also had a great relationship with my skip-level manager. I think that played a big part as well.

Was that work, which some companies would call "glue work," directly valued?

This work was highly valued by leadership at Dropbox. Leadership and many of the very senior engineers were heavily involved in these efforts, especially recruiting, and it was not considered glue work. That being said, it would not have gotten me to Staff on its own. It was a question of finding a good balance between having cultural impact and having something technically strong to showcase.

There is a popular idea that becoming a Staff engineer requires com-

pleting a "Staff Project." Did you have a Staff Project, and if so what was it?

There isn't an explicit expectation, nor is it listed anywhere as a formal requirement, but it is understood that you'll complete a Staff Project to get promoted. I can't think of any Staff promotion that didn't include a really strong project, typically a multi-person project where the engineer was the Tech Lead.

I definitely had a Staff Project. Back in the day, Dropbox was initially a consumer product that people downloaded and installed on their machines. When we launched Dropbox for Business there was a request for both your personal and work Dropbox accounts to work simultaneously, including being able to switch across them without needing to log out and log back in.

The initial implementation was written under immense time pressure, and it ran multiple Dropbox processes. One for your personal account and another for business. My Staff project was to make it so a single Dropbox process could run with multiple users logged in. The hard part was that the project stretched from the kernel all the way to the user interface. I had to understand every single layer of the Dropbox system.

Initially we thought it would take six months, and it ended up taking eighteen months. It took up most of the Desktop Client team's resources for quite a while.

Would you share a piece of advice on reaching Staff that was particularly helpful for you?

Early in my career, my instincts were to ask for projects that I felt I would be able to execute well on instead of projects with more ambiguity that would push me to grow. The advice I got was to push myself out of what I was comfortable with, and to ask for the hard projects on the team. To reach Staff Engineer, you have to know and do more than what you currently know. It's important to always push beyond what you're doing and not be scared of asking for things you think are too hard for you.

This is tied into imposter syndrome, where you might not want to try anything until you're absolutely sure you'll excel at it. But you have to get comfortable with the fact that you might crash and burn. That's okay, you've got to try it.

What about a piece of advice for someone who has just started as a Staff engineer?

People frequently come to me and ask, "What should I do next to reach Staff?" One of the things that I tell them is to be super open and honest with your manager about what you want from your career. A mistake I made early on in my one-on-ones was telling my manager what I thought they wanted to hear, instead of what I actually felt.

They'd ask me if I was interested in a piece of work, and I'd wonder why they were asking, did they *want* me to take the work? So I'd say I was interested even if I wasn't. Or they'd ask me how a project was going, and it might be going horribly, but I'd tell them it was going fine to avoid disappointing them, instead of saying I needed help.

Somewhere along the way I realized that your manager is really on your team. They're looking for a way to make you grow, be productive, be happy and become the best engineer you can be. The way to have an effective relationship with your manager, including having them sponsor you, is to be super honest and open with them.

This became particularly obvious to me when I became a manager myself, because I *wanted* everyone on my team to become a Staff Engineer and to get promoted. I wanted to find reasons to promote them, and worked with them on that.

Did you ever consider engineering management, and if so how did you

decide to pursue the staff engineer path?

I do pendulum a decent amount, because I'm interested in so many things on both sides of the career ladder. I'm interested in growing people, I really like working with recruiting, I'm one of those engineers that actually enjoy interviewing, I like understanding how teams grow. But I also really like writing code, and after I spend some time managing I want to get back into the code and hack around a little bit.

Once I started mentoring and managing I definitely found myself thinking about career growth very differently. The pendulum has helped me see a lot of different perspectives. As a manager you have very explicit responsibilities for things like headcount and performance reviews. Staff engineer responsibilities are really fuzzy and differ across companies. That ambiguity around Staff roles leads many folks to make the lateral switch to management who would have been happier staying as an engineer. That's why it's so valuable to get more information on the Staff role out there for people to read.

What are some resources (books, blogs, people, etc) you've learned from? Who are your role models in the field?

I read a lot, but my reading is very recreational. What's been most impactful for me is having a lot of people who I think of as mentors, usually friends, former managers and folks that I've worked with. I have a decent number of recurring monthly lunches, coffee chats and dinners with people who've worked with me in the past, know me, and I trust. It's those conversations about career challenges and growth that have gotten me to where I am in my career.

Rick Boone - Strategic Advisor to Uber's VP of Infrastructure

This story was recorded in April, 2020. Learn more about Rick on his Linkedin[154].

Tell us a little about your current role: your title, the company you work at, and generally what sort of work does your team do?

I'm the Strategic Advisor to Uber's Vice President of Infrastructure, which means I'm part of the Infrastructure leadership team along with the engineering directors and org-wide Program Managers. Infrastructure Engineering at Uber is about 700 people across six sub-organizations like Metal which handles our data centers and servers, Storage, Developer Platform and so on. I work with the VP on things like technical strategy, cultural strategy and special projects.

Strategic Advisor is a wide ranging role, for example I might work on:

- assessing our technology needs over the next two years
- helping prioritize innovation in the roadmap for the next six months
- digging into important areas without a clear owner and helping streamline the ongoing related projects
- learning how the engineers are feeling before or after a big organizational change
- talking to two teams who need to agree on something but are very far apart and seem like they're having communication issues, figuring out how to help them find an effective path forward

It's just a really, really broad role that's a mix of engineering, culture, psychology, organizational design and strategy. There are two ways that I describe it, both from pop culture. The first is like being the Hand of the King in *Game of Thrones*, and that's the best analogue I have for it. The second is Leo McGarry from *The West Wing*, who always said, "I serve at the pleasure of the President." In my role, I say that I serve at the pleasure of the Vice President of Infrastructure.

Although right now it's just me, previously there were two of us in the Strategic Advisor to VP Infrastructure role, and we would split the work based on our natural affinity to the projects. She often focused more on projects related to managers and leadership while I focused more on IC's and engineering projects - though we still managed to do things in both areas

The Strategic Advisor role is a bit unorthodox; it was created by Matthew Mengerink[155] a little while after he started in the VP of Infrastructure role. To my knowledge, our org, and the office of our CTO, are the only orgs which have a role of this type. Matthew created the role because of the value of having full context from within the engineering teams themselves, and he wanted to create that feedback loop to inform his decision making.

It's a particularly valuable role in Uber's Infrastructure organization because it's a really, really broad organization, and I help serve as a synthesized view across all of it.

How does this role compare to a TPM role?

This is an interesting question, because I was just thinking about the distinction between Chief of Staff and my own role the other day. Within the Infrastructure Leadership Team, we have the strategic advisor and program managers, and in the past, we've also had someone who filled a Chief of Staff role.

The way I see it, the program managers are an organization-scoped operational role. They're working at a high-level, ensuring that the major programs and areas within Infra are progressing along and evaluated at a regular cadence, operationalizing efforts + initiatives, etc. The Chief of Staff role was one which ensured that the entire leadership machine was working well together - that all the people, groups, messaging, etc, involved in running and leading Infra were operating effectively.

My strategic advisor role is more about taking broad domain knowledge, both technical and cultural, getting into the details of the problems on a personal and organizational level, and then mixing in engineering acumen. From that I'll synthesize a set of recommendations or insight which I deliver to either the organizational leader or the entire leadership team. Day-to-day, the vast majority of my work is done directly with the org director and with the PM's - delivering recommendations to the director of the org, and then, with his input and approval, working with the PM's to turn them into a reality.

How do you think about the importance of remaining aligned with your sponsor?

It's funny, because that alignment is key - almost a necessity - for the role. Matthew and I are very aligned on our principles, values, world views, emphasis on emotional intelligence, approach to execution, and philosophies. On so many things we're lined up, such that it's almost a symbiotic relationship.

Alignment with the sponsor is really critical to be effective, but it's more than just the dispassionate connection between Strategic Advisor and Vice President. It's also about the connection between Rick and Matthew as people, and making sure that's a good fit.

In my role we'll often go weeks without being in the same room together, but I still have to operate as if I'm his direct proxy. So I go into a room and think, "What would Matthew do here? What is the question he would want to ask? What guidance has he given on this problem?" Because I can't always run back to him for clarification, it's essential to develop and maintain a deep understanding of his world view. That's essential for me to retain the very deep trust required to be his representative and effectively carry out his strategy and vision. People need to be confident that I'll always give the same answer that

Matthew would give if he were there.

It also means that I have to truly understand his goals, intent, values and principles, to make sure that I'm ready to stake my reputation and credibility on pushing them forward. Often, part of my role involves advocating for or translating his vision and/or implementation to engineers, sometimes when supplemental context isn't always known. When I do this, I have to make sure that I not only understand the logic and value of what he's doing, but that I also believe in it myself - otherwise, advocacy becomes hard, not to mention disingenuous.

This is something I really struggled with a lot when I started in the role. Matthew would constantly tell me, "You're my representative; you should feel free to push on and perform things using my name and role." That was difficult for me because I've never been in a role like that before. Previously I've always operated using my own name and reputation, and now I was operating under the aegis of the Vice President and everything which that carried . Over time I've learned how to be deliberate with using that hammer, since you don't want to overuse it.

I've also learned that I have to let folks know which hat I'm wearing sometimes. I love to mentor people, but sometimes folks aren't sure if they're getting the strategic advisor working for the benefit of the organization and company or the mentor, working for the benefit of that person and their career; I try to let them know which role I'm currently in within a particular conversation. If I meet with someone I'm mentoring, they might want to get advice about changing teams, or even leaving the organization or the company, and they want to know which perspective I'm giving advice from.

What does a "normal" Staff-plus engineer do at your company? Does your role look that way or does it differ?

I think the biggest difference is that other senior-plus engineers work primarily on technical work. They are leaders, so they do get into the realm of emotional intelligence, communication, collaboration, conflict resolution, evangelism and so on, but still 80% of their daily efforts are driven by technical concerns.

Whereas with me, there might be weeks where I'm focused on a project around group psychology or organizational design. Technical concerns are not always the pure focus that drive my day to day - though they are always there, if even just in the background.

How do you stay aware of reality on the ground now that you're developing less?

When I was an engineer I could do this passively, because you're in the code, trying to push commits, dealing with the friction of provisioning and operating services, etc. That approach doesn't work anymore, since I'm not touching code very much; so now, gaining that data and awareness requires an active process.

One thing I've done is continue to sit next to my old team so I can hear them work. Maybe they'll complain about a service's stability, or a gap in our tooling, and it's helpful to keep hearing that.

I also constantly ask folks questions about their developer experience. I keep a list of people in my head of folks who are good at surfacing problems and giving feedback on approaches, and I reach out to them frequently. Sometimes these reach outs are more structured, literally a survey for input, and other times it'll just be a quick message checking in.

I also tell folks to send me non-critical path work that doesn't have a strict timeline, and I try to use that as an opportunity to stay fresh in writing actual code. I have to be careful not to get in the critical path of our actual product though, because I know I won't have much bandwidth to maintain the code going forward.

How have you sponsored other engineers? Is sponsoring other engineers an important aspect of your role?

One of the things that's special about this specific role is that it's essentially a built-in mentorship with the Vice President. When I got started, he asked me, "What do you want to do in five years? What are you aiming for?" At the time, I really didn't have clear answers to those questions. For a long time my perspective has been that being able to write code, in our current time, puts you in one of the best positions in the history of humanity, in terms of job security and trajectory, and that seemed like enough for me.

As I spent time thinking about my goals, what I really came away with was that I love being a visible reference for other engineers, especially other minority engineers, and helping people here at Uber or earlier in their career. I especially enjoy helping people who are just getting into the industry, and might still be a little intimidated by it. That's a huge part of what drives me, and this role has helped me realize and admit that to myself. Before I didn't accept that as a valid purpose, but I realized that if it's what you love, if it's what you're passionate about, then you have to go for it.

Another reason mentorship is important to me because throughout my life and career, I've had six people that I consider key mentors. Each of them, at various times, have provided massive impact and influence upon my life - I would not be anything close to who I am without their past and continued guidance. And I'm both extremely grateful for them and also constantly aware of how much they've guided me. So, I always recognize the power of a mentor and want to make sure I can provide that for others. And sometimes, mentors don't even know how their words or actions change you, the ripple effect they can have, even years later. So, I always try to make myself available for others as a mentor, because you never know when you can have that type of life-changing impact on someone, or how. It might just be the right word, the right perspective, the right push from you, at just the right time for them.

I'll always tell people, "Seriously, if you need me, just come ask for help." This is one of the most exciting parts of what I do, and there are a few different ways I try to make myself available.

One is that I give an Engucation (what happens when you blend engineering and education into a single word) class every month to most new hires in engineering. That class is called "Lessons + Questions" and it's literally just a place where they can ask me anything they want about Uber - technical, cultural, whatever - and I'm as candid as possible. At the end of that, I let people know my email and that they're welcome to reach out. A good number reach out to me after that and I give them advice on their careers, working at Uber, or whatever. Other times I'll have people who just run into me while I'm around the office and ask for advice.

I want to be visible as a Black engineer, showing others that we *are* here and this *is* doable. Once I realized this was an important motivation for me, I knew that I had to get better at public speaking, because that's such an important way to scale myself as a role model. Public speaking used to terrify me. I used to *hate* public speaking. But because it's such a key way to reach large numbers of people, I told myself I had to learn to like it, and since then I've learned to be an effective public speaker and have actually fallen in love with it. It's now one of the most exciting things I do - it's like a roller coaster; everytime I do it, I get nervous, but it's a thrilling, fun type of nervousness and I get a huge rush while I'm doing it.

Do you think about building your external brand?

I have a couple of friends that spend time building their external brand, one of whom is getting back into it right now. He realized that his work at Uber was so intensive that he'd pushed external work to the wayside.

I'm a bit more passive about it. When I'm involved with something that gets written up publicly or I give a public talk, then I'll post a link on LinkedIn, but I don't write my own content at all. I think about doing it, and I'm interested in doing it, but I don't. I tend to think through speaking, so writing this way requires a lot of preparation to organize my thoughts, and I've not spent much time doing it externally so far.

You first got the title strategic advisor at your current company. Were you hired as a strategic advisor? If not, what was the process of getting promoted to that role?

My path was completely unorthodox. It wasn't planned, and there really isn't a reproducible pathway to it, more of a fortunate series of events. Previously Rob Punkunus[156] was in the same role, and when he decided to leave he was asked by Matthew to suggest potential successors. He suggested me and Kate, and both of us ended up serving in the Strategic Advisor role.

Matthew and I had already had several positive interactions before that, where we'd started to identify that we had similar views and values. For example, at one point we had a rash of nasty comments submitted anonymously to our Questions & Answers meeting, and it really bothered me to see our culture heading that direction. I stood up and spoke at one of the Q&As asking folks to find a more constructive way to surface their concerns, and I think that resonated with Matthew.

When he first suggested that I take the role, I had a ton of imposter syndrome about it. I tried to get him to rescind the offer, thinking it wouldn't be a good fit, but ultimately I did accept and have been in the role since.

What two or three factors were most important in you becoming a strategic advisor? How have the companies you joined, your location, or your education impacted your path?

In addition to Rob's recommendation, the most important factor was doing visible work that aligned with Matthew's values. One project I worked on was joining the working group to understand and improve SRE's culture back in 2017. The working group was already planned before Susan Fowler's blog post[157] went out, and our first meeting was coincidentally three days after she posted it. I really think the culture working group did some great work, work which myself and the other group members are extremely proud of and over eighteen months we really moved the culture of a hundred person organization in a meaningful way.

Additionally, I've always just been personally fascinated with things in the realm of both culture and human psychology + behavior. In my career, at the companies I've worked at, culture + group psychology has often been the hidden x-factor that turns organizations from good to great. I'd already been satisfying my own personal curiosity in the area with books and papers on things like behavioral economics, behavioral science, etc, so that natural interest has helped nudge me towards where I'm at now.

Can you remember any piece of advice on reaching Staff that was particularly helpful for you?

Throughout my career people have always told me that I'm much more impactful and have more potential than I realized. I never listened to that, and for me, as well as many other engineers, especially engineers that are minorities, we spend a lot of time doubting ourselves. It's so easy to only see the bad parts. We might not recognize when we're in a meeting and speak passionately about something, and that people are really listening to us. It really helped to have people keep telling me that I didn't realize the impact I was having, that my viewpoints were not only valid, but actually influential in the organization.

Another thing that's helped is having mentors. Specifically I like mentors who are constructively antagonistic. What I mean by that is that they throw me into things that utterly terrify me but they're certain I'm ready for. They've helped push me way beyond what I thought was possible for me. These have generally been managers who I've worked with, but where we've been able to mutually learn from each other.

What about a piece of advice for someone who has just started as a Staff engineer?

This goes back to how I got where I am based on having a broad set of interests in organizational psychology, culture, mentorship and so on, in addition to the technology. I've never been a pure engineer that's just deep in the code 24/7. I've never been that person, and I had to make my peace with that.

For me it's been important to follow my passions. Recently that's been around mentorship, but it's also been around other things like machine learning, which has always been a hobby of mine. I love how machines can generate insights that mimic how people think - it's the perfect marriage of my interests in technology + psychology.

So I have these passions that I stoke, and then when opportunities to align those passions with something the company needs arise, I take them. For example, my previous team at Uber was generating insights into fleet utilization for capacity planning purposes, and that was a great chance to pull together my interest in machine learning and site reliability[158].

Small companies give you the chance to do many different things, but at a certain size companies also give you the unique opportunity to specialize in your passions, and that for me has allowed me to maintain both impact and passion despite never being the person to sit beyond the keyboard and knock out code all day.

Did you ever consider engineering management, and if so how did you

decide to pursue the staff engineer path?

It's something that I think about sometimes, even now it's something I'm thinking about. It's on my list of possibilities, and throughout my career folks have asked, "Have you considered moving into management?"

What I want to focus on right now is becoming effective as a high-level, big-picture leader. Eventually I'd like to develop the people management skill set too, maybe somewhere in the medium future. The thing that appeals to me is that human behavior excites me to no end, and people management is a great opportunity to spend time on that.

What are some resources (books, blogs, people, etc) you've learned from? Who are your role models in the field?

You know, for the first two-thirds of my career I used to love reading as much technical content as I could. I would be on YCombinator or my RSS feed all day reading about distributed systems, reliability, etc. These days I'm much more into reading about behavioral economics, behavioral science, human psychology, organizational strategy and so on. Some people I really enjoy in those realms are Daniel Kahneman[159], Tim Harford[160], Dan Ariely[161]. There are also some amazing podcasts out there - Freakonomics[162], Choice-ology[163], Hidden Brain[164].

Also, last year I started compiling a reading list of books about the human brain and behavior[165] which I share with anyone who's also interested in the topic(s).

I do still keep up with r/linux[166] and r/programming[167] on Reddit, which have replaced RSS feeds for me in discovering new things to read.

Nelson Elhage - Formerly Staff Engineer at Stripe

This story was recorded in April, 2020. Learn more about Nelson on his Twitter[168] and blog[169].

Tell us a little about your current role: your title, the company you work at, and generally what sort of work does your team do?

I was most recently at Stripe. They do online payment processing, and it's a pretty fast growing startup of about two thousand people. Engineering was around six hundred. When I left, I technically didn't have a title. If I had stayed another two months, I would have been a Staff Engineer, because they finally rolled out titles after some years of internal debate.

The team I worked on most recently was called Payment Architecture, which was a team of three or four fairly senior engineers. Payments are the core of Stripe's product, and we looked after the payments codebase. We were particularly focused on the financial infrastructure layers of the codebase, and building the data model and abstractions we needed to support all of Stripe's current and aspirational product lines.

We looked at how code structure fits into organizational structure, including how to structure code within a rapidly growing organization that was adding teams, products, countries, and payments methods. It was particularly important that our architecture support spreading ownership across a number of offices and timezones.

We drove a lot of initiatives around code quality and code architecture, and did some implementation and rewrite projects. For each of those initiatives, we developed metrics and goals, got teams to take on those goals, and then gave teams tools to help them migrate to the new standards.

Was the "Payments Architecture" team a permanent team or more of a project team?

A little bit of both. It wasn't a super tactical team with a narrow project or scope to its mandate. But it was also unlikely to last forever as a team. We were taking an experimental approach to evolving our architecture, with the goal of revising and updating our approach as we went. We hoped that the team would eventually work itself out of its job.

What does a Staff-plus engineer do at your company?

It's hard to say with too much confidence because Stripe was only just introducing titles. It wasn't public who was a Staff Engineer, but you did have a sense of who the senior engineers were based on the people working on the most significant, impactful things.

There are some clear Staff Engineer archetypes. One is working on deep technical projects, maybe scoping out or building new pieces of infrastructure. Before the Payment Architecture team, I worked on building Sorbet[170], which is our static Ruby type checker. I spent about a year with two other senior engineers building that from scratch, which was a good example of the deep, highly leveraged technical work archetype.

There were also Staff Engineers who spent time wrangling cross-cutting projects, serving as a combination of architect and project manager to pull together different parts of the organization to work on a large problem. Typically these problems weren't well-aligned with our current architecture or organization such that they required collaboration across many different teams.

There were also Staff Engineers who worked with one team, or a small group of teams, and they served as the keepers of the team vision. They'd identify what the team was building towards, and where they wanted to be in one to five years. They'd work across the organization to build and share that vision, then work to implement it.

How do you spend your time day-to-day?

This looked very different between the Payment Architecture role and the Sorbet role. Sorbet was more of a "heads down and code" project. On Payments Architecture, there was still some amount of coding because we had a specific approach that we wanted to both try out and to demo the ideas that we were pushing for.

I did a decent amount of project management as well. Things like tending to the task tracker, running the daily stand up, figuring out who needed help or who was blocked. I also spent time being communication glue across the company and engineering organization, especially talking to teams that were interested in the tools and patterns we were building and advising them.

In that effort, I spent time in various meetings figuring out the technical strategy, and also a fair amount of my week writing design documents on the problems we saw along with promoting the shape of architecture that we thought would solve them. Finally, I worked to explain and sell those ideas to leadership and other teams, as a way of setting the agenda and advocating for their investment and prioritization.

Where do you feel most impactful as a Staff-plus engineer?

Certainly the one that's easiest to trace the impact of was Sorbet[170], where in two years a three person team took Stripe from a dynamically typed code base to a substantially statically typed code base. That impacted all of the company's six hundred engineers' daily experience in their editors and development environment.

That said, it's hard to know whether that was truly the most impactful project. There's a more nebulous argument that the architecture strategy work will be more impactful in the long run.

What's something you've done as a Staff-plus engineer that you weren't able or allowed to do in earlier roles?

The question of "allowed" is interesting, and might not be quite the right question because there were very few official policies on who got what kind of role. Most things relied on more informal gauges of seniority.

But that said, both Sorbet and the Payments Architecture team were relatively ambitious projects. Sorbet for example required pulling three senior engineers off of more concrete projects. Starting them required high levels of organizational respect and trust to get permission and support to pull the team off their existing work and having them instead work on these projects for a year.

Do you spend time advocating for technology, practice, process or architectural change?

This is somewhat seasonal around the planning process. Prioritization ultimately means staffing, and staffing decisions happen during planning.

The planning season was a particularly acute period, but I was more or less continually thinking about prioritization at the engineering-wide level. It might be noticing a problem that a lot of engineers were encountering, or seeing something that was slowing teams down. It was a constant, recurring thread that I thought about and it would periodically become an acute priority where I'd spend time advocating for a team to be created or to work on a problem.

How have you sponsored other engineers? Is sponsoring other engineers an important aspect of your role?

That wasn't an angle that I spent a lot of time thinking explicitly about in those terms, and I can't think of clear examples where I would describe that as what I was doing. An adjacent thing that I did a couple of times was helping to bootstrap teams that I wasn't part of. For example, some team would spin up to take over a system that used to be part my capacity, and I would work with them in a close advisory role to give them context and advice.

You first got the Architect title at Oracle after the Ksplice acquisition. What was your process for getting the Architect title?

I don't remember if Ksplice[171] had titles in place pre-acquisition. After the acquisition I spent one year at Oracle and had the title Architect, which I think at the time was their highest individual contributor level. There was definitely some acquisition title inflation going on there. I don't know if I would have reached that title if I had not come in via acquisition.

After Ksplice was acquired by Oracle and you became an Architect, did the work you were doing on a day-to-day basis change from before the acquisition?

I was broadly doing the same style of work. The thing that changed was that I spent a lot more time interfacing with the Oracle Linux organization within Oracle. I was focused on figuring out how our product would integrate with theirs, and also bringing them up to speed on our technology so that they were able to use it. I had previously spent time training new hires, but that was a much slower rate than what happened at Oracle which was, "We're dropping you into this 400-person org, and now training them is a big part of your job."

What two or three factors were most important in you reaching Staff?

The specific path I took was very dependent on coming in quite early at Stripe. I was roughly employee #30. The thing that I did with that though, which I think is not identical to what everyone else did, is I tried to build very broad context and awareness across Stripe. That was comparatively easy to do, when there were 15 engineers; there weren't that many things then.

But I spent a lot of effort as the company grew trying to stay aware of *everything* that was going on in engineering: the interactions between teams, the scaling pain points. I tried to have an unusually global perspective. That helped me know which problems were important to work on and especially what the one level removed important problems were. If I knew the organization had a goal of launching a specific product, I would have the perspective to see the reason why it would be hard is because of these previous architectural decisions, or that this downstream system wasn't currently up to the task.

As the organization got really big, seeing those one level removed dependencies got increasingly hard, and trying to keep a broad view and systems level view helped with that. It also helped me connect teams together, making me a router of information and ideas, as well as an originator of proposals.

Many teams get stuck looking at their section of the world, and have a less developed conception of how their internal customers are integrating with them. This happens because they've never worked on the internal customer teams they support. I helped bring teams the context of how other teams truly used their systems, and connected them to other people across the organization whose perspectives they should gather,

It's hard to keep all this context as the organization grows, but it's even harder for someone who didn't start building that global context when the company was smaller. By starting early, you have a huge competitive advantage relative to someone starting later who tries to reverse engineer the architecture and organizational dependencies.

When I spoke with Keavy McMinn, one interesting point she made was that sometimes it's helpful to be able to see things without the full historical context. Did you ever find that your context made it harder to move forward?

Absolutely. I would notice myself coming into conversations with a team and I was prepared to give them a seven year history of every time someone had attempted the thing that they're doing and why it didn't work. It would take deliberate effort to review that history and ask myself, "Why is this information helpful or relevant to them?"

Sometimes the information isn't useful. On the other hand, if someone tried to do this thing and died on the rocks, there may be some really hard technical problem that's still around. There might be some value in pointing out the rocks, but also there's a lot of value in having the audacity to try again because it's years later and we've become a different organization.

There is a popular idea that becoming a Staff engineer requires completing a "Staff Project." Did you have a Staff Project, and if so what was it?

I'm instinctively a little bit wary of this sort of idea of a staff project, in part because one of the archetypes of Staff Engineers that I've seen are people who don't necessarily run grand projects themselves or do big things. But just are sort of incredibly effective gurus and routers who make the whole engineering organization run better.

Maybe my closest thing to a Staff Project is that I got my final promotion for work on something called the "Data Model Stripe Release Plan." I led this six month long plan to get a bunch of teams to coordinate on a handful of projects addressing the weaknesses in our data models, and advancing the data model in ways that would, aspirationally, be transformative.

I don't think it's a great instance of a Staff Project in some ways. For one, we did good work, but it was much less transformative than anyone hoped due to a combination of reasons. Some of which were in my control and some of which were that the problems were just too hard and the organization didn't have the resources to actually fix them in six months.

While that project wasn't necessarily better work than I did in other halves, it was a very visible, high profile role. It created visibility and increased my standing in the company in important ways.

Can you share a piece of advice on being a Staff engineer that was helpful for you?

One lesson that I learned was the importance of focus and prioritization. That's especially true when you have the broad organizational context that I talked about earlier. It's very easy at any moment to identify thirty different things that you would like to be working on.

Occasionally you can push each of those thirty things forward a little bit. And that's productive for a while, but you need to be careful. If these are things that *aren't* getting worked on and that you think *should* get worked on, you're going to have much better luck picking one of them at a time and really focusing your effort rather than pushing a little across many different projects at once.

One big distinction is whether there are already teams working on those thirty things. If there are already teams working on them, but not in the direction that you think is effective, you can get a lot of leverage out of going to those thirty teams and helping unblock them.

In the end you have to say, "There are all of these things that I wish I could work on, and I'm not going to do all of them. This year I'll pick one or two to work on, and I'm going to deliberately ignore the other for a while, even though I think they're major problems."

What about a piece of advice for someone who has just started as a Staff engineer?

One thing is that I'm a huge believer in the primacy of Conway's Law to guide organizations' technical architecture.

Another is to build and invest in your relationships with engineering leadership: the managers, the directors, and the vice-presidents. I think some of this might be specific to organizational structure, but certainly at Stripe those people often had a lot of implicit power because they were the obvious people to go to with questions. They also have a lot of influence over staffing and prioritization.

It's important to have good relationships with them both so that you can influence them with your ideas, but also so that you can understand what problems they're seeing. You need to know what their incentives are, and what problems they perceive that you don't perceive. Having better alignment with leadership makes a lot of things much easier.

Something else that has been quite valuable for me is estimation. I find it really valuable to be able to look at a system and have the habit of estimating how many gigabytes-per-second is this thing, or how much storage would this data take? You don't have to get it perfect, getting the nearest power of ten is usually enough to be useful.

Did you ever consider engineering management, and if so how did you decide to pursue the staff engineer path?

I considered it but not very seriously. I have a pretty good understanding of myself that, at least for now, I wouldn't really enjoy that work. I think I'd find all the interactions not a sustainable way to spend my time. I occasionally wish I was more interested in it, because I do perceive it as a way to get a lot of power, but I fortunately have enough self awareness to believe, I think correctly, that I wouldn't enjoy it and therefore wouldn't be good at it.

What are some resources (books, blogs, people, etc) you've learned from?

I get that question decently often because I have an unusually broad breadth of general knowledge, and I don't have a good answer for where it came from. I'm pretty voraciously curious about computing, software and architecture. I read lots of different things, and I spend more time reading links on software engineering Twitter than perhaps is healthy.

It's also been really valuable for me to cultivate a good personal network of other senior engineers. I chat with them informally about whatever it is that we're working on and thinking about. When you have personal connections, you can get very unvarnished views of the problems people are seeing and the solutions they're considering.

I've mostly bootstrapped this through the friends-of-friends networks of people I've known professionally or going all the way back to when I was in school. It's not something I sought out post facto.

I read the occasional technical paper, but it's not something I do actively. It's mostly when it's referenced by someone or comes up in some other context. It's definitely not something I make any effort to keep track of systematically or to review the recent publications. I do think that having a decent handle on the quote unquote foundational literature is really handy.

Diana Pojar - Staff Data Engineer at Slack

This story was recorded in April, 2020. Learn more about Diana on her blog[172], Twitter[173], and Linkedin[174].

Tell us a little about your current role: your title, the company you work at, and generally what sort of work does your team do?

I'm a Staff Data Engineer and the Technical Lead for the Data Platform team at Slack. I joined Slack in February 2016 and I was one of the first engineers in the Data Engineering team. I was heavily involved in building many of the tools and infrastructure to make data available for long-term analytics. When I joined, the team had just made the decision to use Thrift as the logging format. If anyone wanted to get insights, they had to schedule cronjobs on top of the read replicas of the production MySQL database.

The purpose of the Data Engineering team at Slack is to enable anyone in the company (data science, engineers, product managers, etc) to access data, so they can compute insights, drive business decisions or build new features. The Data Platform team focuses on building services and frameworks that work at scale to empower everyone that needs to process or use data in the Data Warehouse. Some things that our teams own are: the Data Discovery service that exposes task, table, column lineage and general metadata, the event logging structure and the pipeline that consumes the events and exposes them in raw tables in the Data Warehouse.

What does a Staff-plus engineer do at Slack? How do you spend your time day-to-day?

The role of a Staff-plus engineer depends a lot on what the team needs and also what the particular engineer strengths are. From my experience the responsibilities of a Staff-plus engineer can change over time, but usually their main focus is working on projects/efforts that have strategic value for the company, while driving technical design and up-leveling their team.

There are two big categories that I've seen Staff-plus engineers fall into: focus more on depth (specialist) or focus more on breadth (generalist).

For the first category, folks that focus more on depth are usually experts in a particular domain and most of their time is spent on writing code or working on technical design documents to find solutions in their area of expertise. Companies deal with unique challenges and subject matter experts are needed to drive technical solutions for these extremely hard problems. For example, at Slack, as the company grew and our system needed to scale and perform, there is a principal engineer that his main focus and passion is to detect and fix performance problems.

Folks that focus on breadth usually work more closely with the leadership team, influencing the org or company wide technical vision, improving processes and culture. Due to their breadth, they are more flexible and can work on different areas of the engineering organization based on the company priorities and needs.

Personally, for now, I enjoy and focus more on breadth and how I spend my time depends a lot on what my team and organization needs. I would say that so far this year, about 50% of my time is spent on technical leadership[175] and talking with people about larger technical investments that we should focus on, and 50% of my time is focused on mentoring, reviewing code, writing code, jumping on incidents and fixing critical issues, etc. The ratio does change quarter by quarter.

Where do you feel most impactful as a Staff-plus engineer? What's something you've done as a Staff-plus engineer that you wouldn't have done earlier in earlier roles?

Personally, I feel that it's quite noticeable the increase in trust and respect from people that did not work with me before my promotion / title change. Having the title strongly correlates with one's ability to influence the organization/company roadmap and priorities - basically you get to be in the "room where it happens".

I get to be part of building things that have impact for the direct success of the company. Advocating for such projects and being part of them was not something that would've been achievable in earlier roles.

I'm also able to uplevel others that are more junior and make their voices heard. Having a Staff+ title brings some privilege that others don't have and I try to leverage that to help uplevel my team / peers.

Do you spend time advocating for technology, practice, process or architectural change? What's something you've advocated for?

A significant amount of my time is actually spent on advocating for technical solutions, processes, architectural or cultural changes - it's not only all about writing code. I'm constantly involved in the technical design review process for many of the teams that need to build systems that rely on the Data Engineering tools and services. Besides being involved in advocating for technical projects, an area of my focus is to improve culture or process changes.

One area that is dear to my heart and that I believe I had a significant role in my organization is around Incident Management and Analysis. I've been involved with the company's resilience team to improve our Incident Analysis processes, but for my Data Engineering organization I was very involved in driving our general oncall expectations and structure, while also adopting the company's Incident Response Structure.

How have you sponsored other engineers? Is sponsoring other engineers an important aspect of your role?

Sponsoring is actually an important area for me, as I focus on building amazing relationships with many people that I work with and I strongly believe that we need to lift each other up. Through my journey to get to Staff Engineer and fighting with my own impostor syndrome, I had the opportunity to work with amazing people that sponsored me and had a huge impact on my growth. A couple of people that I worked with and have been my mentors and role models over time are Josh Wills[176], Stan Babourine[177], Bogdan Gaza[178] and Travis Crawford[179].

Mentoring and growing people around me has always been important to me and being in a Staff+ role, you have a type of privilege and power that others don't have and I try my best to use this to help and uplevel people around me.

You first got the title Staff engineer at Slack. Were you hired as a Staff engineer? If not, what was the process of getting promoted to Staff?

I joined Slack as a mid level engineer and after one year I got my Senior promotion. As a Senior Engineer I had the opportunity to work on multiple projects with org/company wide impact, many of them that were directly tied into how our company business metrics are being computed, which were critical for getting the company ready to go public.

After being 2 years in the Senior role, my manager told me that I am operating at the next level and that he believed there was a strong case to make and he planned to put me up for promotion. At Slack, the Staff+ Engineering promotions need to have a promo package put together that illustrates with clear details and measurable information that a person operates at a certain level. The main areas of focus are: Technical Quality, Impact, Collaboration and Execution. We worked together to write and fill in all the necessary details for the promotion package. As an IC, I highly recommend, if it's possible, to work with your manager and write this document together: it should be a team effort. After the packet is ready, the promotion package is evaluated by a special promo committee where some leadership and staff+ engineers from the whole company are present.

What two or three factors were most important in you reaching Staff? How have the companies you joined, your location, or your education impacted your path?

As I look back and contemplate on how I felt and thought about this when I was a junior engineer, the main factor to get to Staff Engineer is to actually believe that **YOU CAN DO IT** and don't let the impostrome syndrome win.

In general, I've always tried to be very intentional with my career choices and usually I spend some time every year to think about what I'm doing and the areas of growth that I want to focus on. I've found this extremely valuable, because it makes me take a step back and assess what I am currently doing, to ask if I'm still growing in my current environment and think about new opportunities.

So at the end of 2015, when I decided I wanted to leave Twitter, I found out that Slack was starting to build their Data Engineering team. Being able to build and design from scratch the systems, services and frameworks was extremely exciting for me. Joining a newly-formed team at Slack was a unique opportunity that definitely contributed to reaching Staff Engineer. It gave me the opportunity to work on projects that had org or company wide impact. For example, the first big project I worked on moved about 25% of the load on the production MySQL database off to the Data Warehouse, saving the company millions of dollars.

Another critical factor that influenced my path to become a Staff Engineer were the people around me, as I was lucky to have amazing role models and mentors in my team. When I joined Slack, I was the 4th person in a very senior team (everyone else was Senior Staff), which contributed to my desire to prove myself and show that I belong. Building a track record of mentoring, visibility and technical quality in every project also contributed to my path towards Staff, I did not see my job as just a job, but I've put a lot of passion into every project or problem we tried to solve.

There is a popular idea that becoming a Staff engineer requires completing a "Staff Project." Did you have a Staff Project, and if so what was it?

No, I did not have an assigned "Staff Project" and that is not something that it's part of the promotion process at Slack. There is a career ladder that describes the general expectations and scope of impact for every level and with Staff+ levels this level of scope starts to expand from org wide impact towards company wide impact.

I usually always try to challenge myself and I was always looking to drive change and impact in my organization. I think the most impactful project that I worked on and contributed to my path towards Staff Engineer was being involved in thinking through and implementing the technical design on how our company business metrics (ex: ARR) are computed to make sure the process is reliable, scalable and most importantly, reproductible. This was a critical initiative as Slack was completing a public company readiness process.

Can you remember any piece of advice on reaching Staff that was particularly helpful for you? Looking back, is there an easier path to Staff that you could have taken?

Something that I felt was extremely helpful was to understand that a Staff+ Engineer's work and responsibility is more than writing code. Basically what got you to senior level will not get you to Staff+. It's important to understand the expectations of this role in your company, but also in the industry as a whole, as there are some differences between companies.

Work with your manager or more senior peers to find projects that will challenge you and increase the scope of your work. Something that was extremely helpful to me is that I started investing in developing my leadership and communication skills more. I also started framing and thinking about certain things in a different way, when I was starting feeling stressed or unsure of my own abilities, that's often a sign that I'm growing and stumbled into an area that offers a lot of growth opportunities.

What about a piece of advice for someone who has just started as a Staff engineer?

Reaching Staff Engineer brings a lot of responsibility and you should always be a strong advocate for your peers. As an IC, I think execution and being hands on are always the "easy" thing to do and the hard things are actually driving change and impact in your organization.

I think that in different moments of your tenure as a Staff engineer, you might see yourself focusing on different things and that is ok and expected. There's not a single clean cut definition of what a Staff Engineer should do.

Did you ever consider engineering management, and if so how did you decide to pursue the staff engineer path?

This is actually a question that I ask myself every couple of years. Every time that I self-reflect and think about the answer to this question, the answer, for now, is no - I don't want to be a manager. I love coding too much and I strongly believe that to be a successful manager you should not write code, and should instead be fully focused on growing your team. I like being involved in technical decisions and thinking about technical solutions way too much to give up this hands-on experience, even though as you get in more senior roles, the time you spend coding will decrease.

Not being an Engineering Manager doesn't mean that you cannot influence and help people grow. As a Staff+ engineer you do need many of the core management skills, even though you are not a manager and I have found reading management books extremely helpful. I actually think that these two roles, even though they are on separate, parallel tracks, they are closer to each other than people think.

It's possible that at some point in time, the answer to this question might change and that is ok.

What are some resources (books, blogs, people, etc) you've learned from? Who are your role models in the field?

I use Twitter extensively, but I'm mostly a consumer and follow many people in tech. I usually follow people that I saw talking at conferences or I worked with and I find their content relevant to me. Here's a couple, in no specific order: Camille Fournier, Lara Hogan, Josh Wills, Vicki Boykis, David Gasca, Julia Grace, Holden Karau, John Allspaw, Charity Majors, Theo Schlossnagle, Jessica Joy Kerr, Sarah Catanzaro, Orange Book.

I also enjoy reading (I read about 50 books each year) and since last year, I always try to leave a mini review on my Goodreads account[180] for every book I read, but here are a couple of books that I found useful:

- Thanks for the Feedback[181]
- Radical Candor[182]
- The Manager's Path: A Guide for Tech Leaders Navigating Growth and Change[183]
- Leadership and Self-Deception: Getting Out of the Box[184]
- The Coaching Habit: Say Less, Ask More & Change the Way You Lead Forever[185]
- First, Break All the Rules: What the World's Greatest Managers Do Differently[186]
- The Courage To Be Disliked: How to free yourself, change your life and achieve real happiness[187]

- Give and Take: A Revolutionary Approach to Success[188]
- Mistakes Were Made (But Not by Me): Why We Justify Foolish Beliefs, Bad Decisions, and Hurtful Acts[189]

That's not an exhaustive list!

Dan Na - Staff Engineer and Team Lead at Squarespace

Story recorded in March, 2020. Learn more about Dan on his blog, Twitter[190], and Linkedin[191].

Tell us a little about your current role: your title, the company you work at, and generally what sort of work does your team do?

I'm a Staff Engineer at Squarespace. Squarespace is the leading all-in-one platform to build a beautiful online presence: websites, domains, online stores, marketing tools, scheduling appointments, etc. I also operate as the Team Lead of the Internationalization Platform team, which is responsible for building and maintaining the foundational primitives of internationalization across Squarespace products. Engineers use the tools and libraries we own to create localized products.

What does a Staff-plus engineer do at Squarespace? How do you spend your time?

I think in practice the day-to-day responsibilities of Staff-plus engineers vary, depending on both your precise role and how your responsibilities map in the organization.

My position as a Team Lead means I'm fully accountable for the output of my team, both from a business and technical perspective. On the business side, I spend a lot of time meeting with different teams and functions across the company. These stakeholders include product, strategy, customer operations, etc. I want to ensure that I have as many inputs as possible to validate that my team's roadmap reflects our company's most important priorities.

On the technical side, I often find myself reviewing technical documents or scoping work in front of a whiteboard for my team's work in flight. My role has evolved to less hands on coding work and more asking probing questions about architectural decisions and deployment strategies. One irony is that as a Staff Engineer I actually code significantly less than I did as a non-Staff. By no means is that universally true across the role, but in the context of my team, closing vim and operating in more of a strategic/oversight role was the highest leverage use of my time. I'm lucky in that my team is already composed of awesome engineers so my specific code contributions are less material to our output.

But many Staff-plus engineers at Squarespace are not Team Leads and code a lot. Others focus on engineering process and culture. In general I'd say Staff-plus Engineer responsibilities are highly contextual.

Where do you feel most impactful as a Staff-plus engineer? What's something you've done as a Staff-plus engineer that you weren't able to or wouldn't have done in earlier roles?

I have a seat at the table at higher level engineering discussions that occur at a level above individual projects and teams. We have recurring staff engineering meetings where we discuss problems that span teams which are both technical and non-technical in nature. As a hypothetical example, I'd feel comfortable surfacing what I perceive as shortcomings in the engineering onboarding process in this type of meeting. It can be hard to attribute a topic like engineering onboarding to a specific team but a lack of formal ownership doesn't make it less important. I think a key responsibility of Staff-plus is a willingness to own all of the things that contribute to (or block) engineering output, which includes both technical strategy and culture.

Regarding something that's changed, on an everyday basis my title affords a high level of credibility at the outset of conversations. While I'm not advocating for a culture that values titles over ideas, I'd be lying if I said it didn't help me escalate or push through issues that I previously might've had a harder time getting through.

Do you spend time advocating for technology, practice, process or architectural change? Can you share a story of influencing your organi-

zation?

I don't really think about advocacy in terms of categories. I mostly just want our engineering team and product to be the best it can be and address things that experience tells me I can help change.

Some examples:

- When I first joined the company we were in the midst of enormous employee growth, and I noticed it felt hard to get to know anyone on other teams unless you happened to work on a project together. As a result I created a slack room — #connect-engineering — that uses a bot to randomly pair two people in engineering for coffee every two weeks. That room has been pairing people for coffee for over two years now.
- I knew based on personal experience that engineering leadership roles can feel isolating and talking to coworkers I could hear some of those feelings of loneliness. As a result some peers and I created an unofficial Engineering Management Book Club, open to Team Leads and Engineering Managers. There are now two self-organized book clubs with ~10 participants each, providing a safe space for both new and experienced leaders to support each other. The feedback about book club has been enormously positive.

To be fair, neither of these examples required a Staff-plus title. But I do think part of being an effective Staff-plus engineer is caring about and addressing cultural gaps as much as technical gaps.

You first got the title Staff engineer at Squarespace. What was the process of getting promoted to Staff?

I was hired as a Senior Software Engineer II (one level below Staff). I was fortunate to land on a team working on a high impact project that I was able to contribute to immediately. The hardest parts about the project concerned a problem space I was already familiar with — wide, sweeping changes across codebases — and I proposed, prototyped and eventually shipped an alternative architecture that I felt would better position the company for success. That became our frontend translation system, which I wrote about on our engineering blog: Building a System for Frontend Translations[192].

I also owned the communication and education effort around the new translation system, presenting the architecture at internal meetings and sending relevant emails about the status of the project. Grouping this technical contribution to some meaningful cultural initiatives — other internal presentations, #connect-engineering, etc. — my manager had a good case for promotion that was agreed upon by the Engineering Directors.

What about a piece of advice for someone who has just started as a Staff engineer?

I feel like progressing up a career ladder is an additive exercise in forcing you to care about more things than you previously cared about. Caring about more things is hard.

As a trivial example: The intern cares about the small aspect of a feature they can build in three months. The full-time engineer on the team cares about the entire lifecycle of that feature. The team lead/manager cares about the suite of features that compose a product. The director cares about the suite of products owned by their organization. And so on.

Every rung up the ladder means you care about another layer of abstraction, in addition to caring about all the layers beneath your current one.

I feel like a Staff Engineering role is similar in that you're leaving the comfort zone of a specific technical domain to a more general problem domain: engineering. And as leaders you're leaving a potential technical comfort zone to the realm of the system of challenges that impact engineering output. What are the biggest problems holding back engineering teams that fall between the cracks of team ownership? Those are your problems now, in addition to all of the problems of your technical domain.

So while Staff is an aspirational title to achieve, it also includes significant added responsibility. You're a leader now, whether you want to be or not.

How have you sponsored other engineers? Is sponsoring other engineers an important aspect of your role?

I think sponsorship is a key responsibility of any senior role and material to the growth of any engineering organization. I suppose the definition of "sponsorship" varies, but to me one tangible way is to provide opportunities for exposure. For example:

- Giving less senior teammates the opportunity to own and present their work at wider meetings.
- Reaching out to a team who just shipped an awesome feature to write a post for our engineering blog.
- Encouraging someone I met in a #connect-engineering coffee who has unique experience or perspective to give an internal presentation.
- Ensuring that meetings are not dominated by the perspectives of a vocal minority and soliciting opinions from everyone in the room.
- Giving public kudos in a large slack room to someone who just did something great that everyone didn't see.

Lara Hogan has a great post on sponsorship in practice: What does sponsorship look like?

Did you ever consider engineering management, and if so how did you decide to pursue the staff engineer path?

Yes, and I still actively consider it. I know it's more convenient to think about the two ladders as mutually exclusive but I don't.

I still enjoy both shipping code and running teams, and I think the ability to do both at a high level is critical for long-term engineering success. Charity Majors has a fantastic blog post on this topic that I recommend reading: "The Engineer/Manager Pendulum".

Charity argues that "manager career path vs engineering career path" is a false dichotomy, and taking time to alternate between both roles makes you better at both. This maps to my own experience. I'm a better manager because I know how terrible it is to be an IC on a poorly planned project, and I'm a better IC because I know how and when to sound an alarm when a project is going poorly.

I think one of the most important strategic skills for building software is the ability to converge towards pragmatic decision making. A failure mode I've seen repeatedly is when a product manager comes with business requirements and an engineer comes with technical pushback and neither are willing to budge. The ability to empathize with both sets of incentives and navigate that tension is the only way to get anything done, and the best way to build that empathy is to sit in both seats.

To specifically answer this question: my previous role prior to joining Squarespace was an Engineering Manager. I love being an Engineering Manager but I wanted to keep my technical skills sharp so I accepted an IC role. Then I was promoted to Staff.

What are some resources (books, blogs, people, etc) you've learned from? Who are your role models in the field?

In the context of engineering leadership, two books stand out.

My favorite engineering leadership book of all time is High Output Management by Andrew Grove[193]. I pick it up from my bookshelf once a year and end up unintentionally re-reading it. Many ideas from Grove's book have significantly shaped how I view work and leadership: "the measure of a manager is the output of the organization underneath them," "delegation is not abdication," the concept of engineering/managerial leverage, etc. In terms of communicating the tactical aspects of engineering leadership I still think Grove's book is best.

On the human side of leadership, I really loved Lara Hogan[194]'s book: Resilient Management[195]. I had the absurdly good fortune of starting my NYC tech career at Etsy in 2013 where Lara was my first engineering manager. Lara is a master of unpacking and addressing the hardest parts about navigating emotions and personalities, fostering psychological safety, and sponsoring coworkers. And having worked directly under her for close to four years, she is totally the real deal and practices what she preaches.

In terms of non-books, I subscribe to and enjoy reading "Irrational Exuberance[196]," where Will Larson regularly blogs about engineering management with a highly pragmatic and strategic perspective. I've also recently discovered and enjoyed reading Marty Cagan's "Insights Blog[197]," mostly because product leadership is a domain I'm less familiar with and am interested in learning more about.

My role models are some of the amazing coworkers I've worked closely with over the years. I sat next to Daniel Espeset[198] for four years at Etsy and learned an immeasurable amount about coupling technical execution with cultural impact. I learned a lot watching Lara do things like advocate for and achieve pay equity across our engineering group. I learn a lot watching current coworkers like Tanya Reilly[199] institute and evolve our engineering processes to match our ever-growing scale. I'm inspired most by people whom I've personally witnessed have the courage to change companies for the better, despite whatever friction they encountered along the way.

Joy Ebertz - Senior Staff Software Engineer at Split

Story recorded in March, 2020. Learn more about Joy on her blog[200], Twitter[201], and Linkedin[202].

Tell us a little about your current role: your title, the company you work at, and generally what sort of work does your team do?

I'm a Senior Staff Software Engineer at Split.io, working on the backend of what we call the COE team. Split is a feature flagging and experimentation framework. We focus on enabling our customers to separate deployment and release in CI/CD and also enabling A/B testing. My team is responsible for most of the main business logic of our web application, including everything from data storage to the APIs. There is a separate team that focuses on the experimentation side, including all of the detailed statistics that goes into that, so we're able to focus more on the main platform.

What does a Staff-plus engineer do at Split? How do you spend your time?

I'm still somewhat new, so I'm still working to define my role, which is part of the beauty of more senior roles. Today, I'm still ramping up, so I'm probably spending around half to three quarters of my time on tasks for my specific scrum team, just like any other engineer here. With the rest of my time, I'm participating in conversations and working with other engineers to define a lot of our longer term architecture and strategy, including our future API and platform strategy, how we want to develop our authorization framework, breaking up and decoupling our builds and more. I've recently also taken over leadership of our backend chapter and now co-lead it with another engineer and we're working to put together a backend technical vision, prioritize tech projects and lead standards discussions. If that wasn't enough, I also continue to write regularly on my blog and speak at conferences.

Where do you feel most impactful as a Staff-plus engineer? What's

something you've done as a Staff-plus engineer that you weren't able to or wouldn't have done in earlier roles?

I feel most impactful when I can facilitate setting a technical vision for an area and get people moving toward that vision. I think we would all agree that we want our code to be better architected than it is or improved in some way. However, I've found that often people have some vague sense of wanting better without having a clear idea of what that thing they want is. I like to help the group decide on a shared understanding of where exactly they're trying to get (it's actually okay if we never get there) and come up with a general game plan of how to get there. This way we're all marching in the same direction. Having a clear idea of what we want allows us to work with Product to get it prioritized. Even if we never get the whole thing prioritized, knowing how to get there, allows us to slowly make changes that will lead us in that direction. For example, if I'm touching a file anyway and can make a few tweaks that brings me closer to that vision, I will. Without knowing that vision, those tweaks would never happen. The vision alone isn't enough, we need everyone to understand that vision and internalize it. Part of the power of those small changes I just mentioned is if everyone is making them as a part of their normal coding. Suddenly we have everyone working toward a common goal.

I think the biggest thing that differs between now and when I was more junior is my sense of ownership and responsibility. I've always been willing to push back or to drive for improvement. However, when I was more junior, I would often just assume that something was someone else's problem. Now, it's all my problem. I may choose to not prioritize something because I think that it's less important than something else, or I may choose to delegate or pass a problem off to someone else, but I still see it as my problem. I no longer ever assume that someone else will handle something. I'm still a big believer in picking my battles, I won't work on everything - that's too much. I also, however, won't assume that anyone else will either, so if it's worth getting done, it's up to me to either do it or to pass it on to someone else.

Do you spend time advocating for technology, practice, process or architectural change? What's something you've advocated for? Can you share a story of influencing your organization?

Yes. All of those. In my current role, I would say this is a huge part of my job. While, as an engineer, I am also contributing on a scrum team, I would say a lot of my job is to keep an eye out for pitfalls I've seen before or larger patterns of problems. I see my job as making all of engineering more efficient - be that through technology, through architecture or through process. However, I should never be making changes for the sake of changes. I've advocated for a number of things over the years, from rewriting our email notification system to rethinking testing to reworking several authorization frameworks.

For some things, like the email overhaul, I didn't do anything big or grand, I just reminded Product every time they wanted to add a notification that our system was ready to fall over and that we really couldn't add any more until we fixed it. As I pushed back, engineers around me also realized that they could push back. At first Product mostly opted to not add more notifications, but eventually they decided to fix the system. In this case, it was mostly a matter of explaining to them the risks of the system and sticking to what I thought was the right course of action in terms of keeping our systems running.

For other things, such as the authorization frameworks, I was tasked with finding a solution. In these cases, even when people want a new/better solution, you still need to convince them that you've picked the right thing. With incredibly complex systems, people will often think they've found things you've forgotten about (and maybe they did), so it's really important to seek feedback early and often and to carefully record and communicate both what you chose and why but also what else you considered and why you didn't chose something else. People need to feel heard and they need to know that you fully considered their concerns. They also want to understand what your thought process was, but even more important, they want to understand that you did thorough research and didn't just pick the first thing to come along. In fact, when I'm vetting someone else's design, this is one of the things I really look for - what else was considered?

How have you sponsored other engineers? Is sponsoring other engineers an important aspect of your role?

Yes. As soon as you get to any sort of more senior role, this is always a part of your role assuming you chose to take advantage of it. Since I'm still new at Split, I haven't had much of a chance to here, but I'm positive that will change. Sometimes sponsoring is the big stuff - recommending people to lead projects or manage a team, but a lot of sponsoring is smaller things - encouraging someone who is a little unsure of themselves, showing off their accomplishments to more senior people they wouldn't normally have access to, finding ways to delegate your work to people who could get a growth opportunity from doing it. I think it's possible to be a senior staff engineer without sponsoring, but I'm not sure it's possible to be a great senior staff engineer without sponsoring. Sponsoring is one of the most powerful ways we can grow those around us and I would say that growing others is one of the most important aspects of our role.

You first got the title Staff engineer at Box. What was the process of getting promoted to Staff?

At Box, we submit a promotion case that outlines how, based on the engineering rubric, we've already been operating at the next level. Our managers also submit their recommendation and the two go to a promotion committee made up of managers and ICs (at least one level above the level we're applying to). They review the case, call in the manager to answer any questions and then make a recommendation. Our VP was able to change any of the decisions (although to my knowledge this never happened). If the answer was no, feedback was given as to why and you could repeal the decision with additional information or try again the following time. Appeals did sometimes go through, so if you disagreed with the feedback, it was worth trying. I liked this process because it allowed the person with the most context on our accomplishments be the one to write them up and it allowed you to go up for a promotion even if your manager didn't agree. On the other hand, I didn't like the process because it subtly discriminates against those with a little less self confidence and those who struggle with self-promotion. It also resulted in managers taking a little less initiative in starting off the promotion process (letting engineers come to them saying they wanted the promotion rather than suggesting it).

What two or three factors were most important in you reaching Staff? How have the companies you joined, your location, or your education impacted your path?

I would say that my location probably hasn't mattered too much. Education helped me a lot in terms of getting interviews when I was more junior, but a lot less so (at least directly) since then. I would say that the three biggest factors for me were company, visibility and opportunities.

I think it's possible to advance at a lot of companies. However, I found that being at a fast-growing startup really helped me out. When I joined Box, engineering was around 30 people and when I left, 8 years later, it was at a few hundred, but much of that growth was in the first half. This allowed me to come into a smaller engineering environment where it was possible to really get to know the environment, people and code. Then, because we were growing, there were lots of leadership opportunities and technical challenges for those motivated and willing to take them. Because we grew, the opportunities grew with me. At the same time, there were also enough people around me for me to learn from (I was previously at a really tiny startup - 2-4 people, where that really wasn't available).

By visibility, I just mean finding some way to be known. I've always worked onsite, which I find makes this a little easier, but I think this is possible even if you are remote (although possibly a bit more challenging). If you do really great work, but no one knows about it, when it comes time for promotion, you'll be passed over. Furthermore, as you become more senior, part of your job becomes mentoring and teaching others and helping your company to create a tech brand - all of these are by definition, visible. Visibility can take a number of forms, but for me I would say that a few things contributed. I was very active in our Slack discussion forums, answering questions for people wherever I could. I also did a lot of blogging and some speaking both internally and externally. Finally, I was active in our women in tech group, which allowed me to form connections with various people throughout engineering.

Finally, opportunities. These can look vastly different as well. For me there was one in particular that was really helpful - I joined our API standards committee. I was actually a bit hesitant to do so at first because I didn't think I was an expert at APIs, but after reading a few (short) books on REST, along with my work on various APIs previously, I had a pretty solid grasp. The powerful thing about this group is that it cross-cut many teams in engineering, which gave me a chance to work with a lot of different engineers (and gave me that visibility I just mentioned). It also allowed me to have something clear to point to in terms of influencing others and being someone who fights for quality. Our projects there had broad impact across engineering and allowed me to think about something (our API, in this case) holistically.

There is a popular idea that becoming a Staff engineer requires completing a "Staff Project." Did you have a Staff Project, and if so what was it?

I actually didn't really have a Staff Project. At the time that I was promoted, I had transitioned back from management around 6 months prior, so I referenced some of my time managing for leadership. At the time, I was leading (from the technical side) the very small Box team on a cross-company collaboration project, which involved understanding another company's development team's requirements and figuring out how to build as little as possible while meeting their needs. I was a member of an engineering-wide API working group responsible for establishing and maintaining our API standards and I had several side projects going on. I would say that all of these contributed to various parts of my promotion and together helped me establish that I could demonstrate all aspects of what they expected.

Can you remember any piece of advice on reaching Staff that was particularly helpful for you? Is there an easier path to Staff that you could have taken?

One piece of advice I got at some point was to amplify my strengths. All of us have strengths and weaknesses and we spend a lot of time talking about 'areas of improvement.' It can be easy to feel like the best way to advance is to eliminate all of those. However, it can require a lot of work and energy to barely move the needle if it's truly an area we're weak in. Obviously, you still want to make sure you don't have any truly bad areas, but assuming you've gotten that, instead focus on amplifying your strengths. How can you turn something you're good at into your superpower? The other thing to think about is how can you use something you're good at to compensate for something you're weak at? For example, I'm a giant introvert and don't particularly like mingling with people I don't know. I'm terrible at networking with strangers. However, I'm good at writing and enjoy doing it. I've used writing on my public blog to meet people I wouldn't otherwise and get exposure more broadly. In fact, I'm sure I've gotten far more from that than I would have by going to many, many meetups.

The other more tactical thing that comes to mind is directly related to the process we have at Box of writing a promotion case. A few things were suggested to me - first to write the promotion case well before I was sure I was ready for the promotion. This allows you to see where there might be gaps and can give you very tangible things to work on. (Or maybe you'll be surprised and realize that you're ready for promotion before you thought you were). The second is to be very aware of where those gaps are. When a promotion committee is reading through promotion cases, all of the cases are going to be very positive. No one says anything negative when they go up for promotion. So instead of looking for negative things, that committee is going to be looking for what isn't said. Where are the blank spots? What seems to be avoided or talked over. Take a look at your case from that light - what things might be missing? What things are you brushing over? Be sure to work on those. Finally, tell your story.

Our promotion cases had templates with pointed questions, but, especially at the higher levels, everyone isn't the same, nor do we want them to be. Instead of just answering the questions, think first about what your strengths are. What are your superpowers? What is your story? Then figure out how to fit that story into the prompts. You'll have a much better overall case if you include your best strengths in it.

It's possible that if I hadn't taken a meander through management, I would have gotten to Staff sooner. That said, I don't regret doing it and I learned a lot about how people think, how organizations are run and how larger projects are prioritized. All of these have continued to help me do my job on the IC track and likely helped me further get promoted to Senior Staff. While I do think it's distinctly possible that it slowed down when I got to Staff, I'm actually less sure for the next level - I think there's a real chance I would have hung out at Staff longer without it. All of this is to say that even though I didn't take the most direct route, I still learned a lot that has helped me out long term.

What about a piece of advice for someone who has just started as a Staff engineer?

The more senior you get, the less your job is about code. Sure, unlike a people manager, you still have a very technical slant and even through principal, you'll likely be doing at least some coding. However, the higher you get, the more your job becomes about mentoring and growing the people around you (and more broadly), building your team through building your company's public tech brand, noticing larger technical trends that can be improved upon or corrected, helping to set the tech vision for your team or the company and advocating for resourcing for tech debt projects. It becomes much more about seeing broader things and getting others on board. Suddenly, communication, leadership and persuasion are even more important than they were previously.

Did you ever consider engineering management, and if so how did you decide to pursue the staff engineer path?

I actually managed for about a year and a half in the middle of my time at Box and found that I hated it (you can find more about that in my blog post on that topic). That said, I found that there is actually a lot of overlap between management and staff+ roles in most companies. Both roles require mentoring others, leading and the ability to persuade people. They require thinking bigger and more attention to longer term - both in terms of technologies and people. While I don't plan to go back to management, I did learn a lot during my time managing[203] and the experience has actually helped me as I've advanced to Staff and beyond.

What are some resources (books, blogs, people, etc) you've learned from? Who are your role models in the field?

I don't tend to follow any particular person, but instead learn from and find inspiration from almost everyone around me. I'll list a few here, but in all honesty, I would say that I've learned from countless different people at all levels (including many more junior than myself).

I had a manager who every time I came to him with a problem, he would always turn it around on me and ask me what I thought I should do. This got to the point where I could hear him telling me to give feedback to someone directly or telling me to figure out how to fix something without me ever having to talk to him. He really taught me that while, as a manager, he was willing to support me, I would learn the most and be the best version of myself if I could do it on my own. He taught me to take responsibility for everything.

As a counterpoint, I would also mention a principal engineer I worked with, who later taught me that I didn't need to try to do everything myself. After I learned to take responsibility, I started to forget that I wasn't alone. Of course I had heard people talk about delegation, but it's one thing to hear about it or think about it in terms of sprint tasks, but it's another to delegate getting something prioritized or delegate figuring out tech vision for a team or delegate following up on an initiative.

There was another co-worker that I worked with who would drive me completely bonkers sometimes because her approach to solving problems was so different from mine. She would ask for clarification when I thought it was obvious and she would ask for detailed explanations when I thought everyone was on the same page. However, she's also one of the smartest engineers I've ever worked with and working with her made me realize that not only can different styles be just as good, but that sometimes putting together two clashing styles can result in much better results than either of us would have gotten on our own. She found holes in things I thought were obvious and while she drove me nuts sometimes, we got some amazing things accomplished and I am better for it.

Damian Schenkelman - Principal Engineer at Auth0

Story recorded in August, 2020. Learn more about Damian on his blog[204], Twitter[205], and Linkedin[206].

Tell us a little about your current role: your title, the company you work at, and generally what sort of work does your team do?

I'm a Principal Engineer at Auth0[207], an Identity as a Service platform. I work in the Systems Architecture group, which today has three Principal Engineers. We work with different teams on strategic initiatives and also shape Auth0's technical strategy[208], architecture decisions, and guidelines.

At the time of writing, I am working with a group of Identity and Access Management[209] (IAM) teams as a tech lead of a large new product feature, as well as driving reliability and scaling related initiatives with other teams.

What does a "normal" Staff-plus engineer do at your company? Does your role look that way or does it differ?

Within Engineering, we are organized in domains (today Identity & Access Management, Developer Experience, Service Management, and Platform). Auth0's Staff Engineers are people that can technically lead teams within a domain. A Staff Engineer would typically be part of a single team in a domain, while also being able to actively contribute to initiatives across the scope of a domain.

Principal is the next level in our ladder. Principal Engineers can either be in a specific team (depth) or work with multiple teams and their scope spans the entire organization (breadth). Today I am operating in "breadth mode." This means both working on specific initiatives and also the definition of technical strategy, technology choices for our Platform, and leading the Design and Architecture workgroup (a.k.a. DNA).

DNA has 6 members (3 permanent Principal, and 3 Staff/Senior II that rotate every 6 months). The workgroup defines decisions and guidelines to help drive Auth0's technology in a specific direction (e.g. avoid language proliferation so we can build libs once and people can switch teams easily) and also collaborate with teams in technical reviews of large initiatives.

The biggest way in which my role differs, because I have been at the company for 6+ years, 3+ of those as a Director of Engineering, is that I have the "broadest scope." I work with both Product and Platform teams on initiatives and also work often with other parts of the company: joining conversations with high profile prospects, working with our legal team on contract language, or collaborating with Marketing.

How do you spend your time day-to-day?

This varies a lot. A typical week involves a lot of meetings, so I am trying a new thing: grouping meetings on Mondays, Wednesdays, and Fridays. Thursdays are completely blocked, and Tuesdays are only for urgent matters. Because we are remote all meetings are over Zoom.

On meeting days I have recurrent: * 1:1s: to catch up with my manager (VP of Engineering), or a team manager or tech lead. Those conversations are great to stay up to date with them and know their challenges. I feel being too detached from that would impact my ability to get things done effectively. * team meetings: Engineering leadership, Design & Architecture workgroup.

Non-recurrent meetings also take place. Some example topics might be:

- specific initiatives I am tech leading
- helping a group of teams figure out how to get something started
- doing a sync design review

On Thursdays (and as much of I can on Tuesdays) I spend my time thinking about:

- current initiatives and how they are going
- what we could/should be doing in the future (next quarter, next year)
- writing docs, guidelines, blog posts
- (not often) doing POCs and/or writing small tools

Where do you feel most impactful as a Staff-plus engineer? A specific story would be grand.

The biggest impact comes from being able to help achieve "people scale," positively influencing the work of as many people as possible internally. The book Scaling Up Excellence[210] provides an easy to understand analogy: scaling is a ground war, not a one-off airstrike. It requires a lot of time, and patience but to get to your goals you need to align the whole company in terms of goals and how to get to them.

As a Principal Engineer, I try to find opportunities/gaps that I believe will set a direction for as many people as possible in the long term. There's a lot more value to align the ~200 people we have in our Product Delivery organization around a certain topic than to code a solution for a problem myself. The former has more impact, it scales better.

Can you think of anything you've done as a Staff-plus engineer that you weren't able to or wouldn't have done before reaching that title?

Before becoming a Principal I was a Director of Engineering at Auth0. The most interesting thing is that as a Principal Engineer people get a lot less defensive when I provide feedback and they seem a lot more open in 1:1s. I think it might be related to the fact that as a Principal Engineer you are not "representing a part of the organization".

In that regard, being an individual contributor feels a lot better.

Do you spend time advocating for technology, practice, process or architectural change? What's something you've advocated for? Can you

share a story of influencing your organization?

A common problem for fast-growing companies is that there's usually some "lack of clarity." In our case, there was a lot of confusion about what was coming in the future and that made us slow and inefficient in making technological decisions. Teams were uncertain if they should be using a particular technology because they didn't know if that technology would be supported in the future, they were uncertain if they should be building a particular product in a certain way because they didn't know if that approach was aligned with our long-term technical strategy, etc. Naturally, this caused a lot of inefficiencies.

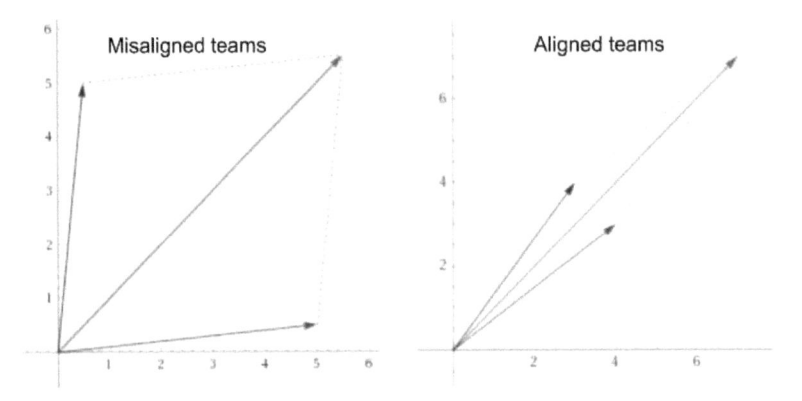

We believed we needed a long-term direction that explained how to approach the technical implementation of problems today and how to bridge the gap between our initial situation and the future vision. More precisely, we needed a documented technical strategy that would detail what we should and shouldn't be doing to be successful in the long run.

After talking to a great number of people I learned that all of them have been exposed to inconsistent information, and rumors, which made them afraid of making decisions, e.g.: "I heard the company is going for X in the future" or "I heard this particular technology Y is not going to be supported by our platform teams." A lot of confusion was caused by a particular rumor that we were going to support a certain customer need and its technical implications. People kept hearing about it, but concrete plans were never announced. I wrote down these issues, connecting all the dots and aiming to translate that information into knowledge. I realized we needed both short and long term ways of solving the problem.

Short term: We had to fill the gap of uncertainty relating to some more urgent and short-term matters. Teams needed to make technical decisions and couldn't wait for a full-fledged technical vision and roadmap. We also realized that once we had that long term vision and decisions, there would naturally be the need to review decisions for specific exceptions. I put together the "design and architecture" (DNA) group, which also wrote guidelines and recommendations, including "approved" technology choices, to guide teams towards independent decisions that don't require review, and also established an RFC review process.

Long term: I came up with a set of topics that I believed the company needed to make decisions about. I tailored my presentations to suit two different audiences – executive and technical. For the executive audience, I developed a succinct presentation, applying non-technical analogies and explanations, and providing actionable solutions. The technical presentation was much more detailed and included many technical terms. I used nemawashi[211] (an informal process of quietly laying the foundation for some proposed change or project, by talking to the people concerned, gathering support and feedback, and so forth) and shared with my VP of Engineering, other execs, my peers, and other senior leaders through to get buy-in before formally making a decision. More specifically, I approached people asking them for their thoughts and opinions securing the buy-in, so that by the time we met to discuss our decisions, it wouldn't be the first time they were seeing the ideas. We finally met, discussed tradeoffs, and arrived at a set of decisions. All decisions were documented in a decision log and we committed specific owners – in writing – to carry them forward.

How do you keep in touch with how things really work as you spend less time on hands-on development?

There are two aspects of this, keeping up with technology in general and keeping up with what goes on at Auth0 and the current "state of affairs" in Engineering teams.

These are the things I do to keep in touch with things related to Auth0:
* Internally: keep an ear to the ground both through Slack and having 1:1s with some tech leads and Engineering Managers. This helps me understand what challenges they are having first hand, and also find patterns or arrive at global solutions instead of local ones. * Externally: talk with customers/prospects to see how they use the product, read tweets and news mentioning Auth0 and the identity space.

I don't feel I am "keeping in touch" as much as I'd like technology-wise, but I do try to. So many new important new things are happening in our industry every month that it is hard to keep up. Accepting the fact that meetings and not being hands-on means that I will likely be less in touch than I'd like with things is important. Once I accepted that I could start prioritizing what was valuable.

I read books, carve out time to do some POCs or read blogs/papers about specific topics, and ask to lead specific initiatives to stay up to date with how we are developing even if I don't code that often.

How have you sponsored other engineers? Is sponsoring other engineers an important aspect of your role?

Yes, a lot! I am a member of our Engineering Leadership team. We meet twice a week to discuss topics around the organization. This, together with keeping an ear to the ground, and being part of meetings about mid-term plans helps me know about (and sometimes propose) opportunities that might be available ahead.

Whenever that happens I typically propose the names of people that I believe would benefit from that opportunity, explain why I think they would be good at it, and, if helpful, offer to mentor them in case there are any perceived skill gaps.

You first got the title Principal engineer at Auth0. Were you hired as a Principal engineer? If not, what was the process of getting promoted to Principal?

My story here is a particular one. I started at Auth0 in May 2014 as the fifth engineer, ~tenth employee. There were no titles, no ladder, nothing like that. Around 2015, I started mentoring and doing 1:1s with a couple of new hires. Towards the end of 2015, I was working on my initiatives, and also leading others, helping with hiring, etc. Late 2015 Matias Woloski[212], Auth0's CTO and co-founder, was looking for someone to lead Engineering teams and he asked me if I would be a Director of Engineering.

I've been privileged enough to be able to approach my career in a way that maximizes learning and opportunities for hard problem-solving. That's the main principle that helps me make decisions. When he offered me, a 25 year old living in Argentina, the opportunity to lead the Engineering organization for a "Silicon Valley," remote-first company that was growing exponentially I naturally said "yes." I had never thought "I want to manage," it just happened because I wanted to learn and solve hard problems.

Things worked out great. I learned a lot about building teams, organizations, leading people, etc. Because I was one of the first engineers, had built a lot of the systems and I enjoyed technical conversations I also did a lot of technical leadership in that role, both with Product and Platform/Infrastructure teams. Towards early 2019 as a Director of Platform, I started thinking that I was not learning as fast as before and that I wanted a broader scope than just working on our platform. After many conversations with Christian McCarrick[213], Auth0's VP of Engineering at the time, I realized that the challenge I wanted to take up next would be being one of Auth0's technical leaders. I transitioned to Principal Engineer in August 2019.

What two or three factors were most important in you reaching Principal? How have the companies you joined, your location, or your education impacted your path?

A quote I love from Seneca is *"Luck is what happens when preparation meets opportunity."* Getting to Principal required getting some things right, but also a lot of luck. I want to call out some of the key factors that got me to Principal and also show how luck played a part in them.

First job: In Argentina it's common to start working while you are in University. When I finished high school I found a job at a fantastic company called Southworks[214]. The two key things about that place were that:

- the company worked on projects with cutting edge technologies, which gave me lots of opportunities to hone my learning skills
- the company worked mainly as a Microsoft US vendor remotely, which meant that not only technical skills were valued, but also we got to practice communication, expectation management, and other interpersonal skills often.

The reason I could work in software right out of high school was that when I was eleven I started telling my mom I wanted to "build video games" and my parents found and paid for a high school that taught programming.

How luck played a part: I was about to take a job at another company when a friend of mine from high school told me her brother worked at Southworks and they were looking to hire junior people. He did a good job selling the company to me and I decided to put the other opportunity on hold to see if I could get into Southworks.

Auth0: I was one of the first engineers at Auth0 and over the years I worked on many parts of its product and infrastructure, which makes it easy for me to help people and provide valuable input on various topics. Being a Director of Engineering also helped me understand many things about our business that help me be a more effective contributor.

How luck played a part: the success of any startup requires a lot of luck at many different points in time. If Auth0 had not grown as it did, I wouldn't have had the opportunities to learn what I did and be where I am. This is particularly important because I live in Argentina where the Software industry is much smaller than it is in the US and most companies don't have dual tracks.

Team sports: I played basketball as a kid and during my teens and I realized early on it felt a lot better to win by scoring any amount of points than to lose scoring lots of points. That shaped how I worked in two ways: * it led me to help team members often to see how we could succeed as a team * it led me to learn and do things that would be required to "cover gaps," which helped me build leadership and interpersonal skills that are very useful as I grew in my career

There is a popular idea that becoming a Staff engineer requires completing a "Staff Project." Did you have a Staff Project, and if so what was it?

I did not. Because of how I grew at Auth0 I kind of "skipped that part". As a Director at a startup, I got the opportunity to technically lead a lot of big, critical initiatives, but there was no specific/explicit "staff/principal project."

I think implicitly the closest thing to a "Staff Project" was the work I led in 2017 & 2018 to increase the reliability and scalability of Auth0, leading some projects to offer higher SLAs for a subset of our key customers.

What piece of advice do you have for someone who has just started as a Staff engineer?

Staff means different things at different places, so the first piece of advice I would give is to talk to as many people as possible to define expectations where they are.

The next thing I would tell people is to be patient. They probably got to where they are because they are fairly technical and got results, but as you grow in the ladder the outcome of your work takes time to develop. You might be working on more things at once, and the impact of them has a longer time horizon. You are also now influencing more people in different roles, and sometimes it takes them longer to "see" the things that you might see clearly. Being patient, progressively influencing people, and teaching others pays off long term.

Finally: get used to writing things down and repeating them to others. Writing down thoughts, plans, reasoning, and standards is the way you will scale yourself. When you document something you make it easy for anyone to access it and read in the future, it is easier to reference. It is a lot better than "just talking about it": it scales better and it also reduces the chances of things being misunderstood. Repetition is also necessary as just publishing written documents is not useful, so you have to share your ideas with people. Hosting AMAs, brown bags, and other sessions to explain what your thoughts are very valuable.

Did you ever consider engineering management, and if so how did you decide to pursue the staff engineer path?

I wasn't planning for it, but when the opportunity came to be Director I took it. However, my thinking is that there's a pendulum where you can go back and forth between the two paths. How easy it will be will depend on the company and how specialized the skills as a Staff/Principal are, but I think it is possible.

Nowadays I am very interested in continuing to develop my technical skills and leadership skills, as that's what I think will bring the most valuable learnings and challenges.

What are some resources (books, blogs, people, etc) you've learned from? Who are your role models in the field?

I try to follow people on Twitter who I think are doing interesting things and from who I can learn. There are so many people doing interesting things and so much to learn! Some of the names that come to mind:

- Aphyr's work with Jepsen[215] and general content about distributed systems is great.
- Tanya Reilly has some very good content like RFC process @ Squarespace[216] and Being Glue[217].
- David Fowler shares a lot of content about the .NET Framework and ASP.NET internals which I find interesting. There's also this video of him sharing how he became the ASP.NET Architect[218].
- At Auth0 I work with Jon Allie[219] who is a fantastic engineer and person. He strives for simplicity, can explain things very clearly, and is extremely humble considering how much he knows.

I haven't found a lot of books or similar content specific to senior "individual contributors" (might be interesting to write one). I recently read Fundamentals of Software Architecture[220] that does a fairly good job at describing that role while also understanding the nuances and gray areas of it.

Some books about management are useful to get organizational awareness and help with mentoring, 1:1s, hiring which are things one typically helps with as a staff-plus engineer. In High Output Management Andrew Grove refers defines the "know-how manager" as "people who may not supervise anyone directly but who even without strict organizational authority affect and influence the work of others", which sounds an awful lot like staff-plus engineers. I strongly recommend Managing Humans[221] as it shares stories that are easy and fun to read, and also helps generate empathy with managers, which is important as a staff-plus engineer. The 7 habits of highly effective people[222] is also a book that has a lot of good lessons for staff-plus engineers.

Accelerate is another great book that helps tie company success to engineering practices and outcomes in a way that is useful to influence stakeholders, especially at an executive level.

Dmitry Petrashko - Tech Advisor to the Head of Infra at Stripe

This story was recorded in May, 2020. Learn more about Dmitry on Twitter[223] or Linkedin[224], and reading his presentations[225].

Tell us a little about your current role: your title, the company you work at, and generally what sort of work does your team do?

I am a Staff engineer and the Technical Advisor to head of Infrastructure at Stripe.

My current team is all of Stripe Infrastructure, which is responsible for foundational infrastructure services at Stripe - Compute, Networking, Storage, Database, Data Engineering, Performance & Efficiency, Observability Services, and Developer Tools. Our work empowers Stripe engineers to focus on product.

The team that I "grew" from was Developer productivity, which builds processes, tools and core libraries used during product development at Stripe, including testing frameworks, linters, typecheckers, build tools, libraries used for gradual rollout, and many others. I started as engineer on that team(while it was still a singular team), eventually becoming a Pillar Tech Lead of that group.

What does a "normal" Staff-plus engineer do at your company? Does your role look that way or does it differ?

A Staff Engineer at Stripe isn't a role, rather it's a level that corresponds to expectation of impact, communication, people and project leadership skills. Staff engineers fill different roles, mine is a current one is Technical Advisor (TA). In that role I partner closely with the Head of Foundation, Rahul Patil, with the goal of researching critical topics ahead of time, diving into critical issues (design, code, analytical), brainstorming technical action items, assisting with urgent technical follow-ups, instrumenting code for data collection, etc. This role is designed to expand Rahul's bandwidth and strategic thinking, but does not directly make technical decisions.

As a stepping stone to that role, I was also a Pillar Tech Lead. As we have more PTLs, the expectations are better defined:

- PTLs help their teams make technical decisions that will play well with each other and with technical decisions made by other groups at Stripe. Teams at Stripe make most technical decisions themselves, but an experienced PTL can help fine tune those decisions to achieve better outcomes. PTLs also work as arbiters in cases where teams cannot reach an agreement amongst themselves on technical topics.
- PTLs guide the technical direction of Stripe, providing input on what are the most important problems to solve and setting the high level technical approaches to solving them.
- PTLs help their organization by representing it to other Pillar Tech Leads and also bring technical decisions made elsewhere back to the teams they work with to create alignment.
- PTLs create opportunities for other engineers to take on impactful projects and help them succeed.

In the PTL role, I used to partner closely with the Head of Developer Productivity and managers of the teams inside the group. We exchanged context and worked towards an agreed goal.

Both of these roles (PTL and TA) are similar in that they partner with engineering manager and share insight into the needs of our users & tools at our disposal to address them, while the EM has a better understanding of Stripe-wide non-technical constraints (e.g. resourcing constraints).

How do you spend your time day-to-day?

On a perfect week I'd spend Monday, Wednesday and Friday in meetings or working groups: either 1:1's or team meetings, collaborating on plans & strategy, both short term and long term. Tuesday and

Thursday of my perfect week would be spent coding alone. In reality, depending on team needs at the time, I may end up having more meetings or more time coding. If I'm working to set up a new project, I'll commonly start by having a week with less meetings: focusing on project briefs, thinking through design, deliverables/milestones and security/reliability implications; followed by a week of socializing the proposal around the company and addressing feedback.

While, from time to time it might seem hard to find time to write code, I believe it's important as it allows me to maintain a strong connection to engineering and be the bridge between business needs/prioritization and engineering constraints that PTLs need to be.

Where do you feel most impactful as a Staff-plus engineer?

Staff Engineers, and Pillar Tech Leads in particular, frequently help set direction for a new project. I feel particularly impactful when I can help improve a proposal that's well intentioned and solves a real need, but the team that drafted it lacks either experience or context to write a good plan to capture the opportunity. In such cases, having a well structured plan can help substantially reduce the scope while getting to most of the value, and thus demonstrate impact sooner. Or, alternatively, see that the proposal in hand addresses more use cases than the team has originally anticipated and refocusing the project towards a usecase that was not known by the team would lead to bigger business impact: in both of these cases, I feel impactful by empowering other engineers.

Can you think of anything you've done as a Staff-plus engineer that you weren't able to or wouldn't have done before reaching that title?

No, Stripe intends the Staff-badge to not be a gate into new opportunities and I believe we're good at it. This is also true about the PTL role. We choose engineers for PTL position that are good at representing opinions of others. Even before I became a PTL I felt that prior PTL, Paul Tarjan[226], always made sure my perspective was presented.

Do you spend time advocating for technology, practice, process or architectural change? What's something you've advocated for? Can you share a story of influencing your organization?

I was hired specifically to introduce typechecking into Ruby at Stripe. This included, together with Nelson[227] and Paul, architecting and implementing the typechecker, Sorbet, and growing the culture around using it.

In the early days of Sorbet, we've carefully chosen what features to add based on usecases that Stripe needs the most. I believe we've succeeded in covering most of usecases that Stripe had with a typesystem and, at the same time, keeping the simplicity: it's very easy to get to a typesystem and culture that promotes complexity and elitism for sake of it and I'm happy that our efforts avoided swinging from untypedness to the other end of spectrum.

Today, in my role as Technical Advisor, I advocate for changes that will have outsized impact, most commonly in terms of Reliability, Scalability, Security and Productivity at Stripe. That can be changing the way data is sharded/stored, or changing the way we address change management. The big difference though is that unlike in Sorbet where I stayed on project for years, I'd be looking to find/grow a person who'll take over the project pretty soon - after organization is bought in, and there's a plan with well articulated milestones and controlled risks. I'll keep having frequent checkings with people driving these important projects with goal to help mitigate these risks and discover opportunities to deliver the project faster, and thus my involvement is visible only in the early stages of a project.

How do you keep in touch with how things really work as you spend less time on hands-on development?

While I was a PTL, I had a least a couple of days a week where I got code. I worked closely with other engineers on my teams and we continuously learn from each other.

As a Technical Advisor, I wasn't able to write code as much as I was as a PTL. I mostly wrote code when it was code-yellow situation[228]. But the success in this role is dependent on having good insights and deep engineering understanding. To do this, I speak to our internal customers and stay on top of designs and, notably, failure thresholds and failure modes of systems of teams that I support.

In my role, it's highly important to understand needs of customers. One helpful resource for that is the Stripe-wide engineer survey that Developer Productivity group organises, where we are looking to find what are the biggest things keeping our engineers from being productive: maybe there's some tool that became slow since the last survey or some use case that had a user base grow that's not well supported. While this survey rarely finds things that we weren't aware of, it's a great tool for relative prioritization: we can compare how many people complain about things and prioritize them accordingly.

Additionally, before the Covid-19-induced lockdown, I used to join random tables for dinners at Stripe. I'd ask 3 questions:

- What are you working on?
- What makes it hard?
- How can infrastructure teams help?

This became a great tool in two ways: 1) connecting me to my users, helping discover their needs; 2) helping mitigate unhappiness of teams that aren't yet supported by having a discussion similar to: "yes, I agree we could help you by doing X, now, lets together look on what we should stop doing to create space for this," where a person would frequently discover that, while they would like us to address their pain point, they don't want it addressed at cost of us deprioritizing our current projects.

As I was transitioning away from role of PTL, I've created a group that's currently called DevProd Assembly that gathers leaders of developer productivity teams. Each member of this group is expected to build a high trust relationship with 2-3 product teams, interview them monthly and aggregate feedback with other members of Assembly.

How have you sponsored other engineers? Is sponsoring other engineers an important aspect of your role?

While sponsoring other engineers isn't required for a Staff Engineer, I believe it helps to succeed as one, as it helps you deliver more impact by creating opportunities for others and helping them succeed.

And yes, there have been multiple projects that I have helped scope, kick-off and derisk, while also helping grow a person to take it over from me when I roll off to the next thing.

There's also a distinction between mentorship and sponsorship and I do both. Mentorship is about helping people grow and deliver impact. Sponsorship is about helping a person get in a position where they could demonstrate their ability to deliver greater impact. In working with my teams, I try to help people work on projects somewhat out of their comfort zone, and in that I sponsor them, and then, I could mentor them to help the project succeed.

You first got the title Staff engineer at your current company. Were you hired as a Staff engineer? If not, what was the process of getting promoted to Staff?

I wasn't hired as a Staff Engineer. I had to get upleveled twice to get to Staff level at Stripe. Both of these uplevels were similar: Stripe uplevels after an employee has already been operating on the next level for quite a while and this adjusts expectations that they are expected to continue operating on that level going forward.

What two or three factors were most important in you reaching Staff?

In order of decreasing importance:

1. Focusing on impact on business and company.
2. Being collaborative: by joining meetings/working groups you should help achieve a better outcome.
3. Technical knowledge.

For me personally, the area that I needed to get good at before getting Staff Engineer was the second item. I was already delivering impact and was considered a person to go to for technical advice. I needed to improve my communication skills and collaboration skills so that I could constructively help people who are outside of my team, who might see me for first time ever and who, despite having good intentions behind their project, may not have the best plan to get it delivered.

A technique that helped me in that was asking for feedback in a private chat immediately after the meeting, in particular after meetings that didn't not go perfectly. This has allowed me to learn what I did that might have contributed to other parties not feeling comfortable in these meetings and, in a few cases, genuinely asking how it could have gone better helped fix the outcome of a meeting that has already gone poorly.

How have where you worked and your education impacted your path?

Companies: I appreciate that Stripe has so many opportunities for impact and this definitely helped me.

Education: I happened to have got a very practical PhD (on how to build fast & maintainable compilers) that almost fully translated to knowledge that's applicable to my work: helping a company to scale engineering. And, while it served me well, I think there's a lot of luck involved: I happened to join the right lab at the right time (when conditions for Scala3 being born became material, I'd been at the lab long enough to not be too "green" but still early enough to not have totally set the direction of my research). I'm unsure if I'd advise others to do a PhD: from my perspective, in practical terms, many of my friends would have learned as much by building systems at Stripe/Google/Facebook for the same 4+ years it takes to complete a PhD. If you'd like to learn how databases work - you'd probably learn this not only at the laboratory that does research on databases, but also at the companies that have some of the highest demands for databases and have teams working to improve them. That said, a PhD was something that was a good tool for me to change my location.

Location: I came to the US from Switzerland to join Stripe. I came to Switzerland from Russia to join one of the best PhD programs in Computer Science. I came to Russia to join one of the best ex-USSR universities from Ukraine. In each of these relocations, I feel, I played geographical arbitrage: I was looking to escape the place where I was among the best to the place where I'd be average. In some of them, I think I wasn't the prime candidate. By joining the people there and learning from them, I grew a lot. It's hard for me to tell if US vs EU is a better location career-wise, but I can definitely tell from my experience that changing locations helped me grow a lot.

There is a popular idea that becoming a Staff engineer requires completing a "Staff Project." Did you have a Staff Project, and if so what was it?

It's a very hard question for me to answer in retrospect. This is because: as far as I know, Sorbet was big enough to be my Staff engineer project, BUT with Nelson and Paul being there and us working closely and very fast with each other, it was very hard to attribute success of the project to specific individuals rather than the whole team.

Around the first performance evaluation into the projects, all three of us got feedback that we should have better ways to prescribe which impact was the result of which individual. While I'd love to say that the fact that we didn't face a similar issue on the next performance evaluation was due to intentional actions, I don't think that is true: I think the project just naturally entered a stage where it was much bigger and thus we didn't need to "quickly iterate in the same 10 files", naturally leading to us having clearer and bigger areas of ownership.

I became the "internal architecture/subtyping" person, as well as "talk to users" person, while Paul became the "change the code to make typechecker like it" person. Nelson clearly knew better how other systems at Stripe work and thus helped integrate the tool with them. All of these played to our strong points: I had prior experience with type checkers (this is what my PhD was about), Paul has a huge skill for programmatic codemods and Nelson is both very knowledgeable in systems in general and has been at Stripe long enough and early enough to know pretty much every system at Stripe. At this point in the project (stabilization, rollout) all of these became huge areas and thus it became much easier to have a person be a directly responsible individual (DRI) for an area, with others helping occasionally.

After Sorbet I had a couple other impactful projects delivered in short timeframe (6 months), that, I believe, sealed the deal of me getting the Staff Engineer level, but, If I was to choose one, I'd still choose Sorbet due to vast scope of project: both technical and cultural.

Can you remember any piece of advice on reaching Staff that was particularly helpful for you?

1. Working with Martin Odersky and Ondrej Lhotak in academia helped me understand how complex systems work together and how to explain that clearly.
2. Brian Goetz helped me understand how much work is behind a simple, yet, robust system to withstand widespread adoption

and design.
3. Paul Tarjan showed me the importance of adjusting my communication style to lead to constructive outcomes for all involved parties.

What about a piece of advice for someone who has just started as a Staff engineer?

At least, at Stripe, Staff Engineers work on very different areas. Make sure you agree with your reporting chain on what is the impact you should be achieving and what are the things you're allowed to compromise on on the way to that impact. Communicate clearly what compromises you're doing and why.

Did you ever consider engineering management, and if so how did you decide to pursue the staff engineer path?

Every time I considered it in the past it was by asking myself and others around me "would it be a way to bring more impact." So far, every time the answer was "seems like no."

That said, I've found that learning some management skills from great managers (in my case, James Iry, Scott MacVicar, Will Larson, Christian Anderson and Shane O'Sullivan) provides huge benefits even in an individual contributor role.

Stephen Wan - Staff Engineer at Samsara

This story was recorded in September, 2020. Learn more about Stephen on his Github[229], Twitter[230], and Linkedin[231].

Tell us a little about your current role: your title, the company you work at, and generally what sort of work does your team do?

I'm a Staff Engineer at Samsara[232].

I started at the company four years ago when the company had been around for a year and we had 50 or so employees. Nowadays, we have over a thousand folks at the company, with engineering teams in the Bay Area, Atlanta, and London.

When I first started, we had yet to form real teams and our ten or so engineers worked on whatever came up. Nine months in, we had doubled up and formed product teams around a few core offerings at the time. I did a brief stint leading a product team before switching over to our budding infrastructure group to start our frontend infrastructure team. Over the years, I've gradually shifted down the stack, also taking stretches on our backend and observability systems.

Today, I work in our Infrastructure & Platform (I&P) group, spending most of my time with the Developer Experience team which builds tools to keep our full-stack development workflow productive.

What does a "normal" Staff-plus engineer do at your company? Does your role look that way or does it differ?

Most of our Staff+ engineers are in specialized roles, either in web infrastructure or device firmware. I suppose that puts me in the majority, but the work our Staff engineers do is varied so it's a bit hard to claim being "normal" in the role.

When looking at parallels between the IC and management tracks, Staff is considered a director-equivalent role. Staff engineers have the option to participate in many processes that are typically reserved for managers. We're invited to the cross-eng director's meeting and, at least in I&P, we're involved in roadmap planning and management syncs. Recently, we've brought in Staff engineers to participate in some promotion calibration meetings.

The level of access gives some sense of having a foot planted on both sides. The role is different enough from Senior levels that it's not quite as much an "individual" software-contributing role, but it's also quite different from our more people-focused management track.

Out of Will's Staff archetypes, I think my role fits somewhere between the Solver and the Tech Lead. Part of the fun for me has been jumping into a different role every 6-12 months, diving into a different part of the system with a different group of folks.

How do you spend your time day-to-day?

It's pretty varied by the day. Right now, I try to make Tuesdays and Thursdays meeting days so that I have dedicated focus time in the rest of the week.

My meeting days typically include 1:1s with folks I'm working closely with as well as staff meetings. I'll also spend some time pairing with individuals on code and design review or more open-ended design discussions.

On other days my focus time is spent in investigation mode, trying to suss out both current issues and paving foundation for future projects. What systems need investment? How have our teams been executing? What upcoming changes should our group prepare for? This time is spent shaping[233] in a broader sense.

Looking back, this focus is distinct from my role prior to Staff. Instead of executing at the individual level working directly on a project or team, the time is centered around a wider lens and over a longer term.

Notably, it's hard for me to guarantee anything longer than a day at a time spent writing code. I don't get counted when we consider engineering roadmap bandwidth, though I do try to reserve at least a day a week for writing some code.

At the micro-level, I keep a document called "what is stephen doing?" that drives my work on the hour-by-hour granularity. There's one main section for the current week and some reminders for future weeks. Every Monday, I start over - unstarted items from the previous week get deleted and few survive to the next week.

That delete-by-default intention ends up helping me keep focused and not feel too strewn out. For a long time, I tried to groom a back-burner list of things to do but it mostly had the effect of stressing me out. Most back-burner items would end up deleted and incomplete anyways, a month later.

Do you spend time advocating for technology, practice, process or architectural change? What's something you've advocated for? Can you share a story of influencing your organization?

Yes. The specific technology or methodology changes quarter to quarter, but advocacy ends up being a big part of my time. On the smaller end, I've helped write culture documents about how we try to approach design documents or code review or code ownership rules.

For a bigger example, I spent a couple quarters helping our product teams adopt Service Level Objectives (SLOs).

At the time, we had a fairly established set of features and customer base, but our measurements for uptime were still primitive. In outages, it was hard to get a sense for customer impact because we lacked the distinctions and definitions to communicate ("What percent of customers are affected? Is it both reads and writes? Is this an outage or an existing bug?"), even though we had plenty of metrics and dashboards to look at.

💣 what is stephen doing?

quarter commitments

- investigation: lightstep/tracing poc
- design partner: 99.9% availability measurement
- design partner: good error handling in frontend
- design partner: org isolation rollout plan with security
- design partner: deploy state migration plan

10/14

- [ ] +Infra and Platform Roadmap Brainstorming
- [ ] product team rotation plan for adam
- [ ] catch up with federation design with will
- [x] ~~terraform splitting chat with kelly~~
- [ ] review dev exp okr draft
- [x] ~~review: https://github.com~~

10/20

- [ ] revise + RFC: Buildkite workload improvements with adam/aashish
  - edit rollout schedule
- [ ] re-evaluate latency monitor false positive/negatives set from 10/9

what is stephen doing?

Though introducing SLOs certainly required new engineering work, I'd guess that the majority of my time on the project was spent writing documentation, talking to people, and doing consultancy-style work with teams. We wanted folks to be able to understand reliability objectives end-to-end: how to define the objective, how to talk about it in outages, how to measure it in systems, how to keep track of it over time, how to react when it becomes unhealthy. That level of depth ends up needing a lot of messaging and massaging to sink in.

As with most of our big "migrations," getting many teams to adopt SLOs came iteratively. We first trialed our new tools with a single team with high-touch support before figuring out the widespread messaging for the rest of the org. I think a key role for me was being able to both talk with engineers about the new tools at a concrete, how-do-I-use-this level, while also convincing director-level folks that it would be worth their effort to speak in SLOs.

This same pattern has held true over most of my projects as a Staff engineer. My role ends up being in brokering deals between groups to sell a change across the organization.

How do you keep in touch with how things really work as you spend less time on hands-on development?

I put in some time programming and doing code review each week, even if it's just to put up a small bug fix. I try to put in time to participate in the same day-to-day rituals other ICs go through - code review, navigating docs, outage situations, etc.

Of course, that's not enough to keep a high-fidelity model in my head - there's just too much happening across too many teams to keep track of. The rest is a lot of intentionally seeking out feedback and hearing first-hand experiences from others.

I've also tried to help bake feedback loops into our organization. I helped get us started on doing half-year dev team surveys with a mix of questions about both our technical systems and engineering culture. The responses from those surveys have been super helpful in keeping a pulse on how the organization is feeling from the ground up.

How have you sponsored other engineers? Is sponsoring other engineers an important aspect of your role?

Yes. I've tried to be intentional about giving away my state, stepping back, and letting others build up expertise.

At the organizational level, I think there are ways to structurally sponsor others, pushing other engineers into taking positions as subject-matter experts. As an example, I worked on introducing a new distributed tracing system late last year. Our core web application is powered by a number of different backend systems and over years, the data flows between these systems became trickier to understand and page performance suffered. We needed a tool to dig ourselves out.

I had worked on early iterations of our performance tools before and knowledge of those systems was largely stuck in my head. In the new project, a concrete goal for me was to bring more folks up to speed. It wasn't enough to lay a technical foundation in the systems design: my teammates on the project would have to own that area of expertise for years to come.

Practically, that meant spending more of my time discussing and pairing with the soon-to-be tracing owners and much less time directly contributing code or design. When we beta tested with a product team, I'd push another engineer to work on a sales pitch, or figure out the demo, or get the team onboarded.

Today, the tracing system is widely used and fully managed by our SRE and Observability group. The folks I worked with at the time are now the go-to group for performance questions.

On a more personal level, there are always small spots where I can help nudge other folks into the spotlight. Sponsorship opportunities can start small. Especially if I'm working with someone earlier in their career, I might suggest that they take on more unknown chunks of a new system design, or write a draft for new documentation, or demo our results at our group-wide meeting.

That small push might be all someone needs to get going, but other times I think it flows nicely into an opportunity to mentor and pair as well. Some things (like building up a slide deck for the first time) can feel intractable until you do them a couple times. There, both the sponsorship and mentorship sides end up feeling impactful.

It also feels like there's some tension to get to the right spot. We want to grow folks into positions where they can own more and make systems decisions, but we also want there to be alignment in how those decisions get made and where we're trying to go. It's hard work - it ends up taking a lot of attention to not gatekeep but get to a satisfying result.

You first got the title Staff engineer at your current company. Were you hired as a Staff engineer? If not, what was the process of getting promoted to Staff?

When I joined the company, we didn't have IC titles. I was leveled into the Staff role when we introduced leveling in early 2019.

I think I had a big advantage from being an early engineer on the team. That history was huge in giving me context on our past decisions - knowing what pitfalls we had already run into and helping land new projects into a good place.

At every stage of growth, we would add more layers of people and management and there'd be a "relearning" period for how the organization worked. Over time, teams would narrow in scope and only be able to see a smaller part of the puzzle. Having a big part of the engineering history in my head not only helped me connect pieces across those divisions, but also gave me a headstart on keeping personal connections over to parts of the organization I stopped working with directly. That breadth naturally lent itself to being able to figure out what could be most impactful for the org.

What two or three factors were most important in you reaching Staff? How have the companies you joined, your location, or your education impacted your path?

My background is somewhat less traditional - I studied Electrical Engineering instead of Computer Science and dropped out of school before completing my degree. That gap forced me to be more self-taught in my experience, but also left me with a lot of imposter syndrome. I failed a lot of software interviews early on for not having the right credentials. Early in my career, that imposter feeling made me really want to learn as much as I could to cover up for what I feared I didn't know.

The summer before I dropped out, I interned at Stripe. I remember, perhaps through rose-tinted glasses, feeling so energized by the engineering culture there: the hyperfocus on customer experience and excitement about building technology to get there. That experience ended up being quite influential to how I wanted a workplace to feel.

Later when I left school, I started working full-time at a smaller startup where I really didn't know what I was doing. The business meandered a bit during my time there, but I was lucky to have worked closely with thoughtful, senior engineers who had a penchant for mentorship. Working there ended up giving me a lot of flexibility on what I wanted to learn which was good for me but probably bad for the company.

As a last bit of background, I worked at a computer camp for a couple summers in high school, teaching school-aged kids basic computer literacy. That teaching mindset certainly left me with more empathy for how folks end up understanding and interacting with computer systems.

By the time I joined Samsara, those experiences gave me a clear sense for how I wanted work to feel - being an early employee gave me the influence to shape the way there.

The final piece of the puzzle was my first three years at Samsara. I was fortunate enough to get to work with so many thoughtful collaborators in that time. I can easily trace back many of the working habits, mental models, and mannerisms that I have today to those individuals. I can't imagine that I'd be in this spot in my career without their influence.

There is a popular idea that becoming a Staff engineer requires completing a "Staff Project." Did you have a Staff Project, and if so what was it?

No, I didn't have a designated Staff Project. Looking back, there were projects over the years that perhaps accumulated into the equivalent of a big Staff project, but it's not something we explicitly talked about in leveling.

As a concept, I'm skeptical of that kind of singularly focused project and worry that they can put folks into a hero mindset[234] when we really want to value engineers that can build the organization, not carry it. I'd be much more excited to see iterative improvement and consistent execution over time: a track record of thoughtful engineering.

I'm happy Samsara seems to agree with that assessment. Our career path document ends up talking much more about that consistent execution over a single large-haul project.

What about a piece of advice for someone who has just started as a Staff engineer?

A couple things come to mind.

Get comfortable talking a lot. I think a big step-change between Senior and Staff roles ends up being the focus on people: reconciling competing priorities, clearing up miscommunication, aligning folks on the same page. Even though they typically don't have direct reports, Staff engineers are working in a system of both the technology and the people: the biggest impact is going to come from influencing both.

Do your best to not get exhausted. As I transitioned into a Staff role, it felt easy to slip into a mindset where I was responsible for everything going on and had to timeslice my focus over too many things. It took me a while to recognize that this role didn't mean I had to work many times harder to be involved in everything, but instead I needed to direct change through others in the organization. Trust folks, flag issues, and expect them to work it out.

Did you ever consider engineering management, and if so how did you decide to pursue the staff engineer path?

Back in 2016, I remember having an initial conversation with my manager about pursuing an IC vs management path. At the time, I still felt early into my professional career and wanted to continue investing in my core technical experience.

I reevaluated that decision every year or so and ended up coming to the same conclusion - that I wasn't done getting my hands dirty on the technical side. Throughout that time, much of the work I was doing was focused around building development experiences for folks at the company. Those efforts ended up pushing me to do more Staff-like work and I naturally progressed from there.

What are some resources (books, blogs, people, etc) you've learned from? Who are your role models in the field?

I tend to prize literature that talks about complicated topics in plain English, both fiction and non-fiction.

I remember reading about novelist Haruki Murakami[235] writing his first novel in English first, then translating it back to Japanese as a way of shaping the style of his expression. He notes, "I could only write in simple, short [English] sentences. Which meant that, however complex and numerous the thoughts running around my head, I couldn't even attempt to set them down as they came. The language had to be simple, my ideas expressed in an easy-to-understand way."

Writing software is a totally different domain, but it feels like the sentiment fits into some tenet that I really value about communicating: having an understanding in your head is half the battle - being able to express that understanding is just as hard and valuable.

I love reading blogs and papers that really go in depth in a technical area. A few that I've come back to over the years include:

- Bob Nystrom's blog posts[236] on programming languages
- Vyacheslav Egorov's blog[237] about compilers and V8 internals (Chrome's JS engine)
- Brandur's blog[238] on various systems topics
- Nelson Elhage's Accidentally Quadratic[239]
- Vicki Pfau's Blog[240] on developing a GameBoy Advance emulator
- fail0overflow's blog[241] and talks about console architecture and exploits
- Bungie's engineering publications[242] on building and producing the original Halo games

As an anecdote, early in my career I had a budding interest in programming language internals and picked up a compilers textbook ("the Dragon book") to learn from. It's a pretty hard book to get through. Maybe it's reasonable to get through it with a professor and a few classmates, but it was truly difficult for me to get a working mental model from a reading. Later, I found Bob Nystrom's Crafting Interpreters[243] which takes a much more practical approach and it felt like a huge breath of fresh air.

I'm also a big fan of reading codebases. Early on in my career, I recall debugging a tricky React problem where some callback wasn't happening in the order I expected. Reading the docs didn't help. Putting in print statements wasn't enough. My mentor at the time got me to read some of the source code to better understand what was going on and that really blew my mind a little bit. I got a bug fix in but also a much stronger understanding of how React worked.

That was really a turning point. Being able to quickly dive in and jump through unfamiliar code has really felt like a superpower and gives me a larger pattern matching library for different approaches to software design. A recent favorite has been reading through the design and code of esbuild[244], a super fast javascript bundler.

Finally, some of my favorite recent non-fiction reads in the last couple years have been on the history of BART[245], the history of Xerox PARC[246], and an overview of modern Japanese culture[247]. In each niche, I've found the history and context fascinating as seemingly small, independent events and decisions have culminated into ways the world works today.

Ending words

Frequently when a group of Staff-plus engineers sit down to chat, they'll spend time commiserating about the industry's broken technical leadership track. It's true; it is broken. What isn't true is that this is inevitable. The industry's views on technical leadership are the summation of the collective daily actions taken by each person operating in, aspiring towards, or managing a Staff-plus engineer role. By changing our habits and approach, we will change the industry.

By improving ourselves, we make the industry better. Make a plan to sponsor someone else in your organization. Synthesize a strategy document, taking the time to make others feel heard. Build a network of peers, and invite more folks into that network. As you do that work, your engineering organization will learn from your example.

Your manager and management chain will learn from your example as well. Many managers have never worked with an effective Staff-plus engineer. They instead view the role through the lens of a previous disaster. Partner with them to understand their priorities and concerns to build alignment. Hold yourself accountable to the same pressures your manager experiences. Work through their fear of what could go wrong, and create excitement for how much can go right.

Does it feel odd to talk about fearing Staff-plus roles? It does, but it's unavoidable. At most companies, the primary factor preventing the adoption of an impactful Staff-plus role is the fear of creating a tyrannical architect. That fear is driven by their previous experiences with inept and poorly managed technical leaders. This fear will only subside as we collectively replenish the groundwater of good Staff-plus role models.

My hope is that reading *Staff Engineer* has given you a map to follow towards a rewarding Staff-plus career or inspired you to keep walking the path of your own that you've already found. The software technology industry is still in its infancy, and what it becomes is wholly in our hands.

Resources

Additional resources on Staff-plus engineering

None of the Staff Engineer I spoke with got there alone. Most got there either through voracious reading or building a powerful network of colleagues. This section is a collection of recommended resources.

Your Network

Almost unanimously, Staff-plus engineers' most valuable learning resources wasn't a book, blog, talk, or paper, but instead their network of peers and mentors. If you only have one hour to develop yourself as an engineer, your best bet would be building a network of people in similar roles.

If you're looking for a Slack community, `#staff-principal-engineering` in the Rands Leadership Slack is a fairly lively room.

What do Staff-plus Engineers do?

- Being a principal engineer at Skyscanner[248] by Nicky Wrightson
- Defining a Distinguished Engineer[249] by Jessie Frazelle
- How I operated as a Staff engineer at Heroku[250] by Amy Unger
- Not all engineering leaders are engineering managers[251] by Tanya Reilly
- The Nuts and Bolts with Tanya Reilly[252]
- On Being A Principal Engineer[253] by Silvia Botros
- On Being a Senior Engineer[254] by John Allspaw

- Staff Engineering[255] by Sam Kleinman
- Thriving on the Technical Leadership Path by Keavy McMinn
- What's a senior engineer's job?[256] by Julia Evans
- What a Senior Staff Software Engineer Actually Does, Part 1: The Role and My Tasks[257] and Part 2: The Mindset and Focus of the Role[258] by Joy Ebertz
- What does Staff level mean at GitLab?[259] by Charlie Ablett

Becoming a Staff-plus Engineer

- Becoming a Staff Engineer – Interview with Kristina Fox, Staff iOS Engineer at Intuit[260] by Kaya Thomas
- On becoming a senior technical leader[261] by Jesse Pollak
- On Mid-Career and Managers[262] by Ryn Daniels
- How does one become a Staff Software Engineer at Google?[263] on Quora
- The Engineer/Manager Pendulum by Charity Majors
- Things to Know About Engineering Levels[264] by Charity Majors

Operating as a Staff-plus engineer

- Being Glue by Tanya Reilly
- Computers can be understood[265] by Nelson Elhage
- Effective Mental Models for Code and Systems[266] by Cindy Sridharan
- "I Wouldn't Start From Here." How to Make a Big Technical Change[267] by Tanya Reilly
- Migrations: the sole scalable fix to tech-debt[268] by Will Larson
- On Mid-Career and Team Dynamics[269] by Ryn Daniels
- Surviving the Organisational Side Quest[270] by Tanya Reilly
- Systems that defy detailed understanding[271] by Nelson Elhage
- Team Objectives[272] by Marty Cagan
- Technical Decision Making[273] by Cindy Sridharan

- Technical Research and Preparation[274] by Keavy McMinn
- The Behind-the-scenes Work of Tech Leadership[275] by Jean Hsu
- Understanding Project Management Will Improve Your Developer Job[276] by Daniel Na
- What Does Sponsorship Look Like? by Lara Hogan
- Where to Start[277] by Keavy McMinn
- Design Docs, Markdown and Git by Caitie McCaffrey

Technical Specifications

- A practical guide to writing technical specs[278]
- Design Docs at Google
- Design Docs, Markdown, and Git
- Documenting Architecture Decisions[279]
- How to write a better technical design document[280]
- Technical Decision-Making and Alignment in a Remote Culture
- Writing Technical Design Docs[281]

Engineering Strategy

- A Framework For Responsible Innovation
- How Big Technical Changes Happen at Slack - Several People Are Coding[282]
- On Drafting an Engineering Strategy[283]
- Defining a Tech Strategy[284]
- Delivering on an architecture strategy
- Stepping Stones not Milestones
- Achieving Alignment and Efficiency Through a Technical Strategy
- The difficult teenage years: Setting tech strategy after a launch[285] by Anna Shipman
- Learning to have an engineering vision[286]

Examples of engineering strategies:

- Run less software by Rich Archibold

There are also many great resources on other facets of strategy as well, for example, Marty Cagan's series on Product Strategy[287].

Books

Although I've found that many folks don't read too many books, when I asked Staff engineers for their most valuable resources, they inevitably mentioned a personal mentor or a book. They had blog posts and tech talks they might mention related to a more specific problem, but they were most changed by this larger, more papery format.

Some books which were recommended:

- A Philosophy of Software Design[288] by John Ousterhout
- Accelerate: Building and Scaling High Performing Technology Organizations by Forsgren, Humble, and Kim
- Becoming a Technical Leader: An Organic Problem-Solving Approach[289] by Gerald Weinberg
- Building Evolutionary Architectures[290] by Ford, Parsons, and Kua
- Escaping the Build Trap: How Effective Product Management Creates Real Value[291] by Melissa Perri
- Good Strategy Bad Strategy: The Difference and Why it Matters by Richard Rumelt
- High Output Management by Andy Grove
- The Manager's Path: A Guide for Tech Leaders Navigating Growth and Change by Camille Fournier
- The Mythical Man-Month[292] by Fred Brooks
- The Phoenix Project by Kim, Behr, and Spafford.
- The Passionate Programmer[293] by Chad Fowler
- The Pragmatic Programmer[294] by Hunt and Thomas
- Resilient Management by Lara Hogan

- Software Design X-Rays: Fix Technical Debt with Behavioral Code Analysis[295] by Adam Tornhill
- Thinking in Systems: A Primer[296] by Donella Meadows

If you're looking for, even more, recommended book lists abound, including my own at Irrational Exuberance's Best Books[297].

Talks

The Staff-plus engineers I've chatted with have generally mentioned giving talks as more valuable to them than listening to talks, but there certainly are some excellent talks out there. Cindy Sridharan[298] (Twitter[299]) is the best source of amazing talks, in particular, her write-ups of Best of 2019 in Tech Talks[300], Best of 2018 in Tech Talks[301], and Best of 2017 in Tech Talks[302].

Papers

Relatively few Staff-plus Engineers are avid readers of Computer Science papers. However, most are familiar with a handful of foundational papers, and the small subset who do spend time reading papers tend to get quite a bit out of it.

If you aspire to join the category of frequent paper readers, there's no better place than Adrian Colyer's the morning paper[303], which will send you a summary of a computer science paper every weekday. If you're more interested in getting some foundational exposure to some well-known papers, first read one of How to Read an Academic Article[304] by Peter Klein or How to Read a Paper[305] by S. Keshav, and then jump into this list of recommended papers:

- Dynamo: Amazon's Highly Available Key-value Store[306]
- On Designing and Deploying Internet-Scale Services[307]
- No Silver Bullet - Essence and Accident in Software Engineering[308]
- Out of the Tar Pit[309]

- The Chubby lock service for loosely-coupled distributed systems[310]
- Bigtable: A Distributed Storage System for Structured Data[311]
- Raft: In Search of an Understandable Consensus Algorithm[312]
- Paxos Made Simple[313]
- SWIM: Scalable Weakly-consistent Infection-style Process Group Membership Protocol[314]
- Hints for Computer System Design[315]
- Big Ball of Mud[316]
- The Google File System[317]
- CAP Twelve Years Later: How the Rules Have Changed[318]
- Harvest, Yield, and Scalable Tolerant Systems[319]
- MapReduce: Simplified Data Processing on Large Clusters[320]
- Dapper, a Large-Scale Distributed Systems Tracing Infrastructure[321]
- Kafka: a Distributed Messaging System for Log Processing[322]
- Large-scale cluster management at Google with Borg[323]
- Mesos: A Platform for Fine-Grained Resource Sharing in the Data Center[324]

Probably the best place to find high-quality papers to read is Papers We Love[325], which also run meetups to discuss papers. A few other resources are the ACM SIGOPS Hall of Fame Award list[326] and Irrational Exuberance's paper collection[327].

Other nice things

As I did the research for these resources, I found some other pieces that didn't quite fit anywhere above, but which I think are good and worth looking at nonetheless:

- Testing in Production, the safe way[328] and Testing in Production: the hard parts[329] by Cindy Sridharan
- A decade in review in tech[330] by Cindy Sridharan
- Boogeyman Problems[331] by Dan Na

If you find more, please send them my way!

Where do Staff-plus engineers fit into the org?

When I work on the organization design of an engineering organization, I think a lot about "organizational mathematics," the guideline that each team should have one manager and six to eight engineers, and each manager of managers should support four to six managers. From those numbers, you can rapidly determine an appropriate structure for your organization that'll work fairly well. It might not be *perfect*, but it'll *work*.

As I've applied that approach to designing multiple organizations, one of the recurring edge cases that have come up is deciding where the senior-most engineers should report. Should they, as the org math dictates, report to managers in the organizational leaf nodes? Or should they, as key leaders in your organization, report to more senior leaders to have better access to the information and authorization they need to excel in their role?

Before answering, it's worth describing the most common configurations you'll find in companies today, in particular how configurations vary across the Staff-plus archetypes:

- **Tech Leads** typically report to a manager responsible for one team. Less frequently, they'll report to a manager responsible for two to four teams. In both cases, they'll operate at the same scope as that manager. *Examples*: Dan Na reported to the manager for the Internationalization Platform.
- **Architects** typically report to a more senior manager, often a manager of managers. Often they'll be responsible for a horizontal-slice across that manager's area of responsibility, for example, data modeling. *Examples*: Keavy McMinn reported to the CTO.
- **Solvers** typically operate in companies that feature a "weak team concept," and often reporting hierarchies are less defined or de-

liberate in such companies. It is *most* common to see them reporting to a team manager, but you'll find a bit of everything. Another common pattern is collecting these folks into an *"Office of the CTO"* or *"Office of the CEO"* where they report to an executive who directs their work. *Examples*: Ritu Vincent is part of an incubator reporting to the CEO.

- **Right Hands** report into a senior leader, often managers responsible for a hundred or more folks, operating with that leader's authority. *Examples*: Rick Boone reported to the VP of Infrastructure; Michelle Bu reported to the Chief Product Officer.

Understanding how these different archetypes typically report differently into the organization helps decode *some* of the seeming arbitrariness of reporting structures.

Office of the CTO

An aside on the "**Office of the CTO**" concept, as many folks haven't encountered it in their work. Typically, the CTO, although sometimes a CEO will do something similar, will have two to eight Staff-plus engineers who report to them directly. These folks are treated as senior leaders in the sense of getting a problem or opportunity to pursue, very little management support, and the proximity to lean on the executive for support when necessary.

Within these offices, you'll find a mix of *Architects, Solvers* and *Right Hands*.

Typically the *Office of the CTO* comes relatively late in a company's evolution and is often introduced as a workaround to an existing organizational problem that is a challenge to address, for example, lack of trust between Staff-plus engineers and management teams, or an inability to delegate by the CTO. If you find yourself reaching for it *early* in a company's evolution, ask yourself if you're avoiding a problem you should be fixing instead of introducing this concept into your structure.

But in practice...

Based on the archetypes, there is usually a theoretically correct place for every engineer to fit into the organization, but you'll find that in practice, few organizations fully align their actual reporting structure with that theoretical structure.

Sometimes this is due to a lack of attention to organizational structure by your management team. In other cases, it's due to a lack of managerial bandwidth to support folks at the correct positions. For example, the "correct" manager is already managing a team of twelve and can't support another engineer effectively. Another common scenario is that the structure is shifting frequently enough that managers are reluctant to change the engineer's manager *again*, especially as manager-changes often lead to abstract, middle-of-the-road performance reviews.

If you find yourself reporting to someone who you believe is the wrong manager, it's a reasonable conversation to have with your manager, but it's worth acknowledging that many managers will react defensively to the implication that they're not the right manager for you. If your manager is mature and you have a strong relationship with them, go ahead and have the conversation. If not, it may be less risky to instead have a more abstract discussion with their skip-level about where Staff-plus engineers report in their organization.

Before you rush to advocate for change, ask yourself what you think would be different if your reporting structure changed. The reporting structure is a form of authority, and generally, folks over-estimate how authority will help them. The classic trap is, of course, that the folks who benefit the most from additional authority–minorities and women–are the folks whose managers are most likely to react defensively to the suggestion of the change.

How should it work?

If you're looking to design a proposal for your management team on how they ought to perform these sorts of organizational adjustments over time, a few things to consider. When possible, **reporting changes should happen immediately.** Delaying forces folks to navigate two transitions, including a particularly challenging intermediate environment between the previous and new roles. It's always lower risk to navigate a single role transition, even if it means agreeing to reduced manager support if your new manager is underwater with their workload.

If you can't make them immediately, **always set a timeline** for reporting to the correct manager after a role change. If you don't have a timeframe to clearly reopen the structure, it's relatively less likely to happen.

Most companies struggle to set up this sort of organizational infrastructure to fully support Staff-plus engineers as genuine leaders, so you should look at this as a problem you want to make progress on *over years*, rather than one that'll get fixed overnight. If you go into it expecting an immediate, permanent solution, you're likely in for some turbulence.

Managing Staff-plus engineers

While getting feedback on *StaffEng*[332], one request was for more content on managing Staff-plus engineers. It doesn't quite fit the theme–that effort is focused on the Staff engineers themselves rather the company or the manager–but it's an interesting topic and a worthy appendix.

Of course, not all aspects of managing Staff-plus folks are unique to the level: there are fundamentals that apply to managing anyone in any role, like doing effective 1 on 1s[333] or giving feedback[334]. For that sort of thing, read Lara Hogan's Resilient Management or Camille Fournier's The Manager's Path[335]. What I wanted to get into here is how managing someone at the Staff-plus level differs from managing, say, a Senior engineer.

These roles vary enough across companies that some aspects of managing your Staff-plus engineers will depend on the Staff archetypes your company emphasizes and where your Staff-plus engineers should fit into the engineering organization, but there are some approaches that will be helpful for you across most configurations.

- **Sponsor and support more than you direct.** If you're giving daily direction to your Staff engineers, you're utilizing them in the wrong roles. If you aren't giving them weekly feedback, you're delaying their growth. If you aren't lending your sponsorship to their initiatives, then you'll train the initiative out of them.
- **Help them rewire their definition of success.** Working in a high-performing product engineering team is a flywheel of positive feedback. Your product manager appreciates your work. Your engineering manager engages the team. Your peers enjoy working together. Your users love your product. Your business loves the user adoption. Conversely, the Staff engineer's flywheel of

feedback is a lot less immediate. You spend more time working through conflict. You work on longer time horizons. You're representing important priorities that require deprioritizing some business or product goals. Many folks don't address this shift and wake up a year later hating their new role, and as their manager, you can help them recognize this shift and find compensating strategies to remain energized.

- **Give feedback.** One particularly important strategy for rewriting their definition of success—and to keep them growing—is to give frequent feedback. If they've picked the wrong battle, tell them, and tell them *why*. If they're prioritizing work you wouldn't, tell them, and tell them *why*. Nothing is more stressful for a high performer than not knowing how they're doing! If you don't give feedback, especially about their best work, they'll keep changing their approach until you do give feedback (often to your regret).
- **Keep them informed**. As a manager, it can be easy to forget how much more access you have to information than the engineers you work with. The reality is that most organizations build their information flows around managers communicating key information to other managers. Your Staff-plus engineers will be hamstrung if you don't find a deliberate, reproducible process for sharing your context with them. Some folks do this at the beginning of their 1:1s, which works OK, but I've come to prefer dropping them into the team's chat channel as they happen and aggregating them into my weekly email update.
- **Involve them in planning and prioritization.** Many engineers get frustrated that "the right work never gets prioritized," and one of the best solutions to this is to proactively involve more engineers in the planning process. This works on two fronts. First, they understand more of the competing work and why that work is important, and second, they'll be present to advocate more ef-

fectively for the sorts of technical work they see missing.
- **Agree on how to stay aligned while acting independently.** As you push Staff-plus engineers you support towards leadership, they're going to start leading more, which will sometimes include surprising you. If leaders you work with *never* surprise you, then you're not delegating enough, but if they frequently surprise you, it may be helpful to explicitly establish your controls.
- **Create space for them to think without detaching them from the day-to-day realities of the organization.** Many folks in these roles are so motivated by impact and "doing the right thing for the business" that they'll grind themselves down without external intervention. If you're their manager, then "external intervention" means you. If you see them spending too much time firefighting and helping unblock urgent work, work with them to protect more time for deep thinking work as well. Conversely, if you see them only doing deep thinking work, they're likely to lose context and potentially the respect of their peers and the business if they don't adjust that mix.
- **Remind them they're a role model.** Much like they do for managers, engineers in an organization watch Staff-plus engineers to learn which behavior and actions are rewarded (and tolerated). This is a great responsibility, but also a huge opportunity for impact: by living positive values, they have the opportunity to create a positive organization around them.
- **Minimize manager overflow.** In the quest for efficiency over effectiveness[336], many companies trap their managers in a staggering amount of coordination and bureaucracy. When you're drowning, you're going to look for help wherever you can, and in many cases, that causes managers to offload management work to their Staff engineers. This is absolutely going to happen sometimes–your relationship with Staff-plus engineers

you manage is a partnership–but try very hard to minimize the amount and ensure it's a temporary overflow rather than a permanent one.

- **Give them unrefined problems.** This is a senior role where you ought to give them a problem space that they narrow into a more specific problem and solution. They have better technical context than you do, and if you point them too precisely at what you think is the problem, you won't benefit from their judgment. Picking precisely the right problem creates at least as much impact as finding precisely the right solution, and is only possible when you create space.
- **Cede space to their leadership.** When you're managing a Staff-plus engineer, find ways to move pieces of your ownership explicitly into their realm of responsibility. For example, how can you enable them to hold their team responsible for technical quality, rather than you doing it? This creates leverage for both of you and a sense of ownership for the Staff-plus engineer.
- **Appreciate them.** Great Staff-plus engineers operate fairly independently, so it can be easy to deprioritize them when the organization is on fire. Ignoring your most important people is the manager version of "snacking"–something that feels important but usually isn't the right priority. So keep your 1:1s, and generally remember to show up for them, especially if they aren't the sort of person to demand it.
- **Build and insist upon alignment with the business.** Some engineers succeed despite harboring a mentality that technical work is more important than the business requiring that work. This mentality is generally toxic, but it is exceptionally toxic when held by a Staff-plus engineer. This is someone who is a role model for the wider organization, and stretching them beyond that perspective is essential for them to remain in a leadership role. Companies undermine and eventually eject

leaders who are misaligned with the business.
- **Hold them responsible for the full role.** While few folks reach Staff-plus roles with major technical weaknesses, it's my lived experience that many folks reach these roles hampered by significant leadership or behavioral challenges. These folks get the title but tend to linger in Staff purgatory where they're expected to lead but are kept away from most leadership opportunities. They're viewed as too unreliable or "expensive to involve." You've got to give these folks feedback on their gaps and hold them accountable to the full role expectations. Don't let them linger as quasi-leaders indefinitely. Maybe they initially got the role via title inflation[337], so you decide to just cover for their gaps instead of fixing it–don't do that, instead, figure out a plan to support them while shifting that responsibility to them[338].
- **Give them access to the room but don't treat it as a status symbol.** Folks often get fixated on status symbols, and one that's particularly common for engineers to focus on is "being in the room." Sometimes meetings *are* where the work happens, but most routine reporting meetings have too many people in them, and you can create a great deal of time and space for both you and the Staff-plus engineer you're supporting by sharding attendance across various meetings rather than doubling up for all of them.

The transition from Senior to Staff-plus engineer is a major one that changes the sort of work being done, whereas previous transitions often only change the work's extent. Many folks struggle with that transition, and many managers aren't sure how to help support the Staff-plus engineers they work with. Certainly, this is an incomplete list of helpful things you can do to support them, but hopefully, it's a useful starting point.

Designing a Staff-plus interview loop

When we talk about designing a Staff-plus engineer interview loop, the first thing to talk about is that absolutely no one is confident their Staff-plus interview loop works well. Many loops end up looking for a senior engineer who's *really* fast at solving problems, which doesn't reflect the actual role. Others focus on communication skills, which *are* a key part of the role but certainly not the entirety of it. A few companies even construct their process to assess whether the candidate *feels* like a member of their existing senior engineering team, conflating excellence with familiarity.

Even if no one feels great about their loop, there is still a body of collective learnings to incorporate into your attempt to design a loop, which is what we'll cover here. We'll start with examining the frequent failure modes of Staff-plus interview loops, discuss the signals that you *do* want to test for in these loops, and finally discuss some interview formats which can be useful for assessing those signals.

Challenges

While technology interviews, in general, are a bit of a mess, interviews for very senior candidates have enough issues of their own to pack a dedicated struggle bus. It's helpful to start with understanding some of the common failure modes before we move into considering what might work better:

- **A senior engineer, but better.** Many interview processes look at Staff-plus engineers as Senior engineers who are a bit better at everything. They're a bit faster. They're a bit clearer in their communication. They're a bit more nuanced in architecture discussions. This stems from most folks being unfamiliar with Staff roles and usually causes Staff-plus engineers to perform poorly on these loops. In particular, most Staff-plus engineers are programming less than Senior engineers, and consequently are *slower* rather than *faster* at rote programming tasks. You'll find some Staff-plus engineers who remain very quick programmers, but you won't find much correlation between that speed and their impact.

- **A senior engineer, but worse.** Conversely, other interview processes recognize that Staff-plus engineers are spending less time programming and anticipate slower performance on some of the more mundane programming exercises. This makes it more likely for Staff-plus engineers to succeed in the loop but doesn't get signal on what makes these sorts of engineers exceptionally impactful. If you don't add additional interviews to capture those strengths, reduced speed on rote work will likely correlate with seniority to some extent, but it correlates more strongly with many other factors.
- **A senior engineer, but they'll accept the offer.** Another failure mode is companies that are struggling to hire Senior engineers and decide to inflate their titles without changing the role expectations. In these cases, the interviews are appropriate to the actual work, but the title isn't. With neither the company nor the candidate fully willing to acknowledge the inflation, all future Staff-plus hiring at the company acquires a veneer of uncertainty.
- **Someone like us.** Many loops focus on whether the Staff-plus candidate *projects* the same wisdom and confidence as the existing Staff-plus engineers at the company, where the interview debrief might include statements like, "They feel like they'd be a natural part of this team." This sort of approach is more likely to anchor on semi-arbitrary features like how they project their confidence than on the candidate's capabilities.
- **Not better than me.** Especially when hiring your first Staff-plus engineers, you'll often find some earlier career interviewers who

undervalue the candidate's strengths and instead anchor on the candidate's capability to perform the interviewer's current role. You'll have an impressive Staff-plus candidate, but the interview panel will be skeptical of their ability to thrive as a mid-level engineer. This seems to be brought up most frequently for women and minority candidates.

- **The reverse filter.** Certain kinds of interviews are signals that you as an organization don't know how to use Staff-plus engineers: whiteboard algorithmic interviews, interviewers are predominantly early career, and so on. Many Staff-plus processes cause the best candidates to opt-out early in the process, often somewhat invisibly to the recruiting metrics.
- **Too title-oriented?** At a certain level of accomplishment, people don't care much about internal leveling, generally because they're already financially secure. This creates a peculiar pressure on folks newly reaching Staff-plus levels to avoid appearing overly career or title motivated, making it harder for folks to attain the title for the first time.

Some of these are quite difficult to address, others are easy as long as you keep them in mind, but all of them are worth considering as you start to design or re-envision your Staff-plus interview process.

Signals

The best interview loops[339] reason forward from the signals you want to capture back to the interview topics and format, which means the first important question to answer is, "Which signals are important for hiring successful Staff-plus engineers?"

The signals I'd recommend focusing on are:

- **Self-awareness**. Are they accountable for mistakes? Have they demonstrated growth in areas where they've previously been

weaker?
- **Judgment.** Are they able to see around corners to identify problems? Are they able to navigate broad, ambiguous problems? Can they effectively mediate between folks in an argument about tradeoffs or design? Can they derisk the execution of difficult problems?
- **Collaboration.** Do they partner well with others? What about folks less experienced than them? More experienced than them? Their managers? Cross-functionally? Executives?
- **Communication.** Are they good listeners who understand the points made by others? Are they able to communicate their ideas clearly? Can they communicate in the formats that your company relies upon (written, verbal, etc)?
- **Development.** Do they grow others around them? Does the "organizational bench" grow in areas they lead or atrophy? Do broken systems and processes get cleaned up?

It's interesting to note that many would not consider these to explicitly be technical skills. Domain expertise is a major factor in success at all of them, but it's exercising that expertise in conjunction with other critical skills and behaviors that transition someone from a tenured Senior engineer into a Staff-plus one.

Formats and structures

The two key questions to ask yourself when designing an interview loop are always:

1. What tasks and behaviors will this person need to succeed on a day to day basis?
2. How can we get them to demonstrate actually doing them?

Most senior candidates become increasingly diplomatic and *asking* them about their work is never as helpful as *watching* them do the work. If mentorship is the most important activity, don't rely on them talking about mentorship, but instead find a way to *see* them mentoring someone. If it's architecture, present your current systems and ask them to bring their questions to see how they react to decisions they disagree with – get away from the ambiguous abstract.

Moving beyond the typical one-on-one discussions and programming interviews, some of the interview formats and structures that I've found particularly effective for evaluating Staff-plus signals are:

- **Structured presentation.** Have the candidate prepare and present for twenty to thirty minutes on a narrow topic to a group of peers. The format gives a great signal on structured thinking, communication, listening to, and answering questions. Depending on the topic you select, you can get strong signals on one or two areas of your choice. This format is particularly effective at hearing how folks talk about their peers and coworkers.
- **Code review.** Prepare a pull request and ask the candidate to provide feedback on it, focusing on empathy, clarity, and usefulness.
- **Data modeling, interfaces, and architecture.** Have the candidate walk through the design of a system, typically with a focus on evolving it to meet changing requirements. These interviews often try to do too much: narrow your focus and add layers to the question to allow you to continue drilling deeper for candidates who make significant progress.
- **Subject matter expertise.** Interviews that test their areas of domain expertise. For example, a frontend engineer might collaborate with a designer and product manager on how technical constraints would impact a proposed design and launch timeline. For backend engineers, you might provide the candidate with a broken piece of software or environment and have them

debug the problem back to a fix.
- **Mentorship panel**. It's challenging to hire Staff-plus candidates if your panel consists entirely of earlier career folks, but it's equally risky to hire a Staff-plus candidate if they haven't demonstrated success mentoring folks earlier in their careers. Have a panel of three to four folks they might be expected to mentor come with questions. Watching folks redirect roughly framed questions into a useful discussion is an especially great insight into their ability to mentor in their new role.

If these formats aren't enough, then start asking around! Most companies have designed bespoke approaches to their Staff-plus loops, and you can learn a great deal from that discussion.

How to pull it together

You might reasonably expect this to end with a precompiled interview loop for your company to use to evaluate Staff-plus engineers, and I hate to disappoint, but I think most of the value comes from thinking through the signals that matter to you and designing formats that get at those signals in a way that resonates to you and your company.

Whatever interviews you end up using, test them, gather candidate feedback, and keep evolving them to be better!

Staff-plus career ladders

There are *so* many different career ladders shared in public these days that there's no reason *not* to read a half-dozen different ones before attempting to design your own.

Some that are particularly worth reading through:

- Rent the Runway[340]
- Kickstarter[341]
- Patreon[342]

You can find even more collected at progression.fyi[343]. Charity Majors has also written a helpful guide of things to know about engineering levels.

I think it's important to recognize that career ladders only apply effectively against populations of individuals. They rarely, if ever, apply cleanly against any individual. This effect becomes particularly pronounced in Staff-plus roles, which are often only populated by a couple of folks. Ladders are essential but don't get caught believing they're a map of how things actually work rather than a mythos of how things are intended to work.

References

[1] *career level*

https://lethain.com/mailbag-beyond-career-level/

[2] *The Manager's Path*

https://www.amazon.com/dp/1491973897

[3] *The Making of a Manager*

https://www.amazon.com/dp/0735219567/

[4] *Resilient Management*

https://resilient-management.com

[5] *An Elegant Puzzle*

https://www.amazon.com/dp/1732265186

[6] *career ladders*

https://lethain.com/perf-management-system/

[7] *individuals, rather than teams, as the atomic unit of planning and ownership*

https://lethain.com/weak-and-strong-team-concepts/

[8] *Hand of the King*

https://awoiaf.westeros.org/index.php/Hand_of_the_King

[9] *Leo McGarry*

https://westwing.fandom.com/wiki/Leo_McGarry

[10] *remaining deeply aligned*

https://lethain.com/staying-aligned-with-authority/

[11] *forty-year career*

https://lethain.com/forty-year-career/

[12] *Tanya Reilly*

https://noidea.dog

[13] *being glue*

https://noidea.dog/glue

[14] *the Lorax*

https://en.wikipedia.org/wiki/The_Lorax

[15] *What does sponsorship look like?*

https://larahogan.me/blog/what-sponsorship-looks-like/

[16] *an organizational restructure*

https://lethain.com/running-an-engineering-reorg/

[17] *Hill-climbing*

https://en.wikipedia.org/wiki/Hill_climbing

[18] *it's hard to prioritize new businesses*

https://en.Wikipedia.org/wiki/The_Innovator's_Dilemma

[19] *to do exploratory work*

https://lethain.com/how-to-invest-technical-infrastructure/

[20] *career level*

https://lethain.com/career-levels-and-more/

[21] *some companies do*

https://www.levels.fyi/

[22] *REPL*

https://en.wikipedia.org/wiki/Read–eval–print_loop

[23] *avoid "snacking"*

https://hunterwalk.com/2016/06/18/the-best-startups-resists-snacks-im-not-talking-about-food/

[24] *career growth*

https://yenkel.dev/posts/how-to-achieve-career-growth-opportunities-skills-sponsors

[25] *current role grows in complexity*

https://lethain.com/growing-with-your-company/

[26] *a strategy shift that fundamentally misunderstands the challenges at hand*

https://lethain.com/grand-migration/

[27] *iterative elimination tournament*

https://lethain.com/iterative-elimination-tournaments/

[28] *like my experience at Digg*

https://lethain.com/digg-v4/

[29] *Twitter's fail whale stability challenges*

https://www.theatlantic.com/technology/archive/2015/01/the-story-behind-twitters-fail-whale/384313/

[30] *hiring funnel*

https://lethain.com/hiring-funnel/

[31] *as impactful as hiring to your company's engineering velocity*

https://lethain.com/productivity-in-the-age-of-hypergrowth/

[32] *only get value from finishing projects*

https://www.amazon.com/dp/B078Y98RG8/

[33] *writing your company's technology strategy*

https://lethain.com/magnitudes-of-exploration/

[34] *be crafting a discerning API*

https://increment.com/apis/api-design-for-eager-discering-developers/

[35] *Camille Fournier*

https://twitter.com/skamille/status/1328763503973429250

[36] *standardized on RFC*

https://blog.pragmaticengineer.com/scaling-engineering-teams-via-writing-things-down-rfcs/

[37] *Design Docs, Markdown, and Git*

https://caitiem.com/2020/03/29/design-docs-markdown-and-git/

[38] *Design Docs at Google*

https://www.industrialempathy.com/posts/design-docs-at-google/

[39] *Technical Decision-Making and Alignment in a Remote Culture*

https://multithreaded.stitchfix.com/blog/2020/12/07/remote-decision-making/

[40] *A Framework for Responsible Innovation*

https://multithreaded.stitchfix.com/blog/2019/08/19/framework-for-responsible-innovation/

[41] *How Big Technical Changes Happen at Slack*

https://slack.engineering/how-big-technical-changes-happen-at-slack/

[42] *Good Strategy, Bad Strategy*

https://www.amazon.com/dp/B004J4WKEC

[43] *Run less software*

https://www.intercom.com/blog/run-less-software/

[44] *Tanya Reilly*

https://twitter.com/whereistanya

[45] *a robust belief in the future*

https://leaddev.com/technical-direction-strategy/sending-gifts-future-you

[46] *A Philosophy of Software Design*

https://www.amazon.com/Philosophy-Software-Design-John-Ousterhout/dp/1732102201

[47] *RAM disk*

https://en.wikipedia.org/wiki/RAM_drive

[48] *Software Design X-Rays*

https://www.amazon.com/Software-Design-X-Rays-Technical-Behavioral-ebook-dp-B07BVRLZ87/dp/B07BVRLZ87/

[49] *Systems thinking*

https://lethain.com/systems-thinking/

[50] *Scrum*

https://en.wikipedia.org/wiki/Scrum_(software_development

[51] *good process is evolved*

https://lethain.com/good-process-is-evolved/

[52] *Accelerate*

https://www.amazon.com/dp/B07B9F83WM/

[53] *better internal documentation*

https://increment.com/documentation/why-investing-in-internal-docs-is-worth-it/

[54] *increasing your best practice adoption-in-progress limit*

https://lethain.com/limiting-wip/

[55] *architecture reviews*

https://lethain.com/scaling-consistency/

[56] *Building Evolutionary Architectures*

https://www.amazon.com/Building-Evolutionary-Architectures-Support-Constant/dp/1491986360/

[57] *Reclaim unreasonable software*

https://lethain.com/reclaim-unreasonable-software/

[58] *size the team*

https://lethain.com/sizing-engineering-teams/

[59] *accidental complexity*

https://en.wikipedia.org/wiki/No_Silver_Bullet

[60] *balances the benefits of exploration against the benefits of standardization*

http://lethain.com/magnitudes-of-exploration/

[61] *discounted cash flow*

https://en.wikipedia.org/wiki/Discounted_cash_flow

[62] *a broad topic about which much has been written*

https://lethain.com/programs-owning-the-unownable/

[63] *the techniques that apply to migrations work for programs as well*

http://lethain.com/migrations/

[64] *weekly email updates*

https://lethain.com/weekly-updates/

[65] *identify the controls*

https://lethain.com/identify-your-controls/

[66] *kicked out of the room*

https://lethain.com/getting-in-the-room/

[67] *the first follower creates a leader*

https://www.cornerstoneondemand.com/rework/ted-talk-tuesday-how-start-movement

[68] *Franklin Hu*

https://twitter.com/thisisfranklin

[69] *helps avoid missteps*

https://lethain.com/learn-to-never-be-wrong/

[70] *show value*

https://lethain.com/showing-value/

[71] *thrives temporarily until that individual leaves*

https://www.amazon.com/dp/B0058DRUV6/

[72] *tactics to build your network*

https://lethain.com/meeting-people/

[73] *Thriving on the Technical Leadership Path*

https://keavy.com/work/thriving-on-the-technical-leadership-path/

[74] *Rands Leadership Slack*

https://randsinrepose.com/welcome-to-rands-leadership-slack/

[75] *Camille Fournier*

https://twitter.com/skamille

[76] *Lara Hogan*

https://twitter.com/lara_hogan

[77] *Josh Wills*

https://twitter.com/josh_wills

[78] *Vicki Boykis*

https://twitter.com/vboykis

[79] *David Gasca*

https://twitter.com/gasca

[80] *Julia Grace*

https://twitter.com/jewelia

[81] *Holden Karau*

https://twitter.com/holdenkarau

[82] *John Allspaw*

https://twitter.com/allspaw

[83] *Charity Majors*

https://twitter.com/mipsytipsy

[84] *Theo Schlossnagle*

https://twitter.com/postwait

[85] *Jessica Joy Kerr*

https://twitter.com/jessitron

[86] *Sarah Catanzaro*

https://twitter.com/sarahcat21

[87] *Orange Book*

https://twitter.com/orangebook_

[88] *including [Aphyr*

https://twitter.com/aphyr

[89] *David Fowler*

https://twitter.com/davidfowl

[90] *The Pyramid Principle*

https://www.amazon.com/Pyramid-Principle-Logic-Writing-Thinking/dp/0273710516/

[91] *nemawashi*

https://blog.toyota.co.uk/nemawashi-toyota-production-system

[92] *managing your software career*

https://www.learninpublic.org/

[93] *distributed office*

https://lethain.com/how-to-start-distributed-engineering-office/

[94] *The Engineer/Manager Pendulum*

https://charity.wtf/2017/05/11/the-engineer-manager-pendulum/

[95] *blog post on that topic*

https://code.likeagirl.io/why-i-left-management-the-engineering-technical-track-vs-management-track-abef5b1d914d

[96] *brag document*

https://jvns.ca/blog/brag-documents/

[97] *well-defined goal*

https://lethain.com/goals-and-baselines/

[98] *glue work*

https://www.slideshare.net/TanyaReilly/being-glue

[99] *goes awry in the promotion process*

http://lethain.com/promo-pathologies/

[100] *its own purpose*

https://www.tablegroup.com/books/dbm/

[101] *disagree and commit*

https://en.wikipedia.org/wiki/Disagree_and_commit

[102] *ohshitgit*

https://ohshitgit.com

[103] *High Growth Engineering*

https://highgrowthengineering.substack.com

[104] *work the policy rather than the exceptions*

https://lethain.com/work-policy-not-exceptions/

[105] *flying wedge*

https://en.wikipedia.org/wiki/Flying_wedge

[106] *Values Oasis*

https://lethain.com/values-oasis/

[107] *refresh your resume*

https://thetechresume.com

[108] *Cracking the Coding Interview*

http://www.crackingthecodinginterview.com

[109] *Salary Negotiation*

https://www.kalzumeus.com/2012/01/23/salary-negotiation/

[110] *blog*

http://blog.michellebu.com/

[111] *Twitter*

https://twitter.com/hazelcough

[112] *Linkedin*

https://www.linkedin.com/in/michellebu/

[113] *Payment Intents API*

https://stripe.com/docs/payments/payment-intents

[114] *"no log":*

https://twitter.com/amyngyn/status/1224160724072558594

[115] *Stripe Radar*

https://stripe.com/radar

[116] *Stripe Elements*

https://stripe.com/payments/elements

[117] *adaptive leadership*

https://www.amazon.com/dp/B004OC071W/

[118] *building a manager voltron*

https://larahogan.me/blog/manager-voltron/

[119] *Draft No. 4, John McPhee*

https://www.amazon.com/dp/B06X18NHC1/

[120] *Creativity Inc., Ed Catmull*

https://www.amazon.com/Creativity-Inc-Overcoming-Unseen-Inspiration-ebook/dp/B00FUZQYBO/

[121] *Impro, Keith Johnstone*

https://www.amazon.com/Impro-Improvisation-Theatre-Keith-Johnstone/dp/0878301178

[122] *Linkedin*

https://www.linkedin.com/in/raskasawilliams/

[123] *Marc Hedlund*

https://twitter.com/marcprecipice

[124] *Dan McKinely*

https://mcfunley.com/

[125] *Coda Hale*

https://codahale.com/

[126] *Kelsey Hightower*

https://twitter.com/kelseyhightower

[127] *"Delivering on an architecture strategy" from Pete Hodgson*

https://blog.thepete.net/blog/2019/12/09/delivering-on-an-architecture-strategy/

[128] *"Stepping Stones not Milestones" from James Cowling*

https://medium.com/@jamesacowling/stepping-stones-not-milestones-e6be0073563f

[129] *blog*

https://keavy.com/

[130] *Twitter*

https://twitter.com/keavy

[131] *Linkedin*

https://www.linkedin.com/in/keavy/

[132] *Fastly*

https://www.fastly.com/

[133] *The Passionate Programmer*

https://www.amazon.com/Passionate-Programmer-Remarkable-Development-Pragmatic-ebook/dp/B00AYQNR5U/

[134] *The Pragmatic Programmer*

https://www.amazon.com/Pragmatic-Programmer-Journeyman-Master/dp/020161622X

[135] *blog*

https://bert.org

[136] *Twitter*

https://twitter.com/bertrandom

[137] *Linkedin*

https://www.linkedin.com/in/bertrandom/

[138] *Slack App Directory*

http://slack.com/apps

[139] *website*

https://sylormiller.com/

[140] *Linkedin*

https://www.linkedin.com/in/ksylor/

[141] *Twitter*

https://twitter.com/ksylor

[142] *Dan Na's talk about pushing through friction*

https://blog.danielna.com/talks/pushing-through-friction/

[143] *Lara Hogan*

https://larahogan.me/

[144] *Dan Na*

https://blog.danielna.com/

[145] *Julia Evans*

https://jvns.ca/

[146] *Ryn Daniels*

https://www.ryn.works/

[147] *Tanya Reilly*

https://noidea.dog/

[148] *Nicole Sullivan*

http://www.stubbornella.org/content/

[149] *Jen Simmons*

https://jensimmons.com/

[150] *Ethan Marcotte*

https://ethanmarcotte.com/

[151] *The Manager's Path*

https://www.amazon.com/dp/B06XP3GJ7F/

[152] *Linkedin*

https://www.linkedin.com/in/rituvincent/

[153] *Guido van Rossum*

https://en.wikipedia.org/wiki/Guido_van_Rossum

[154] *Linkedin*

https://www.linkedin.com/in/kineticrick/

[155] *Matthew Mengerink*

https://eng.uber.com/core-infra-2018/

[156] *Rob Punkunus*

https://www.linkedin.com/in/rob-punkunus-3791273/

[157] *Susan Fowler's blog post*

https://www.susanjfowler.com/blog/2017/2/19/reflecting-on-one-very-strange-year-at-uber

[158] *pull together my interest in machine learning and site reliability*

https://www.youtube.com/watch?v=9ool1BQybaE

[159] *Daniel Kahneman*

https://en.wikipedia.org/wiki/Daniel_Kahneman

[160] *Tim Harford*

https://en.wikipedia.org/wiki/Tim_Harford

[161] *Dan Ariely*

https://en.wikipedia.org/wiki/Dan_Ariely

[162] *Freakonomics*

https://freakonomics.com/archive/

[163] *Choice-ology*

https://www.schwab.com/resource-center/insights/podcast

[164] *Hidden Brain*

https://www.npr.org/podcasts/510308/hidden-brain

[165] *reading list of books about the human brain and behavior*

https://docs.google.com/document/d/1WIqIYuSGfyoU_ZO-xZMDXfaaUmnG2tmnkHiGZQ7pvqg/edit?usp=sharing

[166] *r/linux*

https://www.reddit.com/r/linux/

[167] *r/programming*

https://www.reddit.com/r/programming/

[168] *Twitter*

https://twitter.com/nelhage

[169] *blog*

https://blog.nelhage.com/

[170] *Sorbet*

https://sorbet.org/

[171] *Ksplice*

https://en.wikipedia.org/wiki/Ksplice

[172] *blog*

https://diana.dev/

[173] *Twitter*

https://twitter.com/podiana

[174] *Linkedin*

https://www.linkedin.com/in/dianapojar/

[175] *technical leadership*

https://slack.engineering/technical-leadership-getting-started-e5161b1bf85c

[176] *Josh Wills*

https://www.linkedin.com/in/josh-wills-13882b/

[177] *Stan Babourine*

https://www.linkedin.com/in/stanb/

[178] *Bogdan Gaza*

https://www.linkedin.com/in/bogdangaza/

[179] *Travis Crawford*

https://www.linkedin.com/in/traviscrawford/

[180] *my Goodreads account*

https://www.goodreads.com/user/show/11950463-diana-pojar

[181] *Thanks for the Feedback*

https://www.goodreads.com/book/show/20487821-thanks-for-the-feedback

[182] *Radical Candor*

https://www.goodreads.com/book/show/32809138-radical-candor

[183] *The Manager's Path: A Guide for Tech Leaders Navigating Growth and Change*

https://www.goodreads.com/book/show/34616805-the-manager-s-path

[184] *Leadership and Self-Deception: Getting Out of the Box*

https://www.goodreads.com/book/show/18966789-leadership-and-self-deception

[185] *The Coaching Habit: Say Less, Ask More & Change the Way You Lead Forever*

https://www.goodreads.com/book/show/29342515-the-coaching-habit

[186] *First, Break All the Rules: What the World's Greatest Managers Do Differently*

https://www.goodreads.com/book/show/30109687-first-break-all-the-rules

[187] *The Courage To Be Disliked: How to free yourself, change your life and achieve real happiness*

https://www.goodreads.com/book/show/36752952-the-courage-to-be-disliked

[188] *Give and Take: A Revolutionary Approach to Success*

https://www.goodreads.com/book/show/16158498-give-and-take

[189] *Mistakes Were Made (But Not by Me): Why We Justify Foolish Beliefs, Bad Decisions, and Hurtful Acts*

https://www.goodreads.com/book/show/9530608-mistakes-were-made-but-not-by-me

[190] *Twitter*

https://twitter.com/dxna

[191] *Linkedin*

https://www.linkedin.com/in/danielna/

[192] *Building a System for Frontend Translations*

https://engineering.squarespace.com/blog/2018/building-a-system-for-front-end-translations

[193] *High Output Management by Andrew Grove*

https://www.amazon.com/dp/B015VACHOK/

[194] *Lara Hogan*

http://larahogan.me

[195] *Resilient Management*

https://resilient-management.com/

[196] *Irrational Exuberance*

https://lethain.com/

[197] *Insights Blog*

https://svpg.com/articles/

[198] *Daniel Espeset*

http://www.danielespeset.com

[199] *Tanya Reilly*

http://noidea.dog

[200] *blog*

https://medium.com/@jkebertz

[201] *Twitter*

https://twitter.com/jkebertz

[202] *Linkedin*

https://www.linkedin.com/in/joyebertz/

[203] *learn a lot during my time managing*

https://medium.com/box-tech-blog/no-regrets-my-time-in-management-wasnt-wasted-140b40ded0e6

[204] *blog*

https://yenkel.dev

[205] *Twitter*

https://twitter.com/dschenkelman

[206] *Linkedin*

https://www.linkedin.com/in/damianschenkelman/

[207] *Auth0*

https://auth0.com/

[208] *technical strategy*

https://yenkel.dev/posts/achieving-alignment-and-efficiency-through-a-technical-strategy

[209] *Identity and Access Management*

https://auth0.com/learn/cloud-identity-access-management/

[210] *Scaling Up Excellence*

https://www.amazon.com/dp/B00EGMQIDG/

[211] *nemawashi*

https://en.wikipedia.org/wiki/Nemawashi

[212] *Matias Woloski*

https://twitter.com/woloski

[213] *Christian McCarrick*

https://twitter.com/cmccarrick

[214] *Southworks*

https://www.southworks.com/

[215] *Jepsen*

https://jepsen.io/

[216] *RFC process @ Squarespace*

https://engineering.squarespace.com/blog/2019/the-power-of-yes-if

[217] *Being Glue*

https://www.youtube.com/watch?v=KClAPipnKqw

[218] *ASP.NET Architect*

https://channel9.msdn.com/Shows/Careers-Behind-the-Code/Becoming-the-ASPNET-Architect-with-David-Fowler

[219] *Jon Allie*

https://www.linkedin.com/in/jon-allie-b250296

[220] *Fundamentals of Software Architecture*

https://www.oreilly.com/library/view/fundamentals-of-software/9781492043447/

[221] *Managing Humans*

https://www.amazon.com/Managing-Humans-Humorous-Software-Engineering/dp/1484221575/

[222] *The 7 habits of highly effective people*

https://www.amazon.com/dp/B00GOZV3TM/

[223] *Twitter*

https://twitter.com/darkdimius

[224] *Linkedin*

https://www.linkedin.com/in/darkdimius/

[225] *presentations*

https://d-d.me/site/presentations/

[226] *Paul Tarjan*

https://paultarjan.com/

[227] *Nelson*

https://nelhage.com/

[228] *code-yellow situation*

https://www.usenix.org/conference/lisa18/presentation/kehoe

[229] *Github*

https://github.com/stephen

[230] *Twitter*

https://twitter.com/stpnwn

[231] *Linkedin*

https://www.linkedin.com/in/stephenwan/

[232] *Samsara*

https://www.samsara.com/

[233] *shaping*

https://basecamp.com/shapeup/1.1-chapter-02

[234] *hero mindset*

https://lethain.com/doing-it-harder-and-hero-programming/

[235] *Haruki Murakami*

https://en.wikipedia.org/wiki/Haruki_Murakami

[236] *Bob Nystrom's blog posts*

http://journal.stuffwithstuff.com/category/language/

[237] *Vyacheslav Egorov's blog*

https://mrale.ph/

[238] *Brandur's blog*

https://brandur.org/articles

[239] *Accidentally Quadratic*

https://accidentallyquadratic.tumblr.com/

[240] *Vicki Pfau's Blog*

https://mgba.io/tag/debugging/

[241] *fail0overflow's blog*

https://fail0verflow.com/blog/

[242] *Bungie's engineering publications*

http://halo.bungie.net/inside/publications.aspx

[243] *Crafting Interpreters*

https://craftinginterpreters.com/

[244] *esbuild*

https://github.com/evanw/esbuild/blob/master/docs/architecture.md

[245] *history of BART*

https://www.amazon.com/BART-Dramatic-History-Transit-System/dp/1597143707

[246] *history of Xerox PARC*

https://press.stripe.com/##the-dream-machine

[247] *an overview of modern Japanese culture*

https://www.amazon.com/Making-Common-Policy-Institutional-Studies/dp/0822955105

[248] *Being a principal engineer at Skyscanner*

https://medium.com/@SkyscannerEng/being-a-principal-engineer-at-skyscanner-1830dfa17d30

[249] *Defining a Distinguished Engineer*

https://blog.jessfraz.com/post/defining-a-distinguished-engineer/

[250] *How I operated as a Staff engineer at Heroku*

https://amyunger.com/blog/2020/09/10/staff-engineer-at-heroku.html

[251] *Not all engineering leaders are engineering managers*

https://leaddev.com/not-all-engineering-leaders-are-engineering-managers

[252] *The Nuts and Bolts with Tanya Reilly*

https://engineering.squarespace.com/blog/2020/the-nuts-and-bolts-with-tanya-reilly

[253] *On Being A Principal Engineer*

https://blog.dbsmasher.com/2019/01/28/on-being-a-principal-engineer.html

[254] *On Being a Senior Engineer*

https://www.kitchensoap.com/2012/10/25/on-being-a-senior-engineer/

[255] *Staff Engineering*

https://tychoish.com/post/staff-engineering/

[256] *What's a senior engineer's job?*

https://jvns.ca/blog/senior-engineer/

[257] *What a Senior Staff Software Engineer Actually Does, Part 1: The Role and My Tasks*

https://medium.com/box-tech-blog/what-a-senior-staff-software-engineer-actually-does-f3fc140d5f33

[258] *Part 2: The Mindset and Focus of the Role*

https://medium.com/box-tech-blog/what-a-senior-staff-software-engineer-actually-does-d55308fcdd41

[259] *What does Staff level mean at GitLab?*

https://about.gitlab.com/blog/2020/02/18/staff-level-engineering-at-gitlab/

[260] *Becoming a Staff Engineer – Interview with Kristina Fox, Staff iOS Engineer at Intuit*

https://elpha.com/posts/4j56np6p/becoming-a-staff-engineer-interview-with-kristina-fox-staff-ios-engineer-at-intuit

[261] *On becoming a senior technical leader*

https://blog.coinbase.com/on-becoming-a-senior-technical-leader-14106f1383b8

[262] *On Mid-Career and Managers*

https://www.ryn.works/blog/on-mid-career-and-managers

[263] *How does one become a Staff Software Engineer at Google?*

https://www.quora.com/How-does-one-become-a-Staff-Software-Engineer-at-Google-What-might-a-new-grad-entering-the-company-do-to-grow-their-career-to-reach-that-level

[264] *Things to Know About Engineering Levels*

https://charity.wtf/2020/09/14/useful-things-to-know-about-engineering-levels/

[265] *Computers can be understood*

https://blog.nelhage.com/post/computers-can-be-understood/

[266] *Effective Mental Models for Code and Systems*

https://medium.com/@copyconstruct/effective-mental-models-for-code-and-systems-7c55918f1b3e

[267] *"I Wouldn't Start From Here." How to Make a Big Technical Change*

https://noidea.dog/blog/getting-there-from-here

[268] *Migrations: the sole scalable fix to tech-debt*

https://lethain.com/migrations/

[269] *On Mid-Career and Team Dynamics*

https://www.ryn.works/blog/on-mid-career-and-team-dynamics

[270] *Surviving the Organisational Side Quest*

https://noidea.dog/blog/surviving-the-organisational-side-quest

[271] *Systems that defy detailed understanding*

https://blog.nelhage.com/post/systems-that-defy-understanding/

[272] *Team Objectives*

https://svpg.com/team-objectives-overview/

[273] *Technical Decision Making*

https://medium.com/@copyconstruct/technical-decision-making-9b2817c18da4

[274] *Technical Research and Preparation*

https://keavy.com/work/technical-preparation/

[275] *The Behind-the-scenes Work of Tech Leadership*

https://blog.coleadership.com/behind-the-scenes-tech-leadership/

[276] *Understanding Project Management Will Improve Your Developer Job*

https://blog.danielna.com/understanding-project-management-will-improve-your-developer-job/

[277] *Where to Start*

https://keavy.com/work/where-to-start/

[278] *A practical guide to writing technical specs*

https://stackoverflow.blog/2020/04/06/a-practical-guide-to-writing-technical-specs/

[279] *Documenting Architecture Decisions*

https://cognitect.com/blog/2011/11/15/documenting-architecture-decisions

[280] *How to write a better technical design document*

https://www.range.co/blog/better-tech-specs

[281] *Writing Technical Design Docs*

https://medium.com/machine-words/writing-technical-design-docs-71f446e42f2e

[282] *How Big Technical Changes Happen at Slack - Several People Are Coding*

https://slack.engineering/how-big-technical-changes-happen-at-slack-f1569d25ee7b

[283] *On Drafting an Engineering Strategy*

https://www.paperplanes.de/2020/1/31/on-drafting-an-engineering-strategy.html

[284] *Defining a Tech Strategy*

https://sarahtaraporewalla.com/agile/design/architecture/Defining-a-Tech-Strategy

[285] *The difficult teenage years: Setting tech strategy after a launch*

https://medium.com/ft-product-technology/the-difficult-teenage-years-setting-tech-strategy-after-a-launch-7f42eb94a424

[286] *Learning to have an engineering vision*

https://unwiredcouch.com/2018/01/03/engineering-vision.html

[287] *Product Strategy*

https://svpg.com/product-strategy-overview/

[288] *A Philosophy of Software Design*

https://lethain.com/notes-philosophy-software-design/

[289] *Becoming a Technical Leader: An Organic Problem-Solving Approach*

https://www.amazon.com/dp/B004J4VV3I/

[290] *Building Evolutionary Architectures*

https://lethain.com/building-evolutionary-architectures/

[291] *Escaping the Build Trap: How Effective Product Management Creates Real Value*

https://www.amazon.com/dp/B07K3QBWG1/

[292] *The Mythical Man-Month*

https://www.amazon.com/dp/0201835959/

[293] *The Passionate Programmer*

https://www.amazon.com/dp/B00AYQNR5U/

[294] *The Pragmatic Programmer*

https://www.amazon.com/dp/020161622X

[295] *Software Design X-Rays: Fix Technical Debt with Behavioral Code Analysis*

https://www.amazon.com/dp/B07BVRLZ87

[296] *Thinking in Systems: A Primer*

https://www.amazon.com/dp/1603580557

[297] *Irrational Exuberance's Best Books*

https://lethain.com/best-books

[298] *Cindy Sridharan*

https://medium.com/@copyconstruct

[299] *Twitter*

https://twitter.com/copyconstruct

[300] *Best of 2019 in Tech Talks*

https://medium.com/@copyconstruct/best-of-2019-in-tech-talks-bac697c3ee13

[301] *Best of 2018 in Tech Talks*

https://medium.com/@copyconstruct/best-of-2018-in-tech-talks-2970eb3097af

[302] *Best of 2017 in Tech Talks*

https://medium.com/@copyconstruct/best-of-2017-in-tech-talks-8f78b34ff0b

[303] *the morning paper*

https://blog.acolyer.org/

[304] *How to Read an Academic Article*

https://organizationsandmarkets.com/2010/08/31/how-to-read-an-academic-article/

[305] *How to Read a Paper*

https://blizzard.cs.uwaterloo.ca/keshav/home/Papers/data/07/paper-reading.pdf

[306] *Dynamo: Amazon's Highly Available Key-value Store*

https://s3.amazonaws.com/systemsandpapers/papers/amazon-dynamo-sosp2007.pdf

[307] *On Designing and Deploying Internet-Scale Services*

https://s3.amazonaws.com/systemsandpapers/papers/hamilton.pdf

[308] *No Silver Bullet - Essence and Accident in Software Engineering*

https://s3.amazonaws.com/systemsandpapers/papers/Frederick_Brooks_87-No_Silver_Bullet_Essence_and_Accidents_of_Software_Engineering.pdf

[309] *Out of the Tar Pit*

https://s3.amazonaws.com/systemsandpapers/papers/outofthetarpit.pdf

[310] *The Chubby lock service for loosely-coupled distributed systems*

https://s3.amazonaws.com/systemsandpapers/papers/chubby-osdi06.pdf

[311] *Bigtable: A Distributed Storage System for Structured Data*

https://static.googleusercontent.com/media/research.google.com/en//archive/bigtable-osdi06.pdf

[312] *Raft: In Search of an Understandable Consensus Algorithm*

https://s3.amazonaws.com/systemsandpapers/papers/raft.pdf

[313] *Paxos Made Simple*

https://s3.amazonaws.com/systemsandpapers/papers/paxos-made-simple.pdf

[314] *SWIM: Scalable Weakly-consistent Infection-style Process Group Membership Protocol*

https://s3.amazonaws.com/systemsandpapers/papers/swim.pdf

[315] *Hints for Computer System Design*

https://s3.amazonaws.com/systemsandpapers/papers/acrobat-17.pdf

[316] *Big Ball of Mud*

https://s3.amazonaws.com/systemsandpapers/papers/bigballofmud.pdf

[317] *The Google File System*

https://s3.amazonaws.com/systemsandpapers/papers/gfs.pdf

[318] *CAP Twelve Years Later: How the Rules Have Changed*

https://www.infoq.com/articles/cap-twelve-years-later-how-the-rules-have-changed

[319] *Harvest, Yield, and Scalable Tolerant Systems*

https://s3.amazonaws.com/systemsandpapers/papers/FOX_Brewer_99-Harvest_Yield_and_Scalable_Tolerant_Systems.pdf

[320] *MapReduce: Simplified Data Processing on Large Clusters*

https://s3.amazonaws.com/systemsandpapers/papers/mapreduce.pdf

[321] *Dapper, a Large-Scale Distributed Systems Tracing Infrastructure*

https://s3.amazonaws.com/systemsandpapers/papers/dapper.pdf

[322] *Kafka: a Distributed Messaging System for Log Processing*

https://s3.amazonaws.com/systemsandpapers/papers/Kafka.pdf

[323] *Large-scale cluster management at Google with Borg*

https://s3.amazonaws.com/systemsandpapers/papers/borg.pdf

[324] *Mesos: A Platform for Fine-Grained Resource Sharing in the Data Center*

https://s3.amazonaws.com/systemsandpapers/papers/mesos.pdf

[325] *Papers We Love*

https://paperswelove.org/

[326] *ACM SIGOPS Hall of Fame Award list*

https://www.sigops.org/awards/hof/

[327] *Irrational Exuberance's paper collection*

https://lethain.com/some-of-my-favorite-technical-papers/

[328] *Testing in Production, the safe way*

https://medium.com/@copyconstruct/testing-in-production-the-safe-way-18ca102d0ef1

[329] *Testing in Production: the hard parts*

https://medium.com/@copyconstruct/testing-in-production-the-hard-parts-3f06cefaf592

[330] *A decade in review in tech*

https://medium.com/@copyconstruct/a-decade-in-review-in-tech-1cde76c9b43c

[331] *Boogeyman Problems*

https://blog.danielna.com/boogeyman-problems/

[332] *StaffEng*

http://staffeng.com

[333] *doing effective 1 on 1s*

https://marcorogers.com/blog/my-approach-to-1-on-1s

[334] *giving feedback*

https://smallbigideas.substack.com/p/own-your-feedback-part-1

[335] *The Manager's Path*

https://www.oreilly.com/library/view/the-managers-path/9781491973882/

[336] *efficiency over effectiveness*

https://www.amazon.com/dp/B004SOVC2Y/ref=dp-kindle-redirect?_encoding=UTF8&btkr=1

[337] *title inflation*

https://charity.wtf/2020/11/01/questionable-advice-the-trap-of-the-premature-senior/

[338] *while shifting that responsibility to them*

https://hbr.org/1999/11/management-time-whos-got-the-monkey

[339] *best interview loops*

https://lethain.com/designing-interview-loops/

[340] *Rent the Runway*

https://docs.google.com/spreadsheets/d/1k4sO6pyCl_YYnf0PAXSBcX776rNcTjSOqDxZ5SDty-4/edit##gid=0

[341] *Kickstarter*

https://gist.github.com/jamtur01/aef437a79fee5a9cefdc##junioreng

[342] *Patreon*

https://levels.patreon.com

[343] *progression.fyi*

https://www.progression.fyi

Printed in Poland
by Amazon Fulfillment
Poland Sp. z o.o., Wrocław